NEW MUTANTS

A DATE WITH THE DEVIL

COLLECTION EDITOR
JENNIFER GRÜNWALD
ASSISTANT EDITORS
ALEX STARBUCK &
NELSON RIBEIRO
EDITOR, SPECIAL PROJECTS
MARK D. BEAZLEY

SENIOR EDITOR, SPECIAL PROJECTS
JEFF YOUNGQUIST
SENIOR VICE PRESIDENT OF SALES
DAVID GABRIEL
SVP OF BRAND PLANNING & COMMUNICATIONS
MICHAEL PASCIULLO
BOOK DESIGN
JEFF POWELL

EDITOR IN CHIEF
AXEL ALONSO
CHIEF CREATIVE OFFICER
JOE QUESADA
PUBLISHER
DAN BUCKLEY
EXECUTIVE PRODUCER
ALAN FINE

NEW MUTANTS: A DATE WITH THE DEVIL. Contains material originally published in magazine form as NEW MUTANTS #33-37. First printing 2012. ISBN# 978-0-7851-5232-3. Published by MARVEL WORLDWIDE, INC., a subsidiary of MARVEL ENTERTAINMENT, LLC. OFFICE OF PUBLICATION: 135 West 50th Street, New York, NY 10020. Copyright © 2011 and 2012 Marvel Characters, Inc. All rights reserved. $19.99 per copy in the U.S. and $21.99 in Canada (GST #R127032852); Canadian Agreement #40668537. All characters featured in this issue and the distinctive names and likenesses thereof, and all related indicia are trademarks of Marvel Characters, Inc. No similarity between any of the names, characters, persons, and/or institutions in this magazine with those of any living or dead person or institution is intended, and any such similarity which may exist is purely coincidental. **Printed in the U.S.A.** ALAN FINE, EVP - Office of the President, Marvel Worldwide, Inc. and EVP & CMO Marvel Characters B.V.; DAN BUCKLEY, Publisher & President - Print, Animation & Digital Divisions; JOE QUESADA, Chief Creative Officer; DAVID BOGART, SVP of Business Affairs & Talent Management; TOM BREVOORT, SVP of Publishing; C.B. CEBULSKI, SVP of Creator & Content Development; DAVID GABRIEL, SVP of Publishing Sales & Circulation; MICHAEL PASCIULLO, SVP of Brand Planning & Communications; JIM O'KEEFE, VP of Operations & Logistics; DAN CARR, Executive Director of Publishing Technology; SUSAN CRESPI, Editorial Operations Manager; ALEX MORALES, Publishing Operations Manager; STAN LEE, Chairman Emeritus. For information regarding advertising in Marvel Comics or on Marvel.com, please contact John Dokes, SVP Integrated Sales and Marketing, at jdokes@marvel.com. For Marvel subscription inquiries, please call 800-217-9158. Manufactured between 3/5/2012 and 4/2/2012 by R.R. DONNELLEY, INC., SALEM, VA, USA.

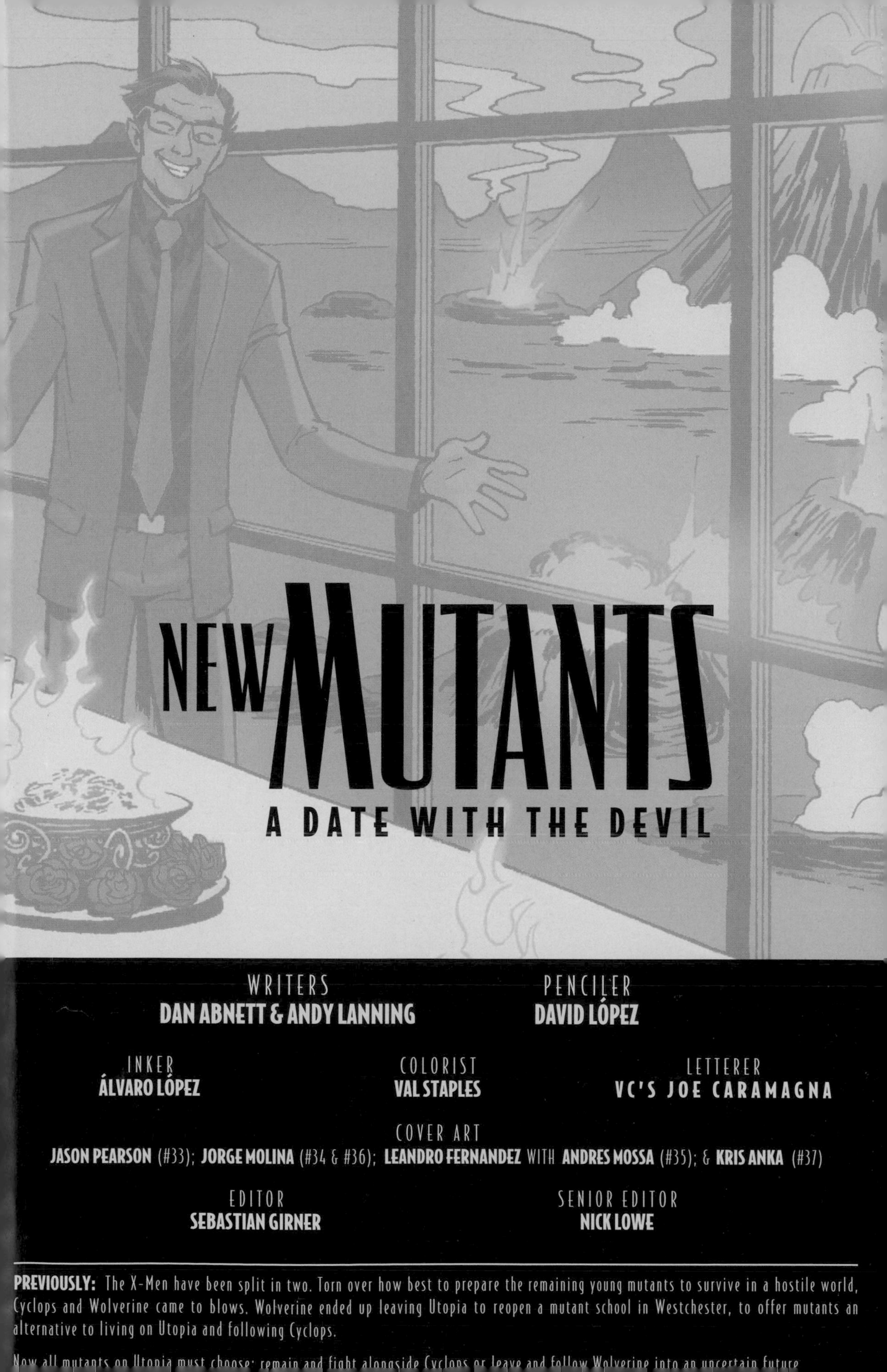

NEW MUTANTS

A DATE WITH THE DEVIL

WRITERS
DAN ABNETT & ANDY LANNING

PENCILER
DAVID LÓPEZ

INKER
ÁLVARO LÓPEZ

COLORIST
VAL STAPLES

LETTERER
VC'S JOE CARAMAGNA

COVER ART
JASON PEARSON (#33); **JORGE MOLINA** (#34 & #36); **LEANDRO FERNANDEZ** WITH **ANDRES MOSSA** (#35); & **KRIS ANKA** (#37)

EDITOR
SEBASTIAN GIRNER

SENIOR EDITOR
NICK LOWE

PREVIOUSLY: The X-Men have been split in two. Torn over how best to prepare the remaining young mutants to survive in a hostile world, Cyclops and Wolverine came to blows. Wolverine ended up leaving Utopia to reopen a mutant school in Westchester, to offer mutants an alternative to living on Utopia and following Cyclops.

Now all mutants on Utopia must choose: remain and fight alongside Cyclops or leave and follow Wolverine into an uncertain future.

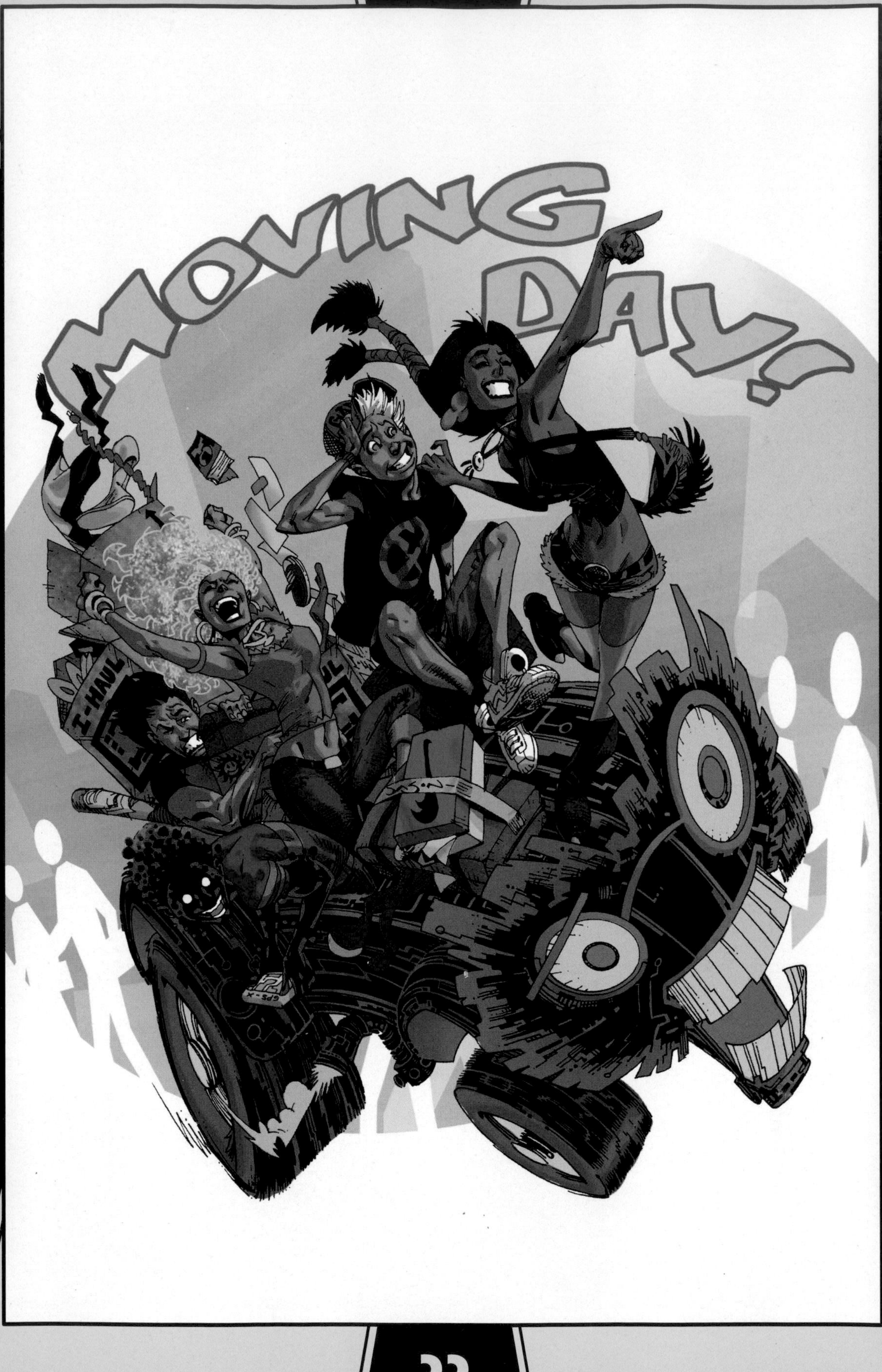
MOVING DAY!
U-HAUL

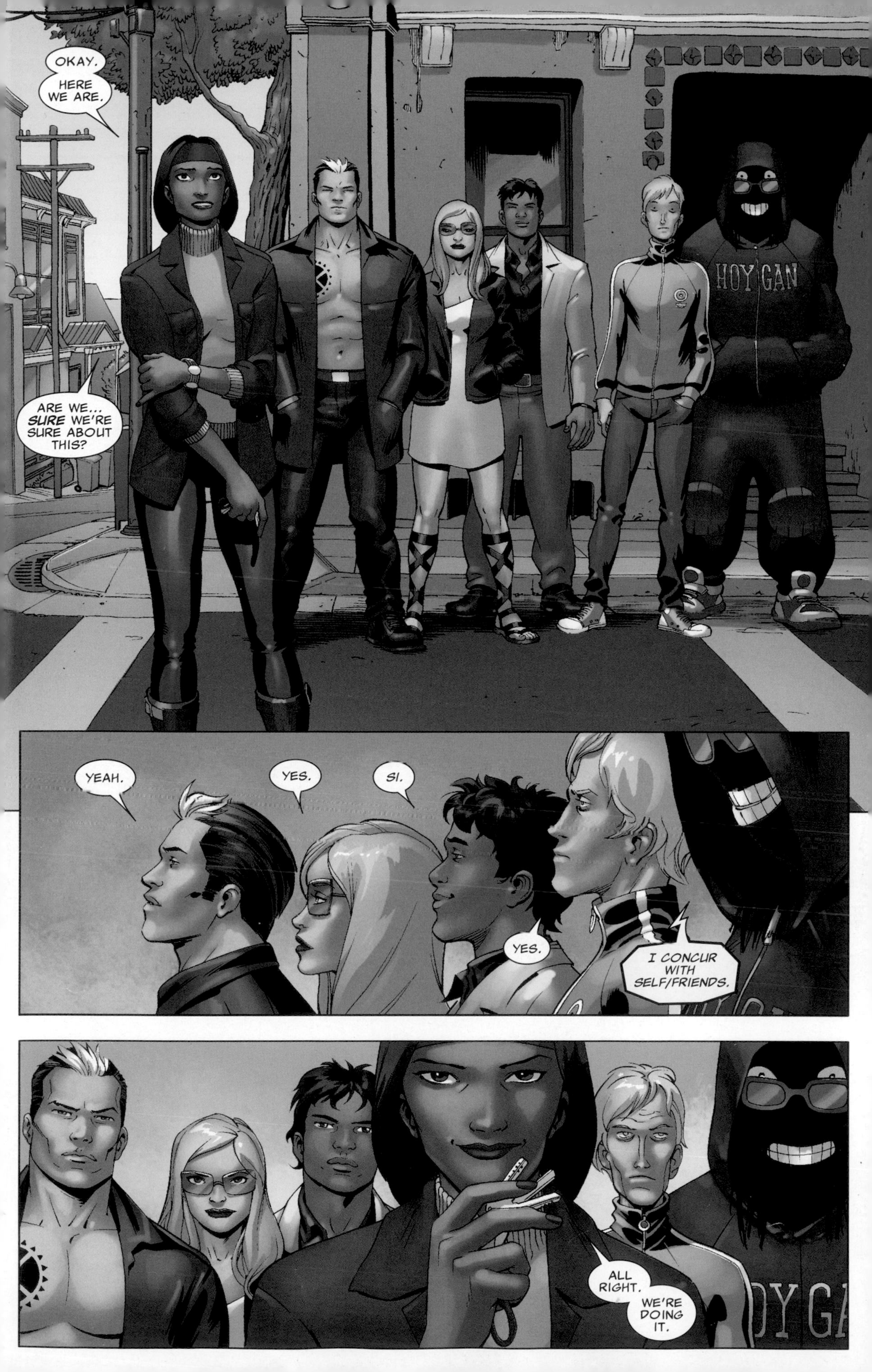
OKAY. HERE WE ARE.
ARE WE... **SURE** WE'RE SURE ABOUT THIS?
YEAH.
YES.
SI.
YES.
I CONCUR WITH SELF/FRIENDS.
ALL RIGHT. WE'RE DOING IT.
HOY GAN

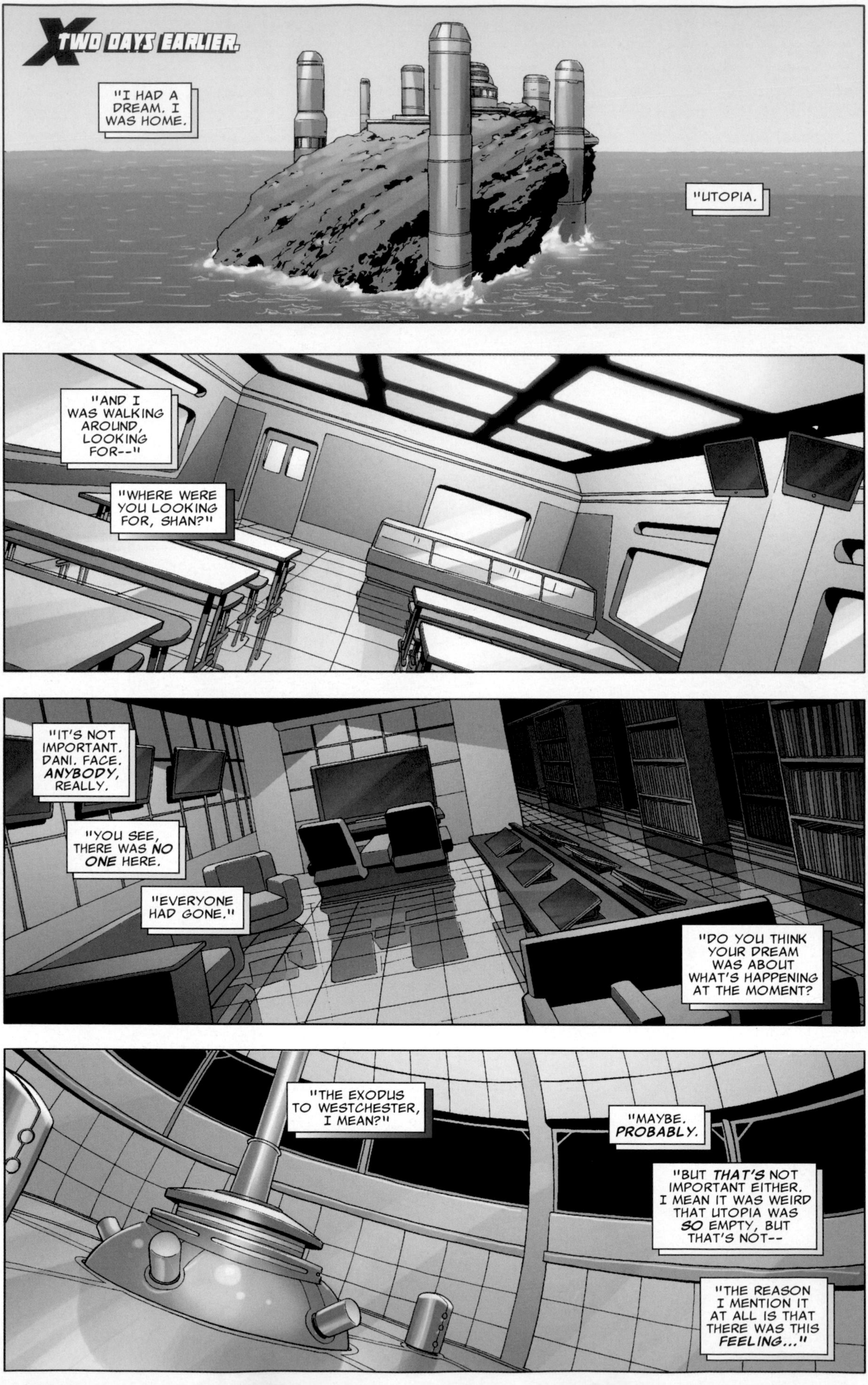
TWO DAYS EARLIER.
"I HAD A DREAM. I WAS HOME.
"UTOPIA.
"AND I WAS WALKING AROUND, LOOKING FOR--"
"WHERE WERE YOU LOOKING FOR, SHAN?"
"IT'S NOT IMPORTANT. DANI. FACE. ANYBODY, REALLY.
"YOU SEE, THERE WAS NO ONE HERE.
"EVERYONE HAD GONE."
"DO YOU THINK YOUR DREAM WAS ABOUT WHAT'S HAPPENING AT THE MOMENT?
"THE EXODUS TO WESTCHESTER, I MEAN?"
"MAYBE. PROBABLY.
"BUT THAT'S NOT IMPORTANT EITHER. I MEAN IT WAS WEIRD THAT UTOPIA WAS SO EMPTY, BUT THAT'S NOT--
"THE REASON I MENTION IT AT ALL IS THAT THERE WAS THIS FEELING..."

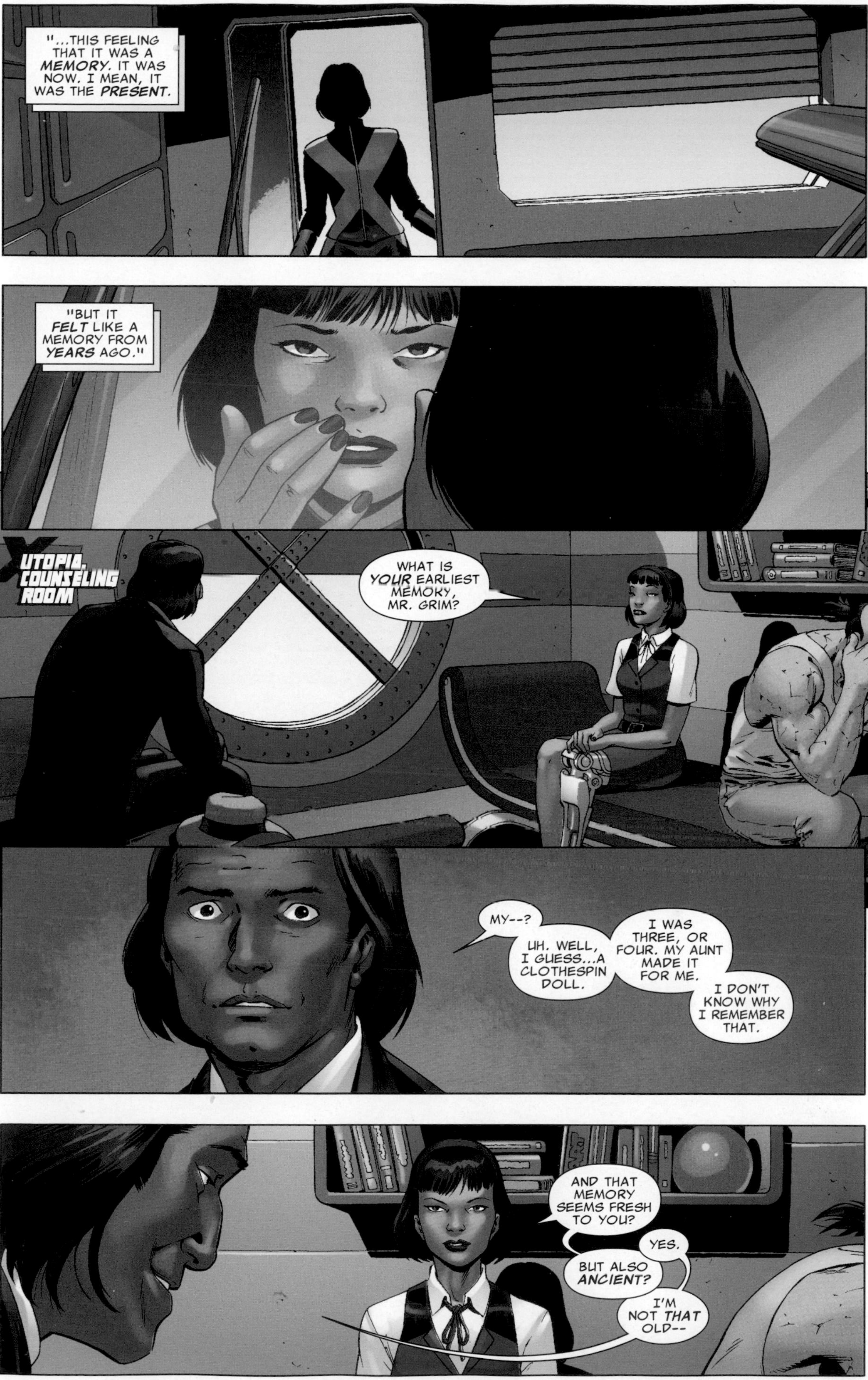
"...THIS FEELING THAT IT WAS A MEMORY. IT WAS NOW. I MEAN, IT WAS THE PRESENT.
"BUT IT FELT LIKE A MEMORY FROM YEARS AGO."
UTOPIA, COUNSELING ROOM
WHAT IS YOUR EARLIEST MEMORY, MR. GRIM?
MY--?
UH. WELL, I GUESS...A CLOTHESPIN DOLL.
I WAS THREE, OR FOUR. MY AUNT MADE IT FOR ME.
I DON'T KNOW WHY I REMEMBER THAT.
AND THAT MEMORY SEEMS FRESH TO YOU?
YES.
BUT ALSO ANCIENT?
I'M NOT THAT OLD--

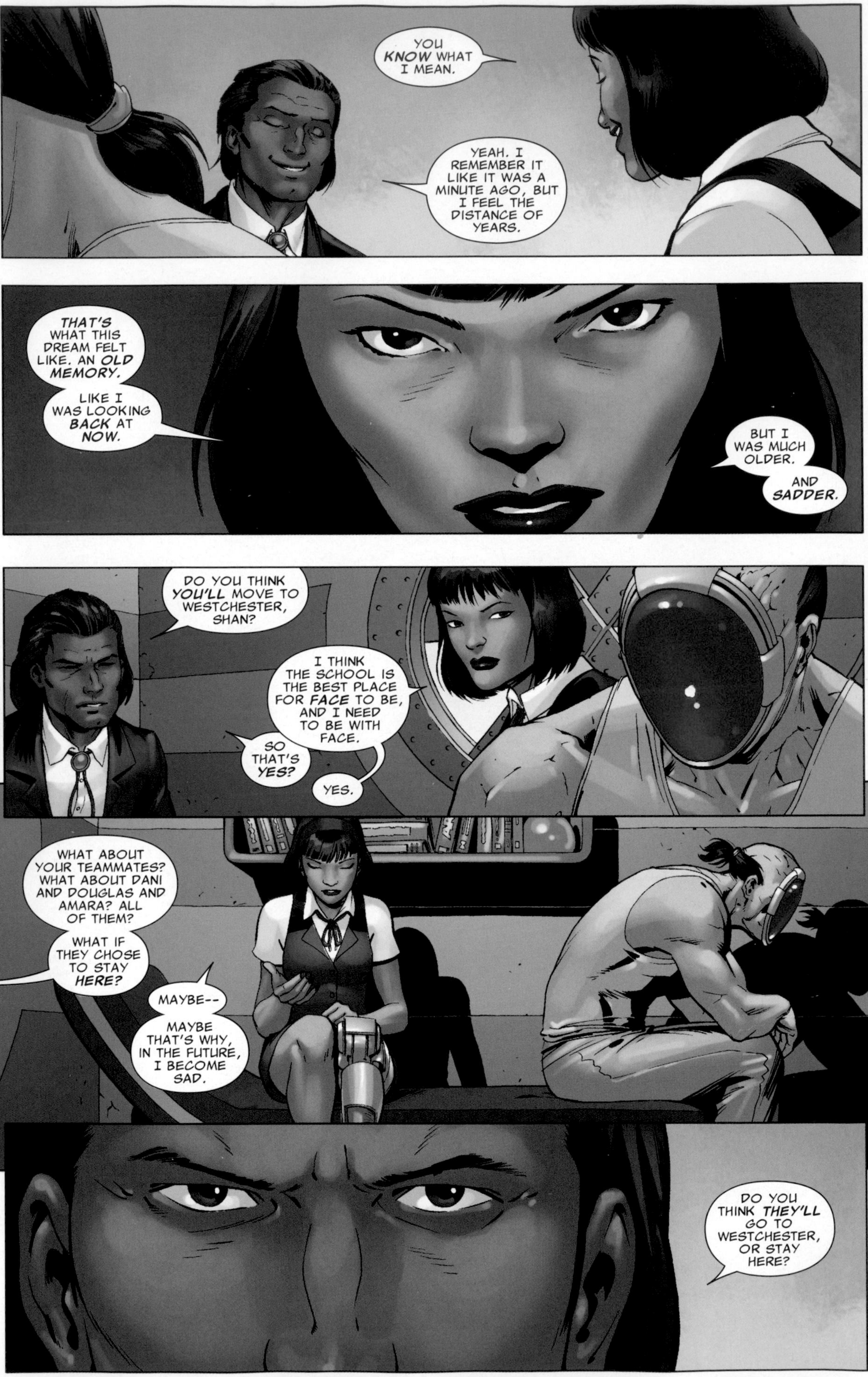

YOU KNOW WHAT I MEAN.
YEAH. I REMEMBER IT LIKE IT WAS A MINUTE AGO, BUT I FEEL THE DISTANCE OF YEARS.
THAT'S WHAT THIS DREAM FELT LIKE. AN OLD MEMORY.
LIKE I WAS LOOKING BACK AT NOW.
BUT I WAS MUCH OLDER.
AND SADDER.
DO YOU THINK YOU'LL MOVE TO WESTCHESTER, SHAN?
I THINK THE SCHOOL IS THE BEST PLACE FOR FACE TO BE, AND I NEED TO BE WITH FACE.
SO THAT'S YES?
YES.
WHAT ABOUT YOUR TEAMMATES? WHAT ABOUT DANI AND DOUGLAS AND AMARA? ALL OF THEM?
WHAT IF THEY CHOSE TO STAY HERE?
MAYBE--
MAYBE THAT'S WHY, IN THE FUTURE, I BECOME SAD.
DO YOU THINK THEY'LL GO TO WESTCHESTER, OR STAY HERE?

"I DON'T KNOW."

WHAT DO YOU THINK? GO OR STAY?

I THINK THERE USED TO BE ROOM TO PLAY A LITTLE SOCCER HERE.

SINCE THAT SENTINEL ATTACK, THERE'S BARELY ENOUGH SPACE FOR KEEPY-UPPY.

THERE'S SPACE IN WESTCHESTER.

YOU KNOW, I COULD JUST GET ME A PLACE IN THE CITY. LIVING LARGE.

I COULD AFFORD THAT.

I KNOW.

I AM INDEPENDENTLY WEALTHY. I HAVE INDEPENDENT WEALTH.

I KNOW.

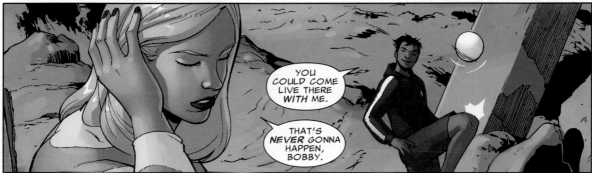

YOU COULD COME LIVE THERE WITH ME.

THAT'S NEVER GONNA HAPPEN, BOBBY.

OKAY. JUST SAYING.

WHERE ARE YOU GOING?

TO GET MY BALL BACK.

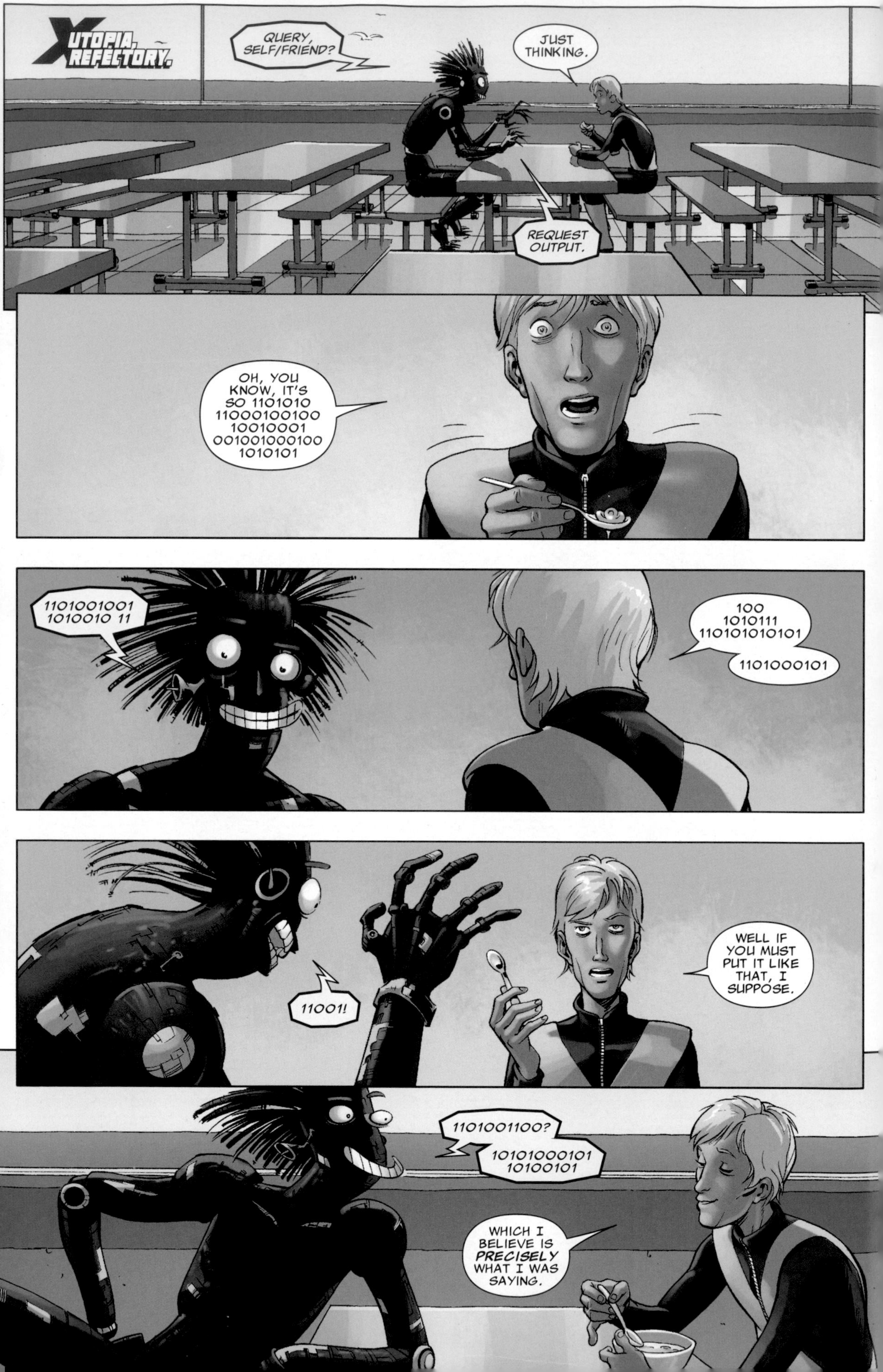
UTOPIA, REFECTORY.
QUERY, SELF/FRIEND?
JUST THINKING.
REQUEST OUTPUT.
OH, YOU KNOW, IT'S SO 1101010 11000100100 10010001 001001000100 1010101
1101001001 1010010 11
100 1010111 110101010101
1101000101
11001!
WELL IF YOU MUST PUT IT LIKE THAT, I SUPPOSE.
1101001100?
10101000101 10100101
WHICH I BELIEVE IS PRECISELY WHAT I WAS SAYING.

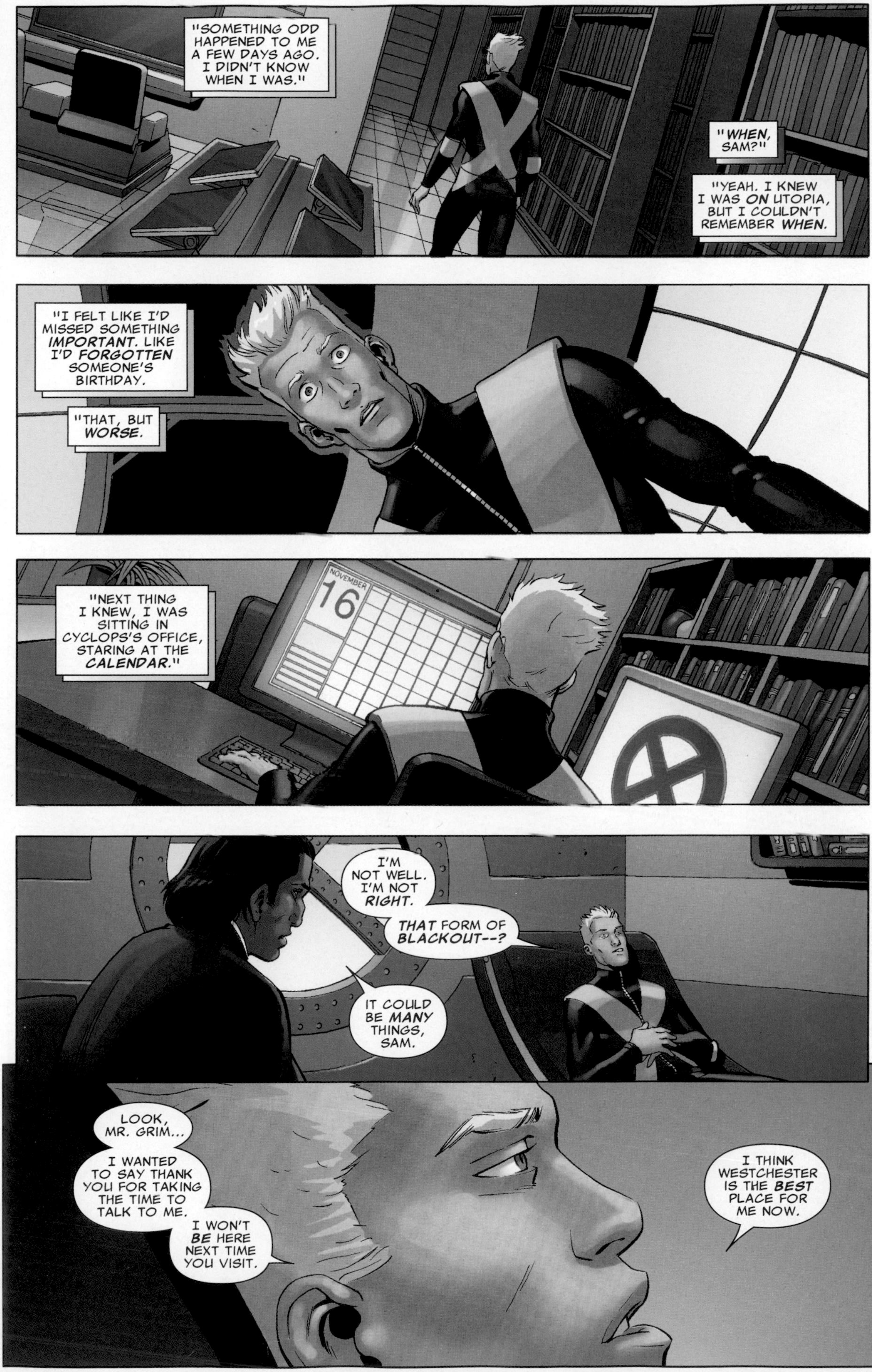
"SOMETHING ODD HAPPENED TO ME A FEW DAYS AGO. I DIDN'T KNOW WHEN I WAS."
"WHEN, SAM?"
"YEAH. I KNEW I WAS ON UTOPIA, BUT I COULDN'T REMEMBER WHEN.
"I FELT LIKE I'D MISSED SOMETHING IMPORTANT. LIKE I'D FORGOTTEN SOMEONE'S BIRTHDAY.
"THAT, BUT WORSE.
"NEXT THING I KNEW, I WAS SITTING IN CYCLOPS'S OFFICE, STARING AT THE CALENDAR."
NOVEMBER
16
I'M NOT WELL. I'M NOT RIGHT.
THAT FORM OF BLACKOUT--?
IT COULD BE MANY THINGS, SAM.
LOOK, MR. GRIM...
I WANTED TO SAY THANK YOU FOR TAKING THE TIME TO TALK TO ME.
I WON'T BE HERE NEXT TIME YOU VISIT.
I THINK WESTCHESTER IS THE BEST PLACE FOR ME NOW.

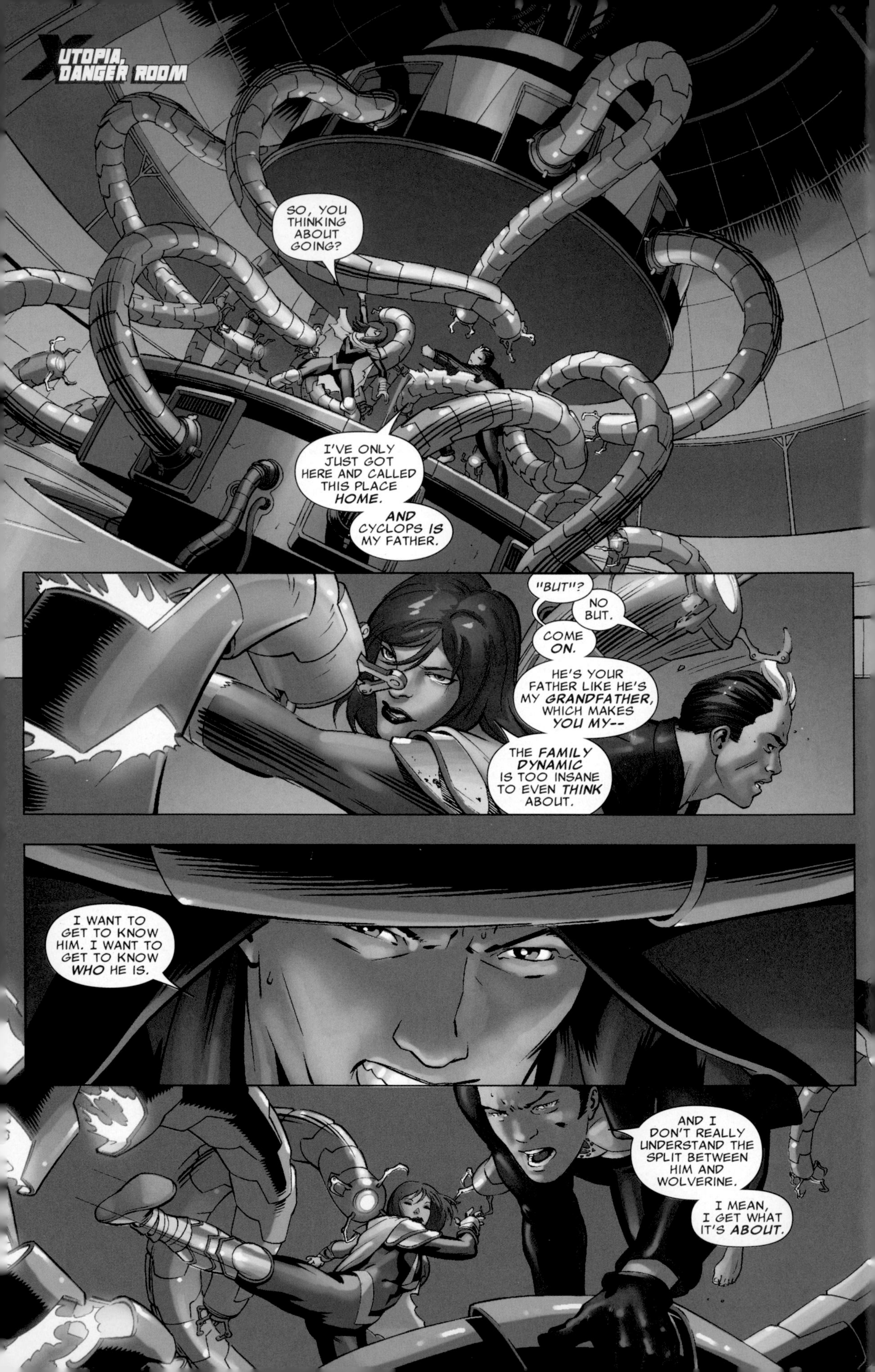
UTOPIA, DANGER ROOM
SO, YOU THINKING ABOUT GOING?
I'VE ONLY JUST GOT HERE AND CALLED THIS PLACE HOME.
AND CYCLOPS IS MY FATHER.
"BUT"?
NO BUT.
COME ON.
HE'S YOUR FATHER LIKE HE'S MY GRANDFATHER, WHICH MAKES YOU MY--
THE FAMILY DYNAMIC IS TOO INSANE TO EVEN THINK ABOUT.
I WANT TO GET TO KNOW HIM. I WANT TO GET TO KNOW WHO HE IS.
AND I DON'T REALLY UNDERSTAND THE SPLIT BETWEEN HIM AND WOLVERINE.
I MEAN, I GET WHAT IT'S ABOUT.

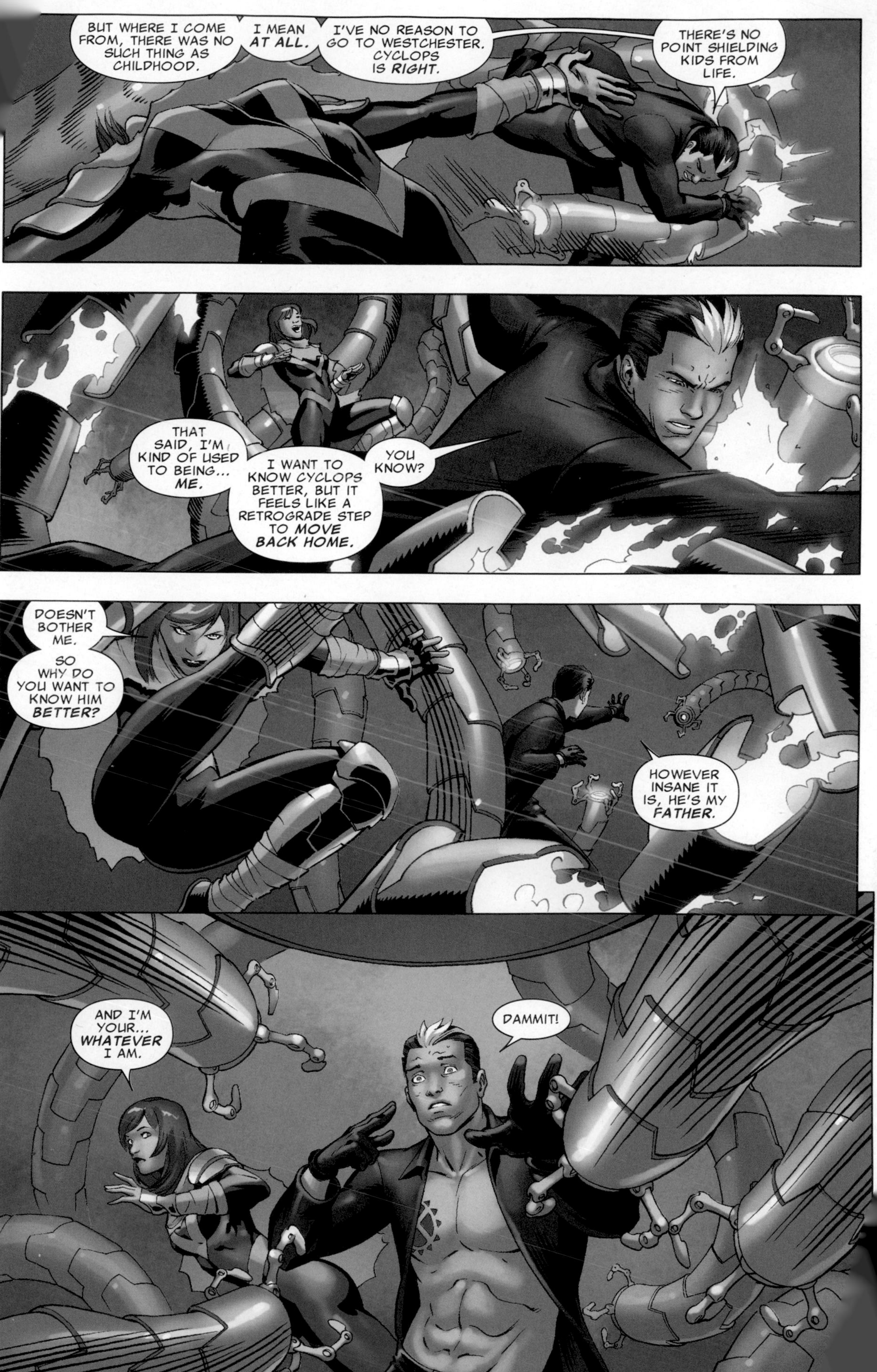
BUT WHERE I COME FROM, THERE WAS NO SUCH THING AS CHILDHOOD.
I MEAN AT ALL.
I'VE NO REASON TO GO TO WESTCHESTER. CYCLOPS IS RIGHT.
THERE'S NO POINT SHIELDING KIDS FROM LIFE.
THAT SAID, I'M KIND OF USED TO BEING... ME.
I WANT TO KNOW CYCLOPS BETTER, BUT IT FEELS LIKE A RETROGRADE STEP TO MOVE BACK HOME.
YOU KNOW?
DOESN'T BOTHER ME.
SO WHY DO YOU WANT TO KNOW HIM BETTER?
HOWEVER INSANE IT IS, HE'S MY FATHER.
AND I'M YOUR... WHATEVER I AM.
DAMMIT!

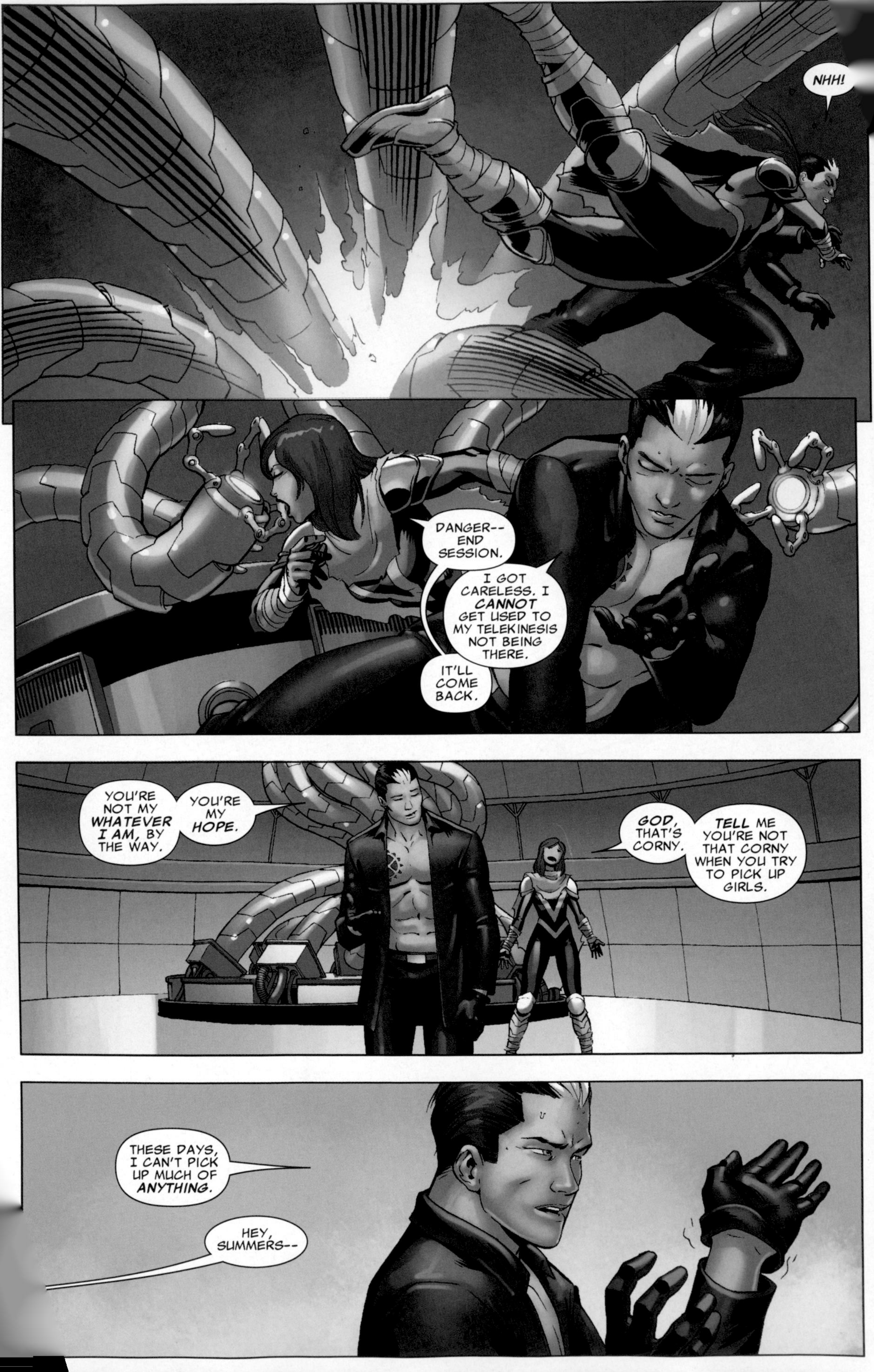
NHH!
DANGER-- END SESSION.
I GOT CARELESS. I CANNOT GET USED TO MY TELEKINESIS NOT BEING THERE.
IT'LL COME BACK.
YOU'RE NOT MY WHATEVER I AM, BY THE WAY.
YOU'RE MY HOPE.
GOD, THAT'S CORNY.
TELL ME YOU'RE NOT THAT CORNY WHEN YOU TRY TO PICK UP GIRLS.
THESE DAYS, I CAN'T PICK UP MUCH OF ANYTHING.
HEY, SUMMERS--

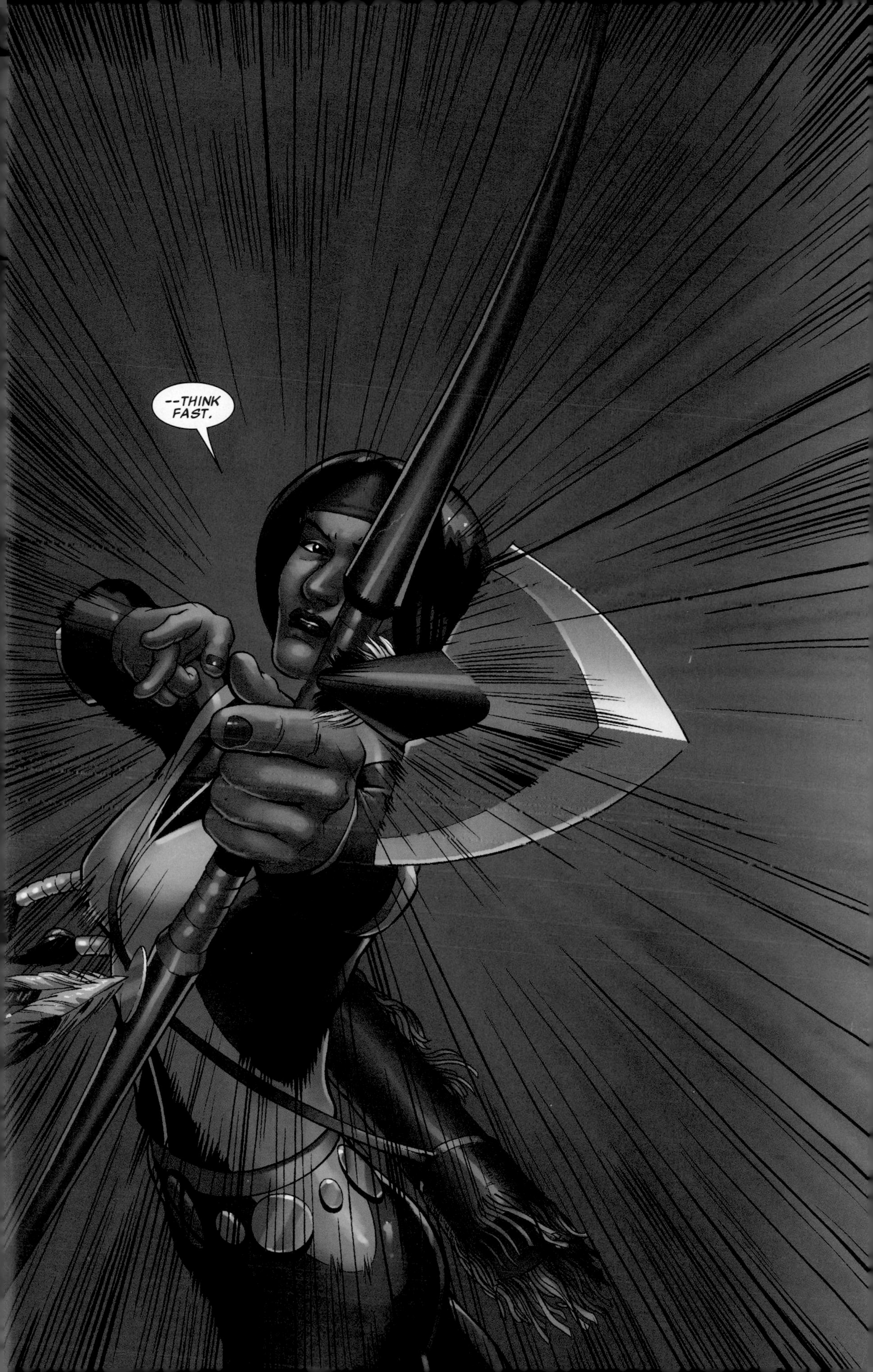
--THINK FAST.

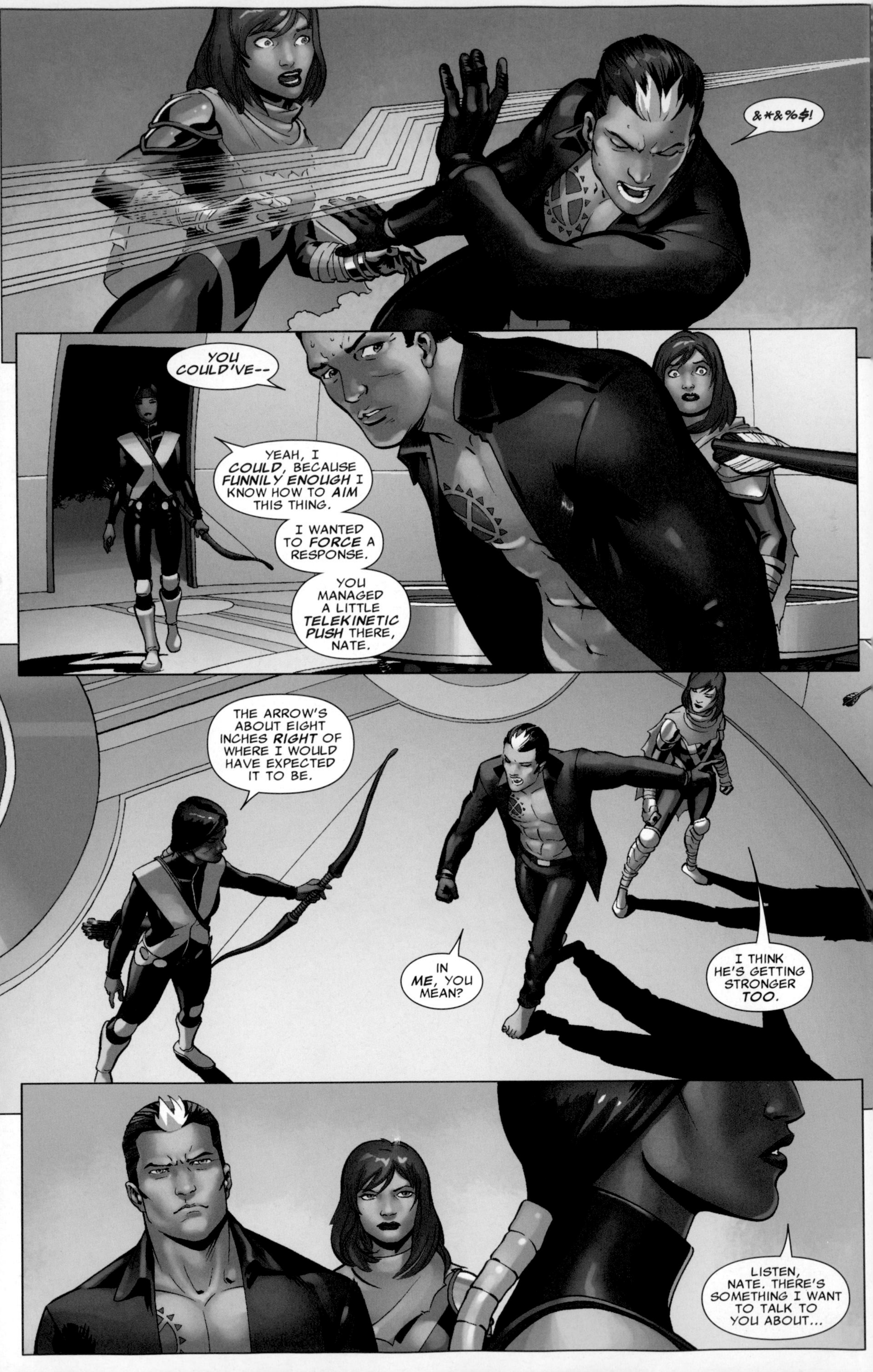
&*&%$!
YOU COULD'VE--
YEAH, I COULD, BECAUSE FUNNILY ENOUGH I KNOW HOW TO AIM THIS THING.
I WANTED TO FORCE A RESPONSE.
YOU MANAGED A LITTLE TELEKINETIC PUSH THERE, NATE.
THE ARROW'S ABOUT EIGHT INCHES RIGHT OF WHERE I WOULD HAVE EXPECTED IT TO BE.
IN ME, YOU MEAN?
I THINK HE'S GETTING STRONGER TOO.
LISTEN, NATE. THERE'S SOMETHING I WANT TO TALK TO YOU ABOUT...

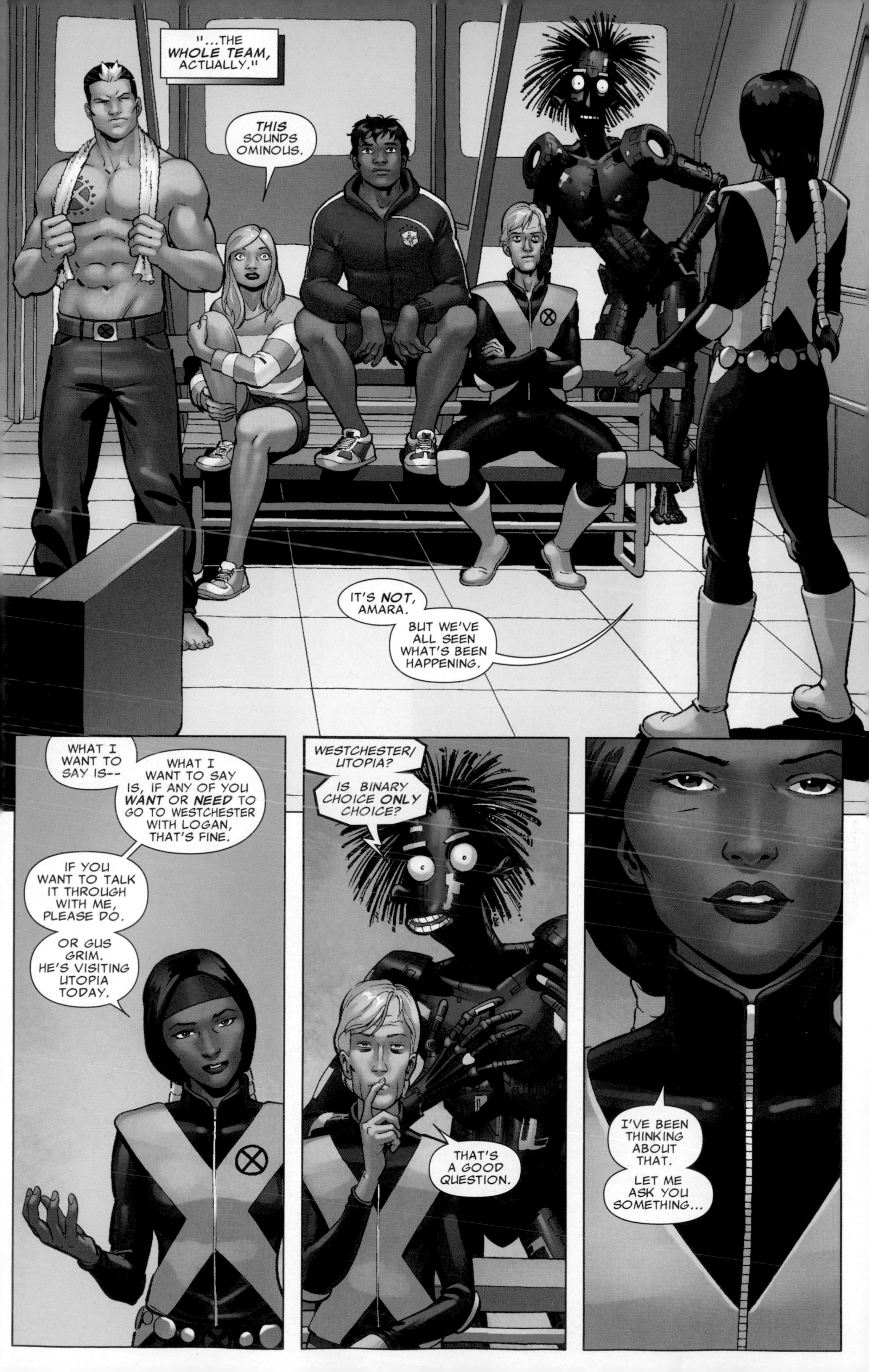

"...THE WHOLE TEAM, ACTUALLY."
THIS SOUNDS OMINOUS.
IT'S NOT, AMARA.
BUT WE'VE ALL SEEN WHAT'S BEEN HAPPENING.
WHAT I WANT TO SAY IS--
WHAT I WANT TO SAY IS, IF ANY OF YOU WANT OR NEED TO GO TO WESTCHESTER WITH LOGAN, THAT'S FINE.
IF YOU WANT TO TALK IT THROUGH WITH ME, PLEASE DO.
OR GUS GRIM. HE'S VISITING UTOPIA TODAY.
WESTCHESTER/ UTOPIA?
IS BINARY CHOICE ONLY CHOICE?
THAT'S A GOOD QUESTION.
I'VE BEEN THINKING ABOUT THAT.
LET ME ASK YOU SOMETHING...

SO?

SO...

AS I UNDERSTAND IT, CYCLOPS AND THIS WOLVERINE GUY GOT INTO IT.

OVER WHAT THE *X-MEN* SHOULD BE.

IT WAS UGLY. DON'T ASK.

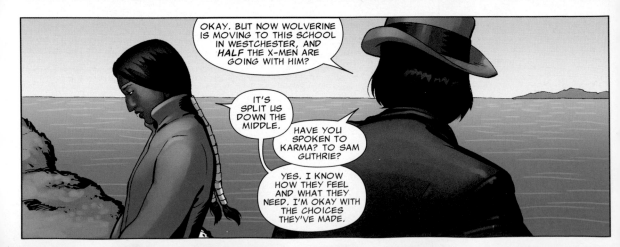

OKAY. BUT NOW WOLVERINE IS MOVING TO THIS SCHOOL IN WESTCHESTER, AND *HALF* THE X-MEN ARE GOING WITH HIM?

IT'S SPLIT US DOWN THE MIDDLE.

HAVE YOU SPOKEN TO KARMA? TO SAM GUTHRIE?

YES. I KNOW HOW THEY FEEL AND WHAT THEY NEED. I'M OKAY WITH THE CHOICES THEY'VE MADE.

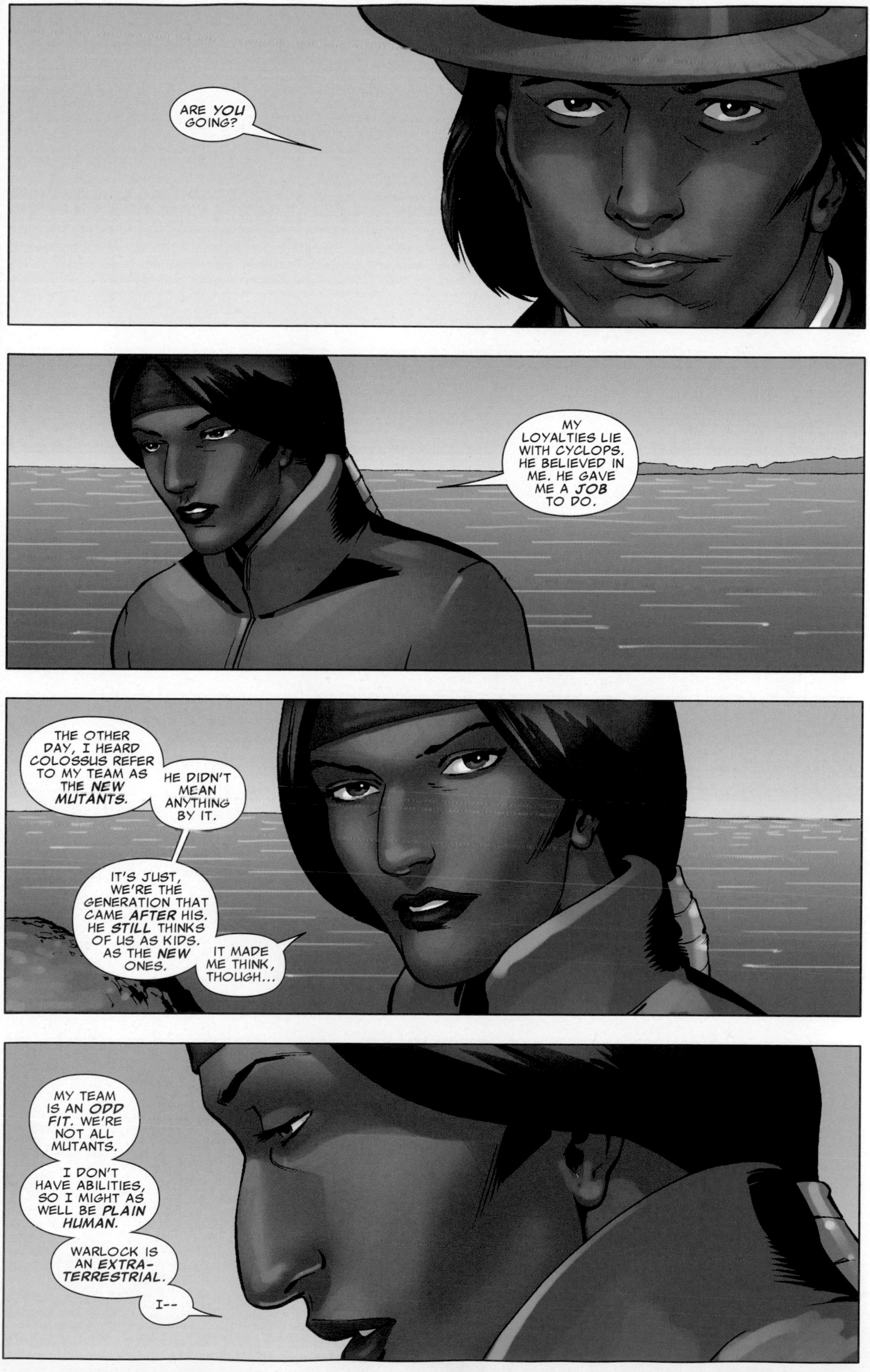
ARE YOU GOING?
MY LOYALTIES LIE WITH CYCLOPS. HE BELIEVED IN ME. HE GAVE ME A JOB TO DO.
THE OTHER DAY, I HEARD COLOSSUS REFER TO MY TEAM AS THE NEW MUTANTS.
HE DIDN'T MEAN ANYTHING BY IT.
IT'S JUST, WE'RE THE GENERATION THAT CAME AFTER HIS. HE STILL THINKS OF US AS KIDS. AS THE NEW ONES.
IT MADE ME THINK, THOUGH...
MY TEAM IS AN ODD FIT. WE'RE NOT ALL MUTANTS.
I DON'T HAVE ABILITIES, SO I MIGHT AS WELL BE PLAIN HUMAN.
WARLOCK IS AN EXTRA-TERRESTRIAL.
I--

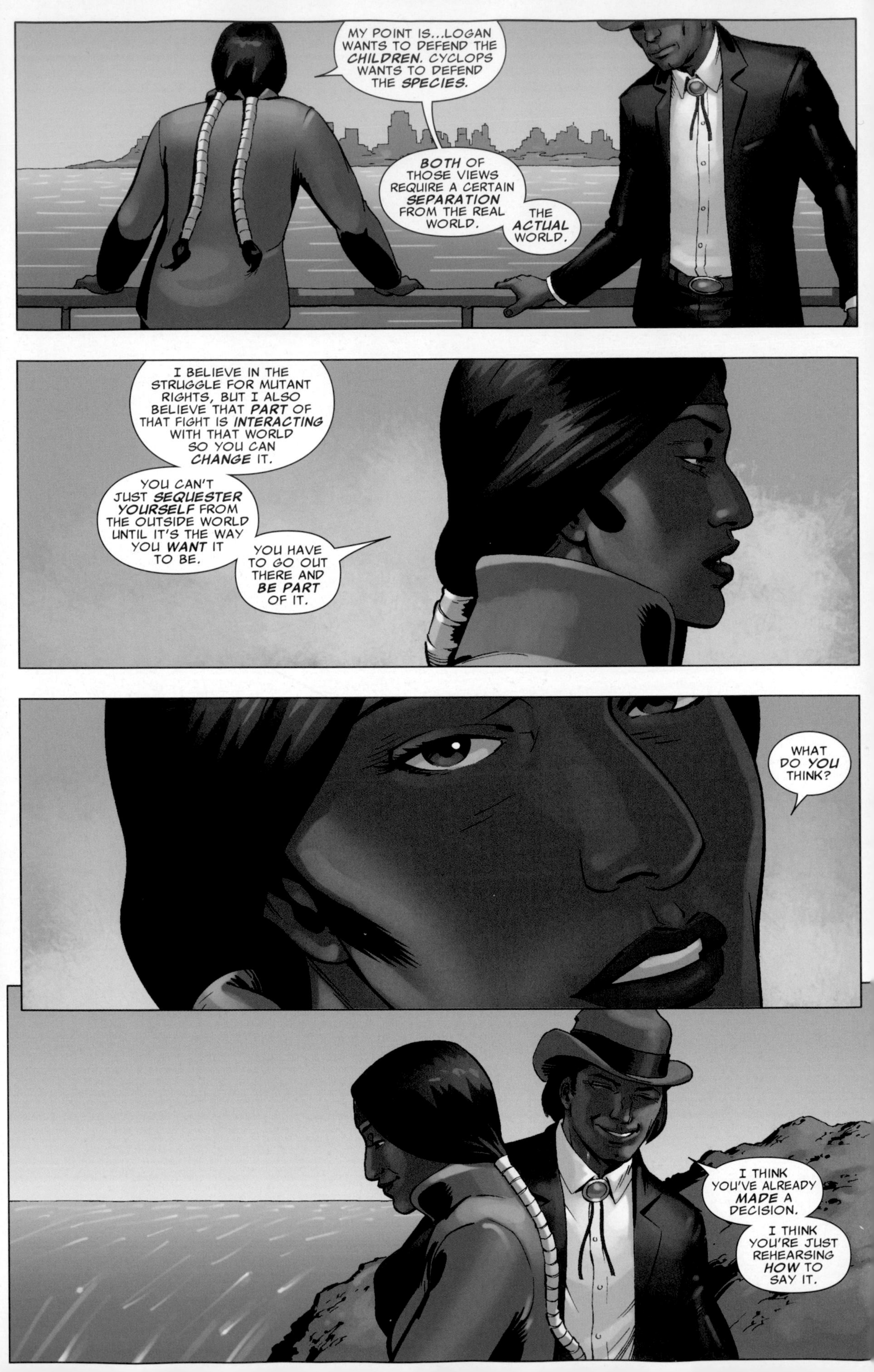
MY POINT IS...LOGAN WANTS TO DEFEND THE CHILDREN. CYCLOPS WANTS TO DEFEND THE SPECIES.
BOTH OF THOSE VIEWS REQUIRE A CERTAIN SEPARATION FROM THE REAL WORLD.
THE ACTUAL WORLD.
I BELIEVE IN THE STRUGGLE FOR MUTANT RIGHTS, BUT I ALSO BELIEVE THAT PART OF THAT FIGHT IS INTERACTING WITH THAT WORLD SO YOU CAN CHANGE IT.
YOU CAN'T JUST SEQUESTER YOURSELF FROM THE OUTSIDE WORLD UNTIL IT'S THE WAY YOU WANT IT TO BE.
YOU HAVE TO GO OUT THERE AND BE PART OF IT.
WHAT DO YOU THINK?
I THINK YOU'VE ALREADY MADE A DECISION.
I THINK YOU'RE JUST REHEARSING HOW TO SAY IT.

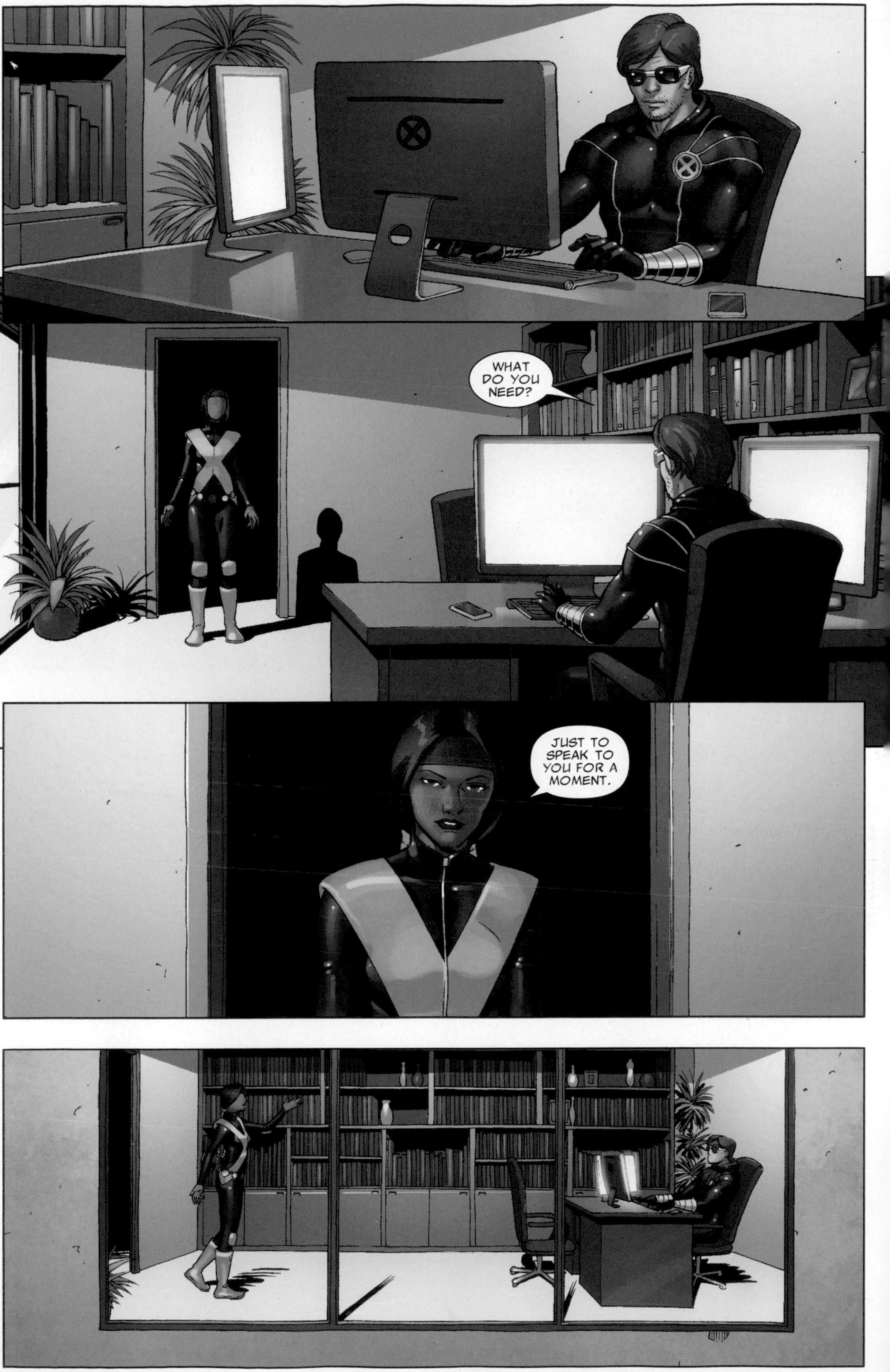
WHAT DO YOU NEED?
JUST TO SPEAK TO YOU FOR A MOMENT.

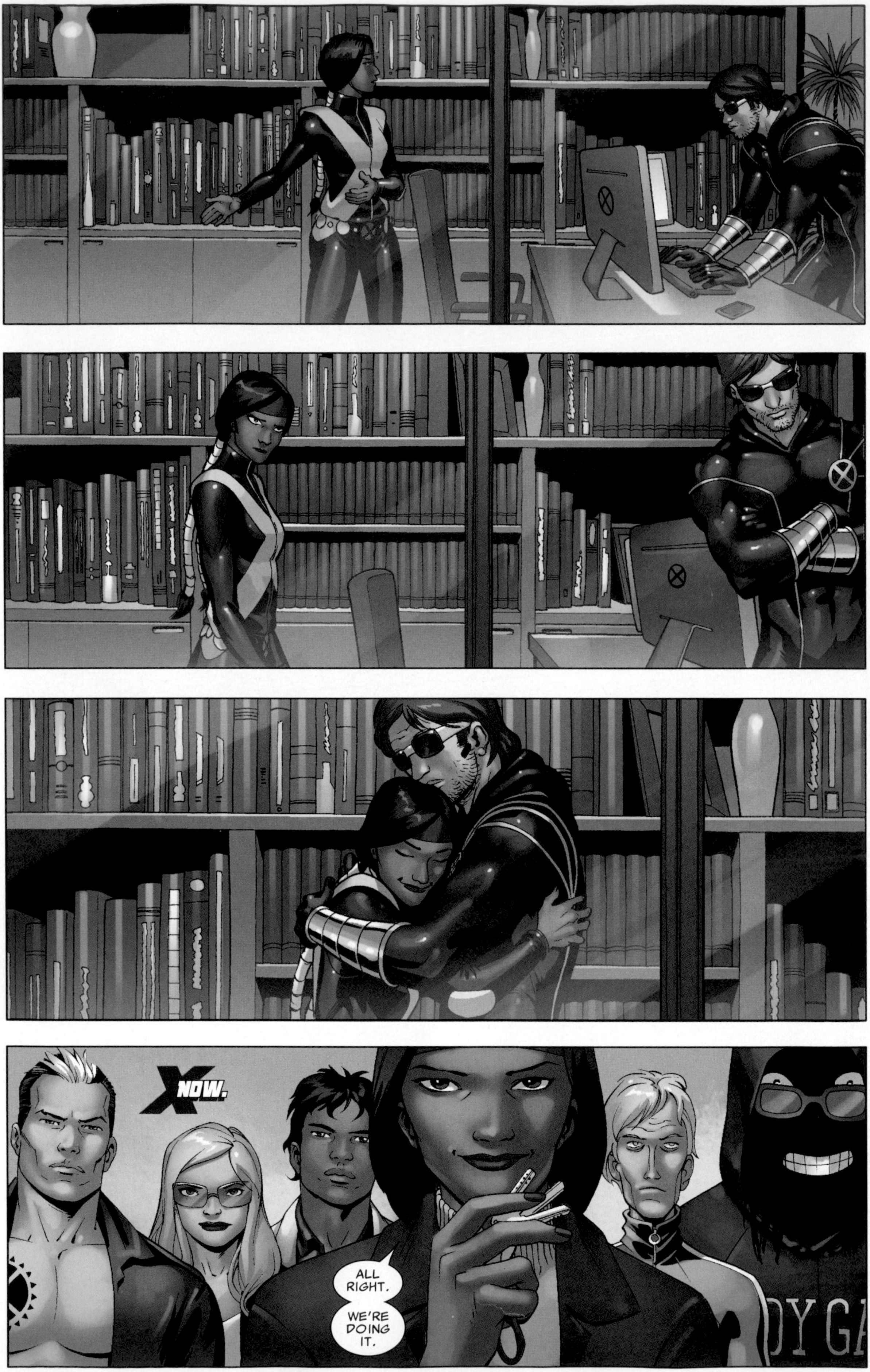
X NOW.
ALL RIGHT.
WE'RE DOING IT.

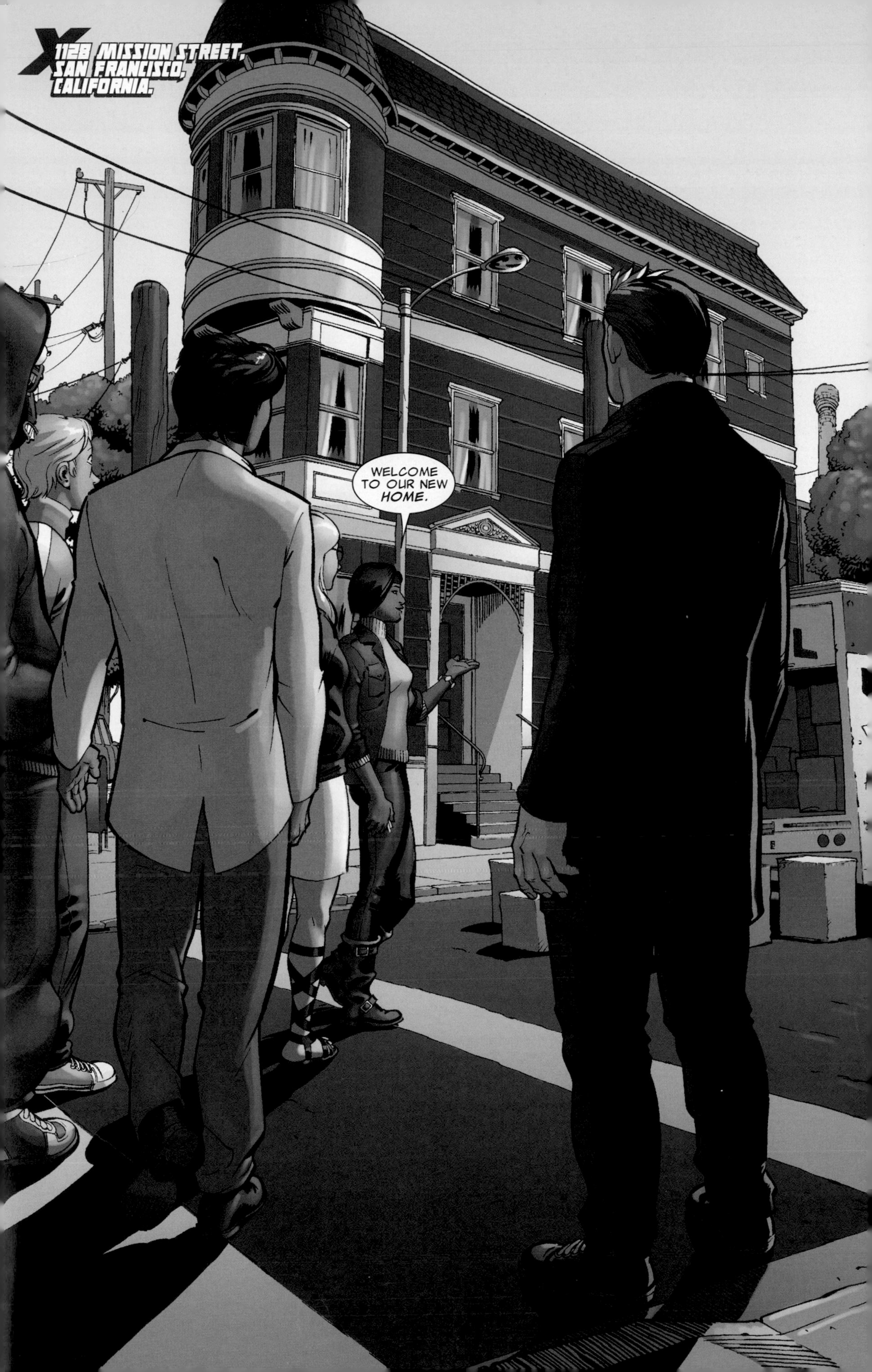
1128 MISSION STREET, SAN FRANCISCO, CALIFORNIA.
WELCOME TO OUR NEW HOME.

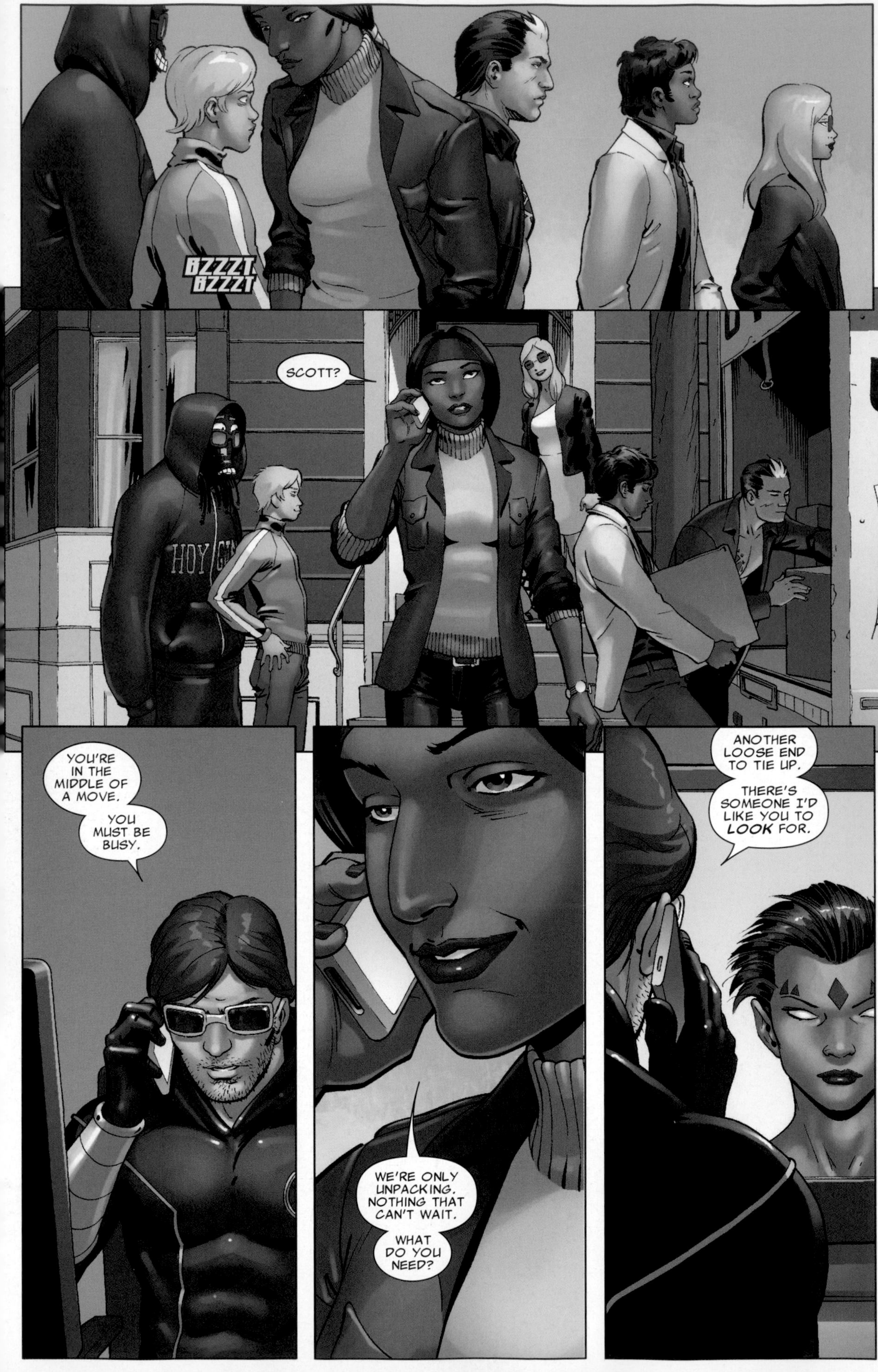
BZZZT
BZZZT
SCOTT?
YOU'RE IN THE MIDDLE OF A MOVE.
YOU MUST BE BUSY.
WE'RE ONLY UNPACKING. NOTHING THAT CAN'T WAIT.
WHAT DO YOU NEED?
ANOTHER LOOSE END TO TIE UP.
THERE'S SOMEONE I'D LIKE YOU TO LOOK FOR.

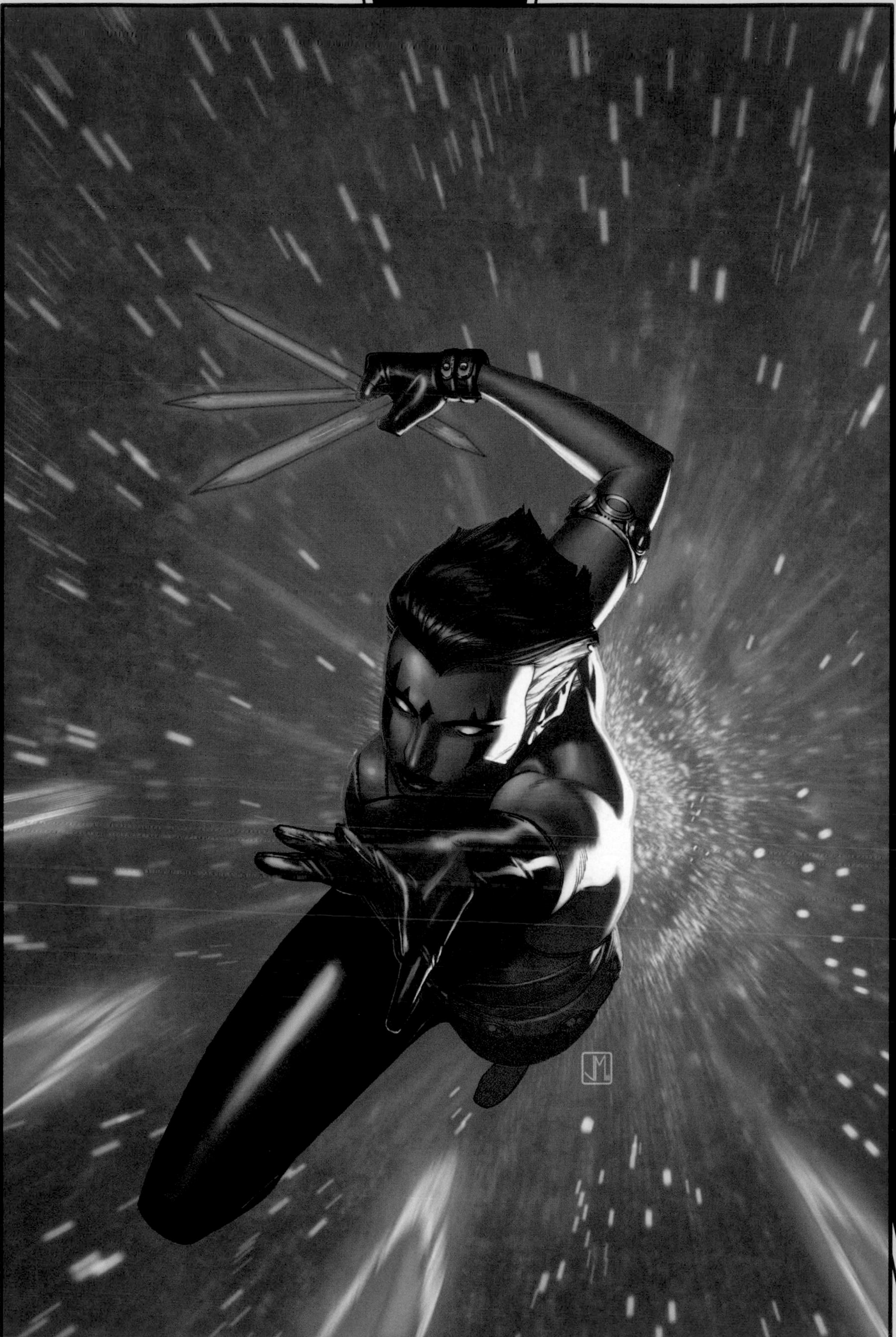

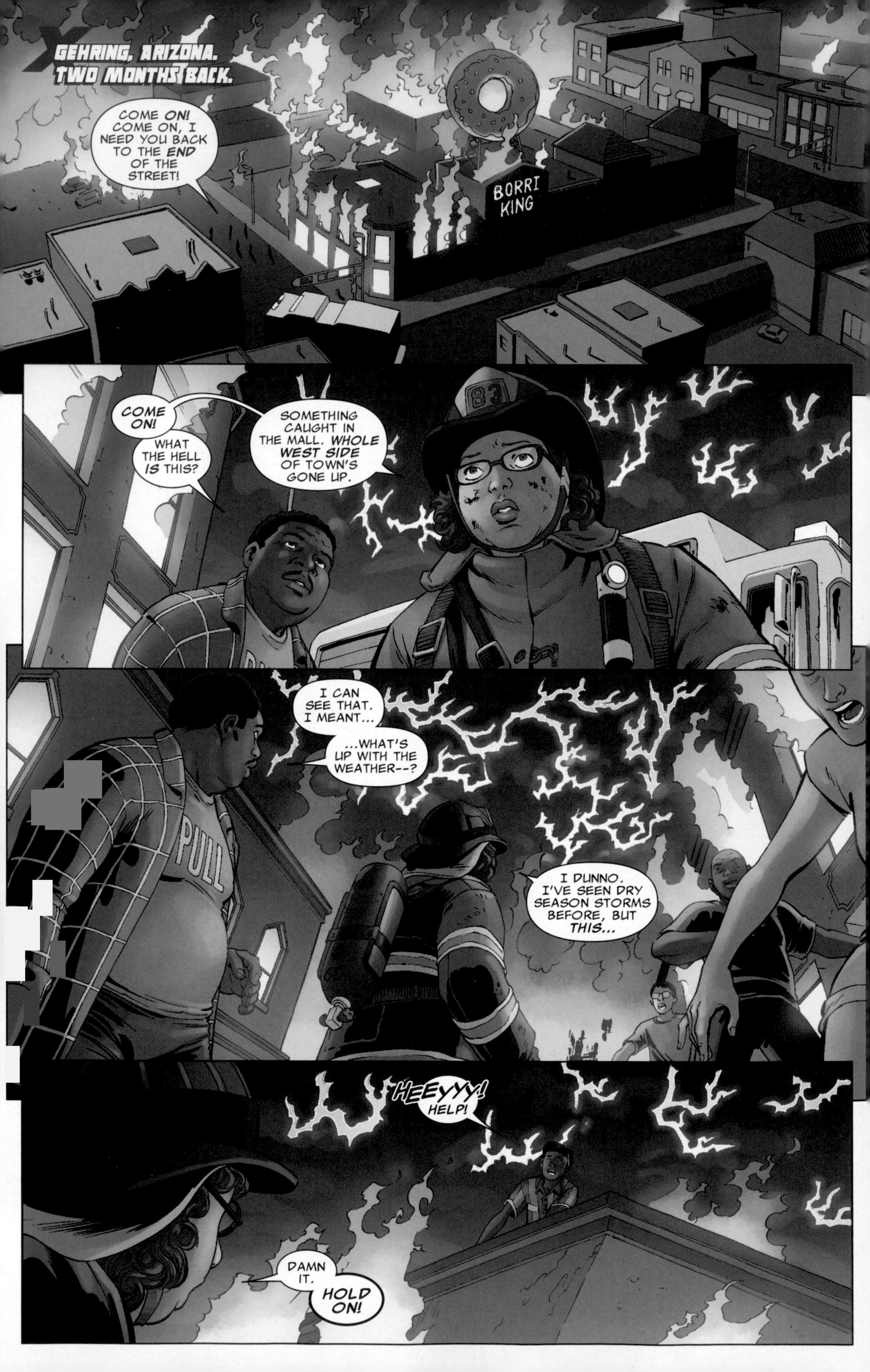
GEHRING, ARIZONA. TWO MONTHS BACK.
COME ON! COME ON, I NEED YOU BACK TO THE END OF THE STREET!
BORRI KING
COME ON!
WHAT THE HELL IS THIS?
SOMETHING CAUGHT IN THE MALL. WHOLE WEST SIDE OF TOWN'S GONE UP.
I CAN SEE THAT. I MEANT...
...WHAT'S UP WITH THE WEATHER--?
PULL
I DUNNO. I'VE SEEN DRY SEASON STORMS BEFORE, BUT THIS...
HEEYYY! HELP!
DAMN IT.
HOLD ON!

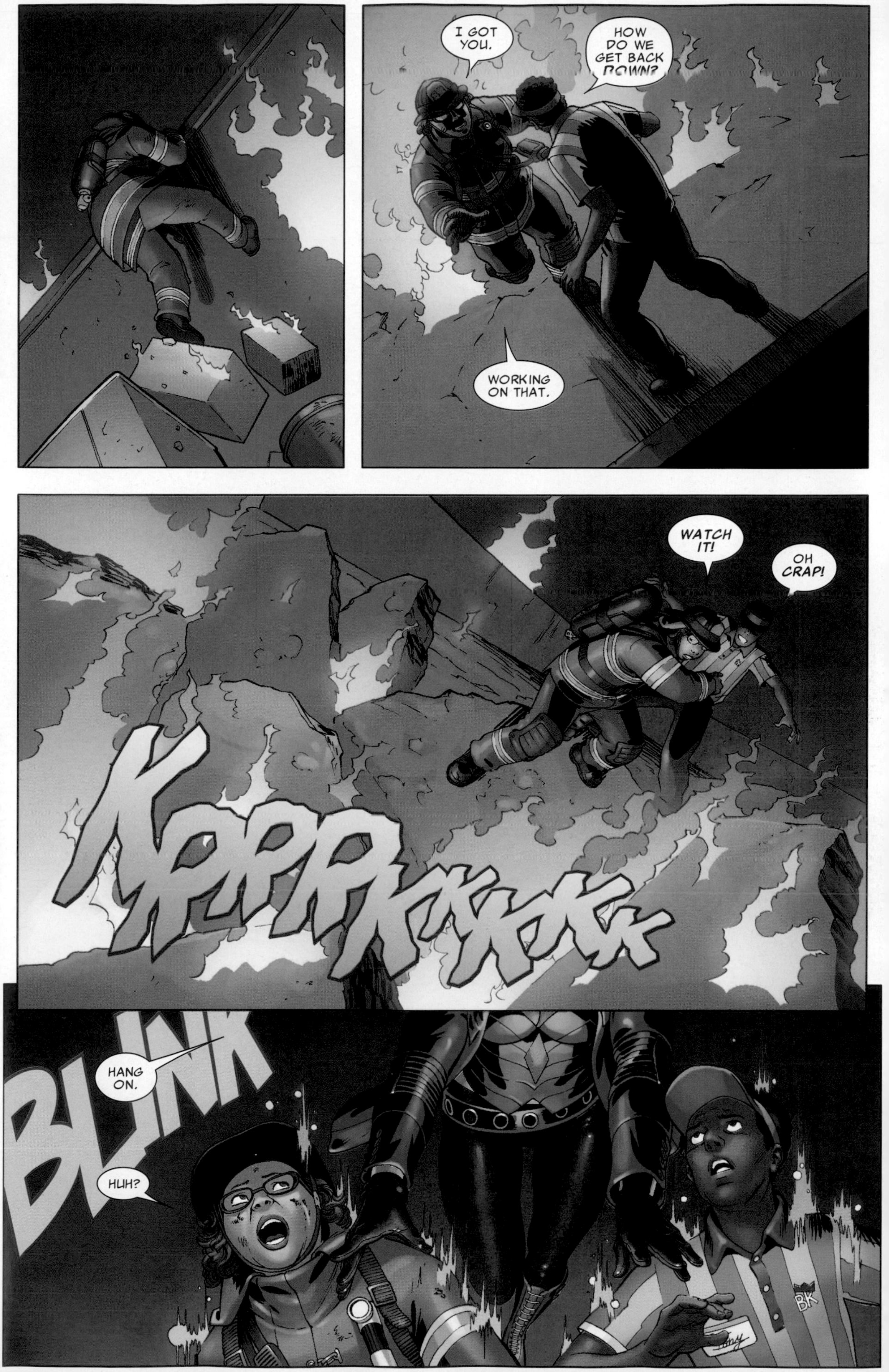
I GOT YOU.
HOW DO WE GET BACK DOWN?
WORKING ON THAT.
WATCH IT!
OH CRAP!
BLINK
HANG ON.
HUH?

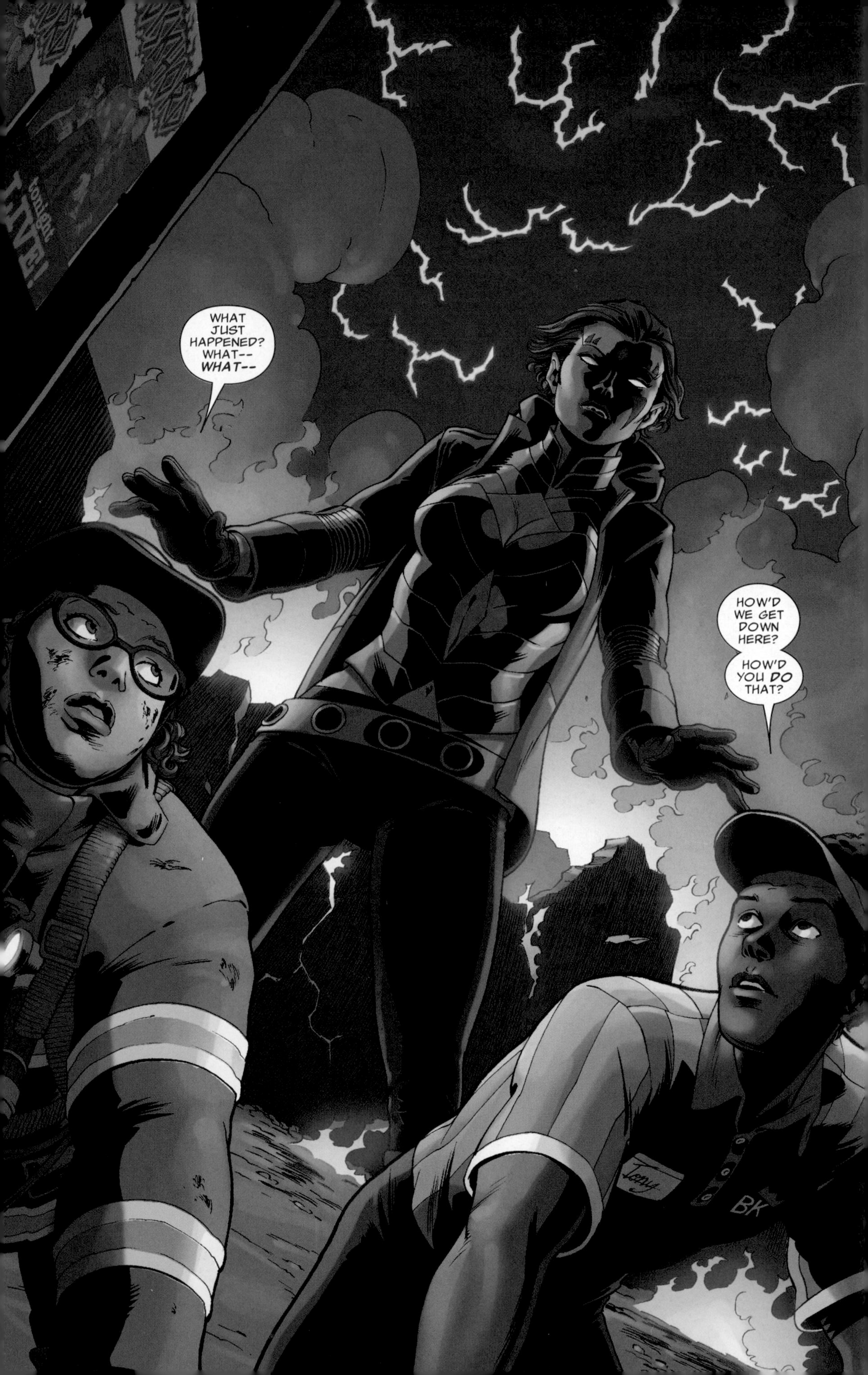
WHAT JUST HAPPENED? WHAT-- *WHAT--*
HOW'D WE GET DOWN HERE?
HOW'D YOU *DO* THAT?

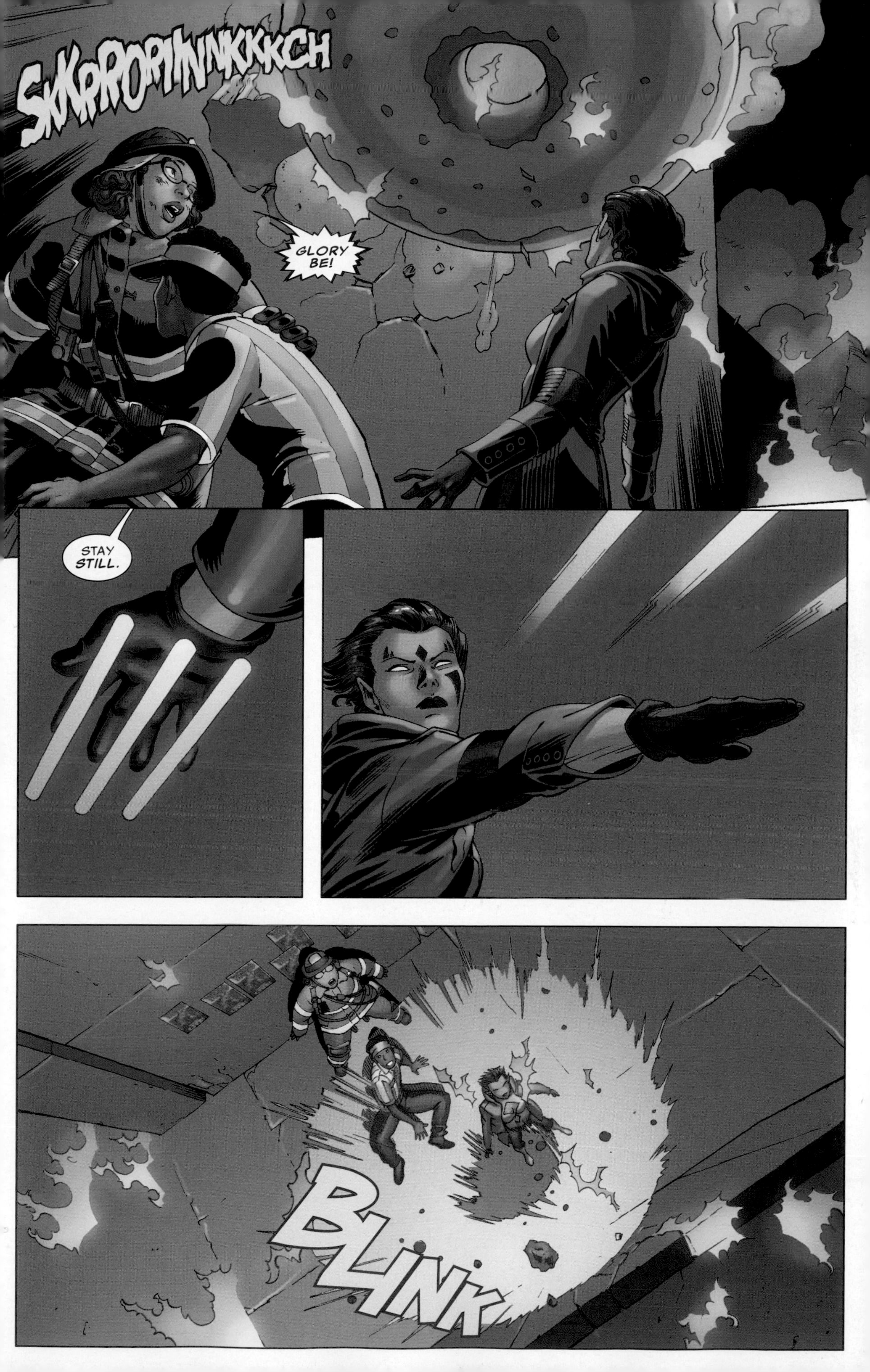
SKKPROPINNKKKCH
GLORY BE!
STAY STILL.
BLINK

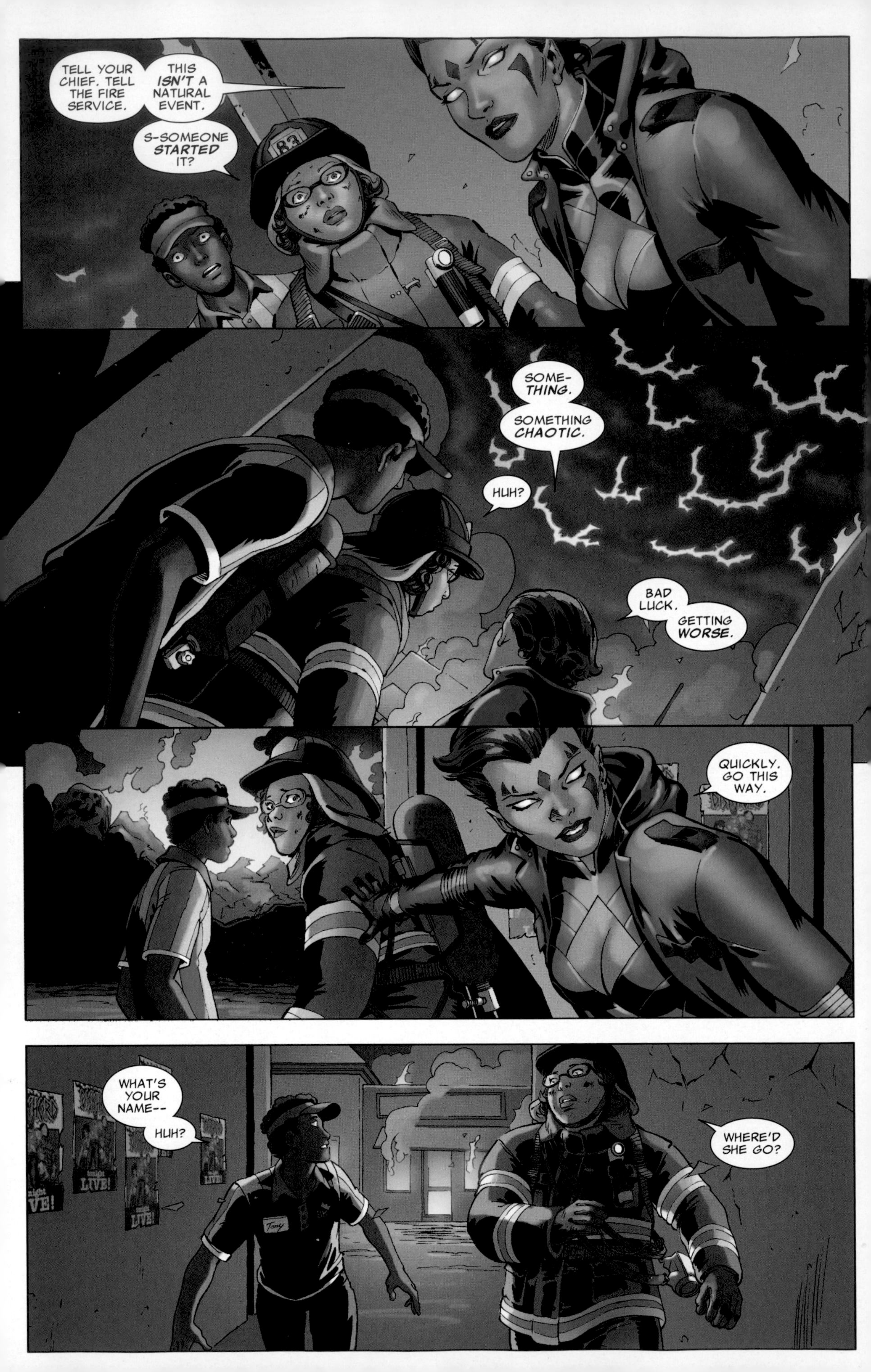
TELL YOUR CHIEF. TELL THE FIRE SERVICE.
THIS ISN'T A NATURAL EVENT.
S-SOMEONE STARTED IT?
SOME-THING.
SOMETHING CHAOTIC.
HUH?
BAD LUCK.
GETTING WORSE.
QUICKLY. GO THIS WAY.
WHAT'S YOUR NAME--
HUH?
WHERE'D SHE GO?

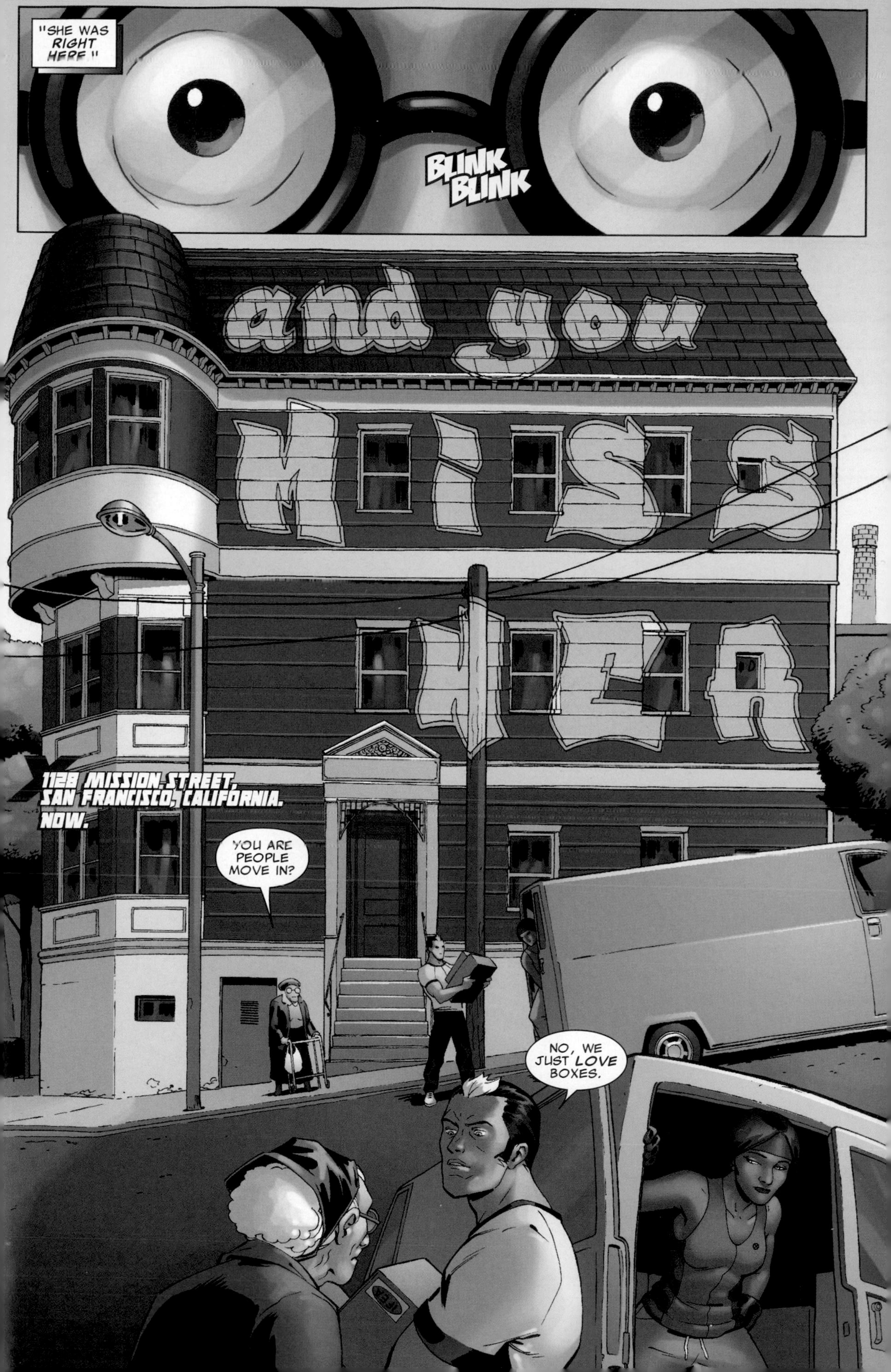
"SHE WAS RIGHT HERE."
BLINK BLINK
and you miss her
1128 MISSION STREET, SAN FRANCISCO, CALIFORNIA. NOW.
YOU ARE PEOPLE MOVE IN?
NO, WE JUST LOVE BOXES.

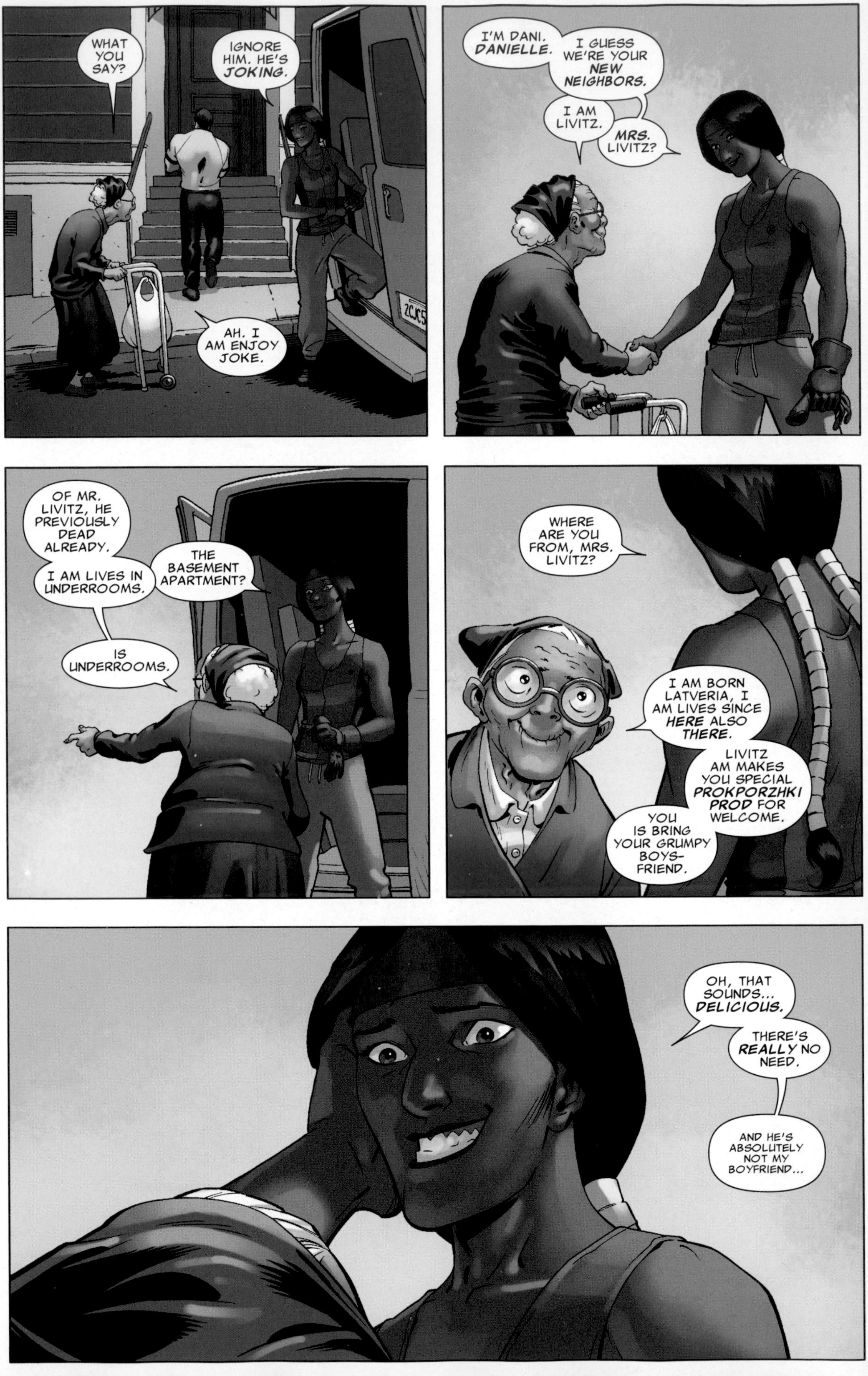
WHAT YOU SAY?
IGNORE HIM. HE'S JOKING.
AH. I AM ENJOY JOKE.
I'M DANI. DANIELLE.
I GUESS WE'RE YOUR NEW NEIGHBORS.
I AM LIVITZ.
MRS. LIVITZ?
OF MR. LIVITZ, HE PREVIOUSLY DEAD ALREADY.
I AM LIVES IN UNDERROOMS.
THE BASEMENT APARTMENT?
IS UNDERROOMS.
WHERE ARE YOU FROM, MRS. LIVITZ?
I AM BORN LATVERIA, I AM LIVES SINCE HERE ALSO THERE.
LIVITZ AM MAKES YOU SPECIAL PROKPORZHKI PROD FOR WELCOME.
YOU IS BRING YOUR GRUMPY BOYS-FRIEND.
OH, THAT SOUNDS... DELICIOUS.
THERE'S REALLY NO NEED.
AND HE'S ABSOLUTELY NOT MY BOYFRIEND...

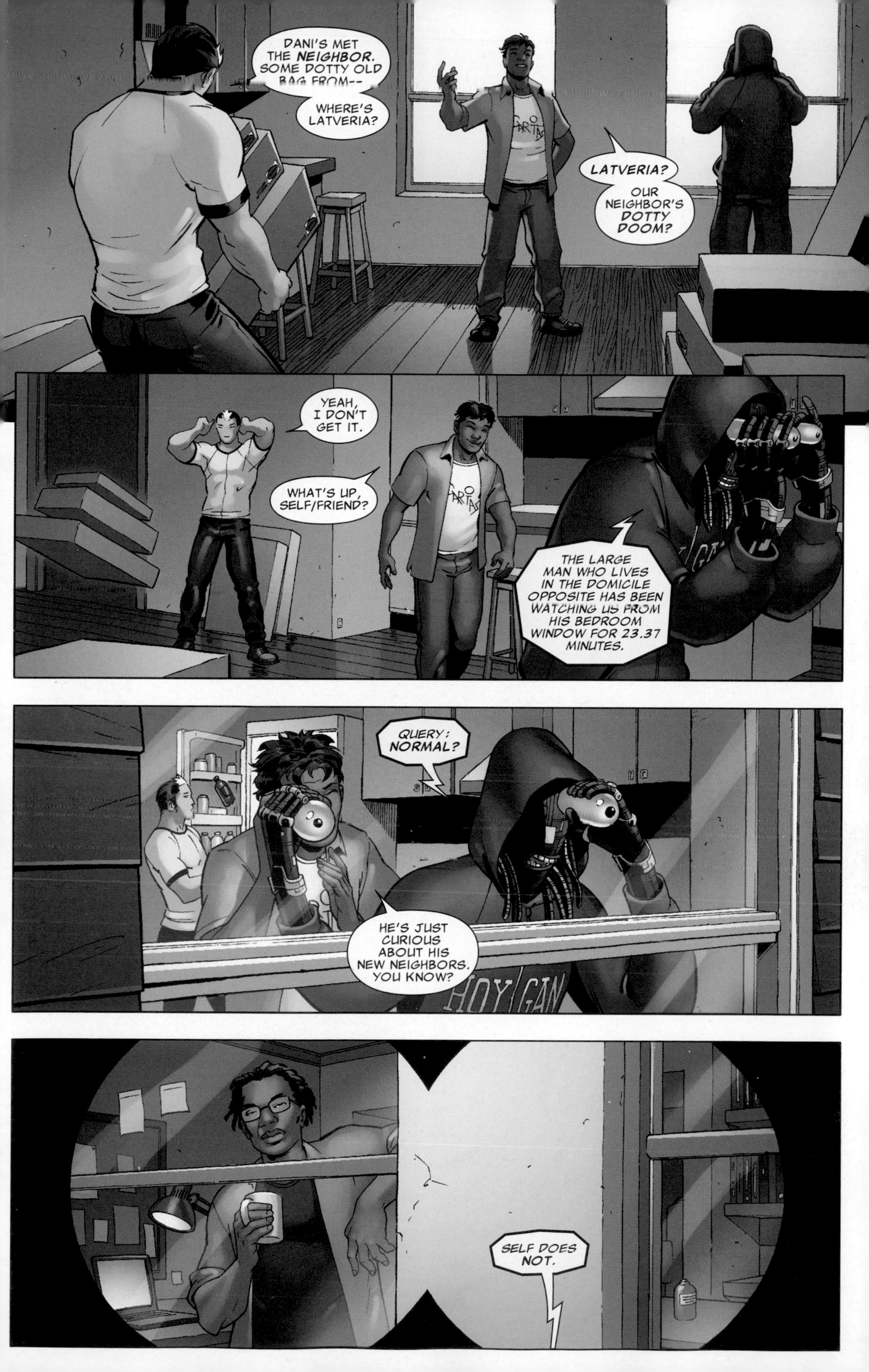
DANI'S MET THE NEIGHBOR. SOME DOTTY OLD BAG FROM--
WHERE'S LATVERIA?
LATVERIA?
OUR NEIGHBOR'S DOTTY DOOM?
YEAH, I DON'T GET IT.
WHAT'S UP, SELF/FRIEND?
THE LARGE MAN WHO LIVES IN THE DOMICILE OPPOSITE HAS BEEN WATCHING US FROM HIS BEDROOM WINDOW FOR 23.37 MINUTES.
QUERY: NORMAL?
HE'S JUST CURIOUS ABOUT HIS NEW NEIGHBORS. YOU KNOW?
SELF DOES NOT.

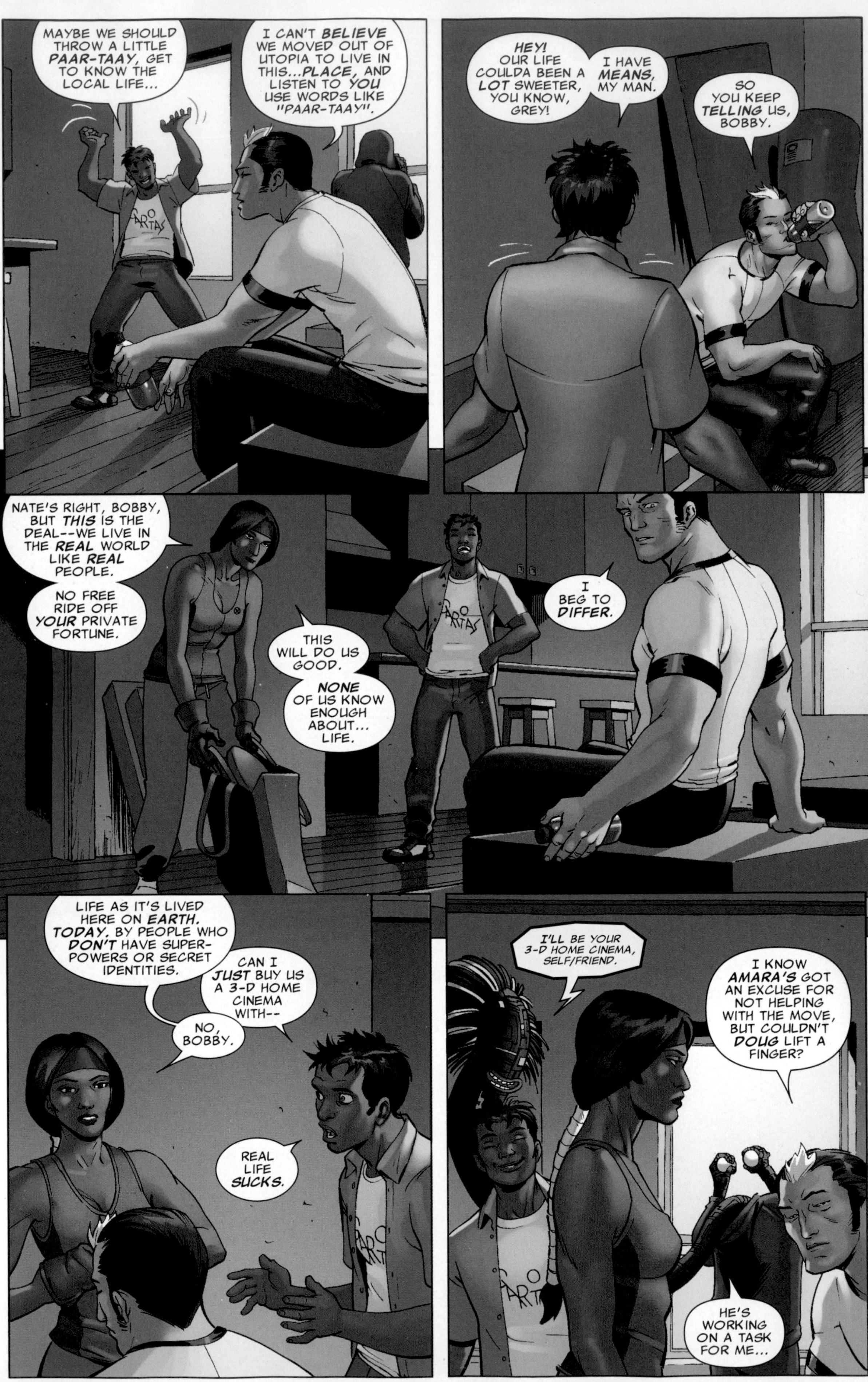
MAYBE WE SHOULD THROW A LITTLE PAAR-TAAY, GET TO KNOW THE LOCAL LIFE...
I CAN'T BELIEVE WE MOVED OUT OF UTOPIA TO LIVE IN THIS...PLACE, AND LISTEN TO YOU USE WORDS LIKE "PAAR-TAAY".
HEY! OUR LIFE COULDA BEEN A LOT SWEETER, YOU KNOW, GREY!
I HAVE MEANS, MY MAN.
SO YOU KEEP TELLING US, BOBBY.
NATE'S RIGHT, BOBBY, BUT THIS IS THE DEAL--WE LIVE IN THE REAL WORLD LIKE REAL PEOPLE.
NO FREE RIDE OFF YOUR PRIVATE FORTUNE.
THIS WILL DO US GOOD.
NONE OF US KNOW ENOUGH ABOUT... LIFE.
I BEG TO DIFFER.
LIFE AS IT'S LIVED HERE ON EARTH. TODAY. BY PEOPLE WHO DON'T HAVE SUPER-POWERS OR SECRET IDENTITIES.
CAN I JUST BUY US A 3-D HOME CINEMA WITH--
NO, BOBBY.
REAL LIFE SUCKS.
I'LL BE YOUR 3-D HOME CINEMA, SELF/FRIEND.
I KNOW AMARA'S GOT AN EXCUSE FOR NOT HELPING WITH THE MOVE, BUT COULDN'T DOUG LIFT A FINGER?
HE'S WORKING ON A TASK FOR ME...

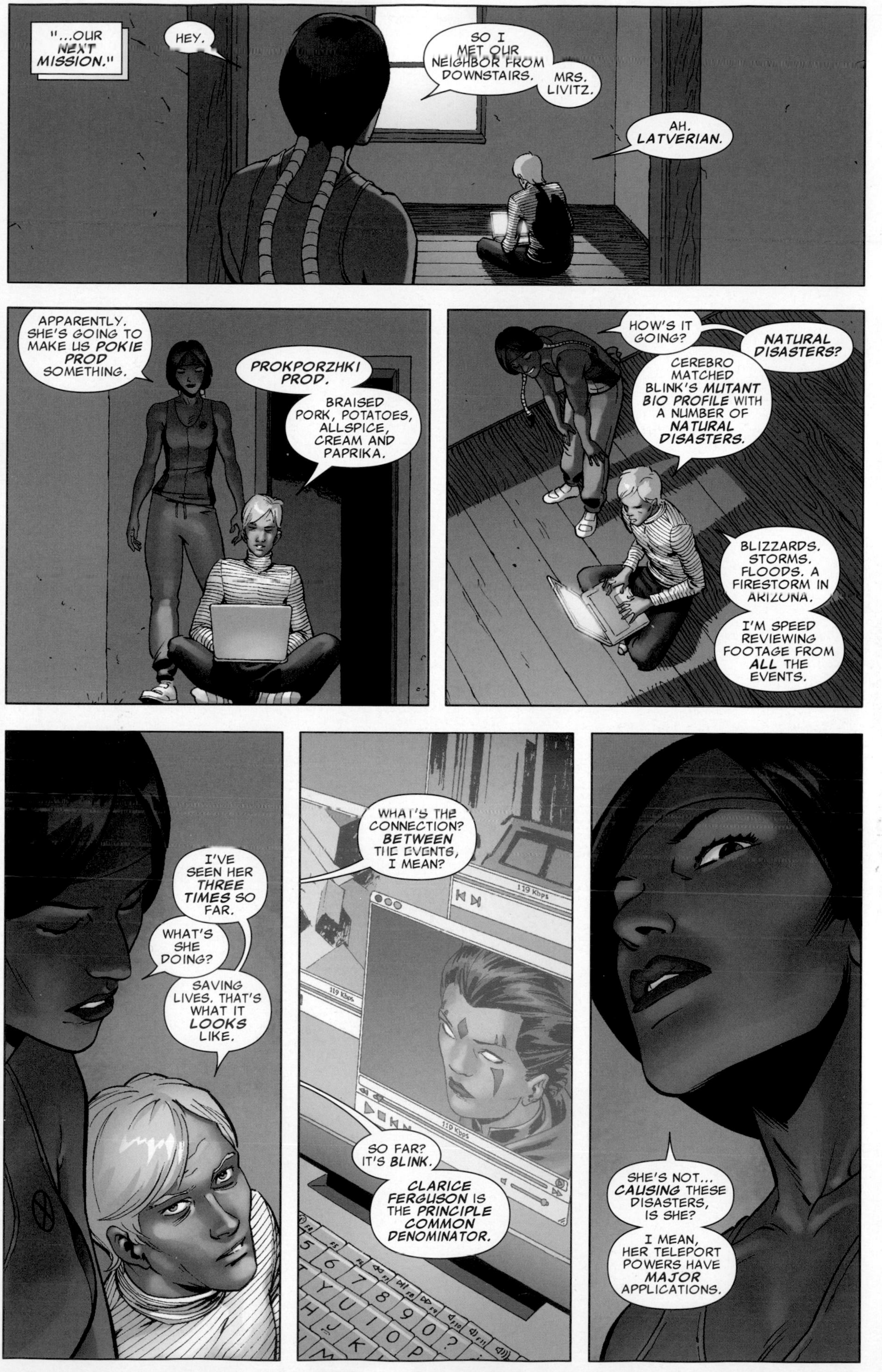
"...OUR NEXT MISSION."
HEY.
SO I MET OUR NEIGHBOR FROM DOWNSTAIRS.
MRS. LIVITZ.
AH. LATVERIAN.
APPARENTLY. SHE'S GOING TO MAKE US POKIE PROD SOMETHING.
PROKPORZHKI PROD.
BRAISED PORK, POTATOES, ALLSPICE, CREAM AND PAPRIKA.
HOW'S IT GOING?
NATURAL DISASTERS?
CEREBRO MATCHED BLINK'S MUTANT BIO PROFILE WITH A NUMBER OF NATURAL DISASTERS.
BLIZZARDS. STORMS. FLOODS. A FIRESTORM IN ARIZONA.
I'M SPEED REVIEWING FOOTAGE FROM ALL THE EVENTS.
I'VE SEEN HER THREE TIMES SO FAR.
WHAT'S SHE DOING?
SAVING LIVES. THAT'S WHAT IT LOOKS LIKE.
WHAT'S THE CONNECTION? BETWEEN THE EVENTS, I MEAN?
SO FAR? IT'S BLINK.
CLARICE FERGUSON IS THE PRINCIPLE COMMON DENOMINATOR.
SHE'S NOT... CAUSING THESE DISASTERS, IS SHE?
I MEAN, HER TELEPORT POWERS HAVE MAJOR APPLICATIONS.

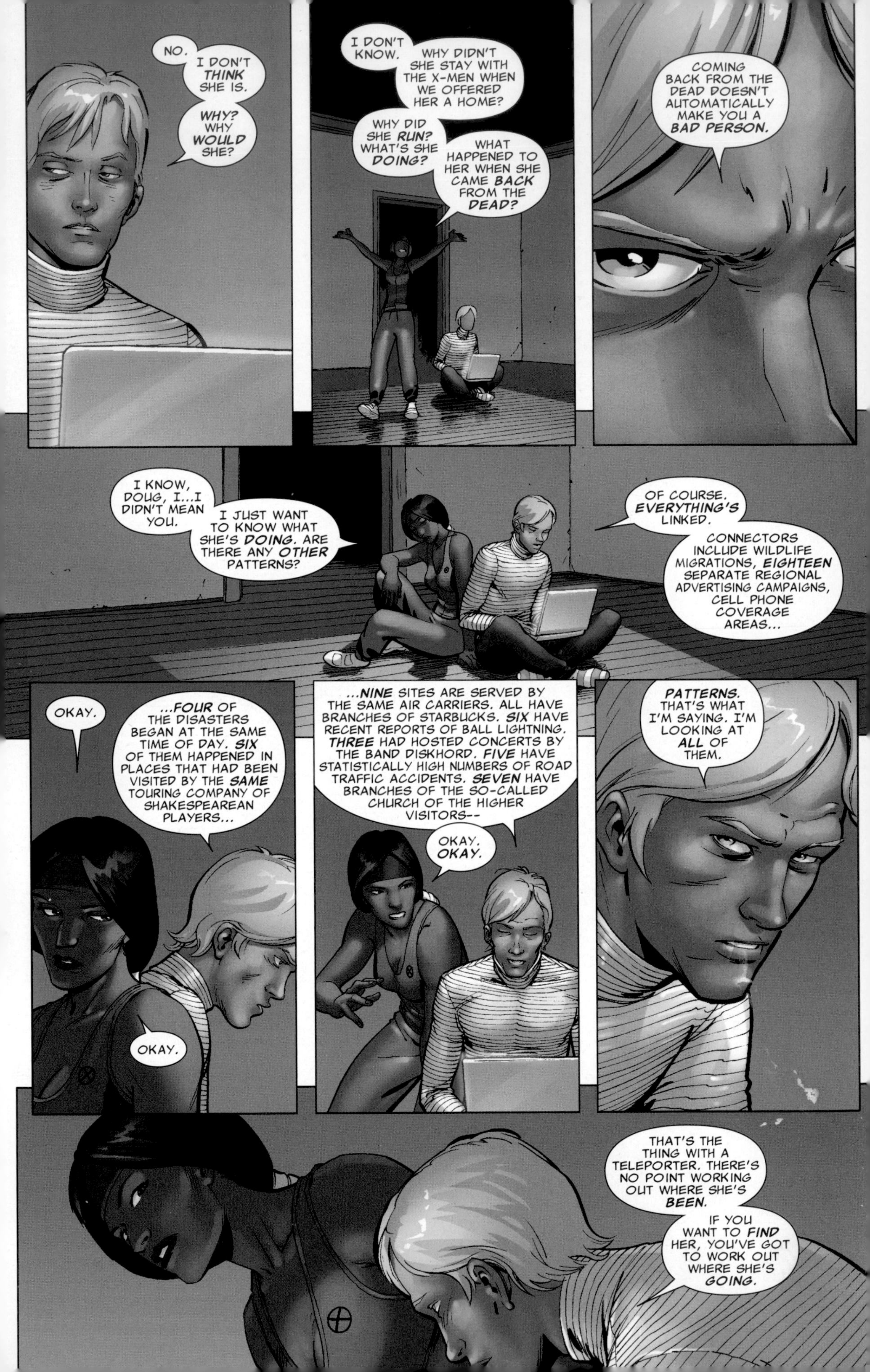
NO.
I DON'T THINK SHE IS.
WHY? WHY WOULD SHE?
I DON'T KNOW.
WHY DIDN'T SHE STAY WITH THE X-MEN WHEN WE OFFERED HER A HOME?
WHY DID SHE RUN? WHAT'S SHE DOING?
WHAT HAPPENED TO HER WHEN SHE CAME BACK FROM THE DEAD?
COMING BACK FROM THE DEAD DOESN'T AUTOMATICALLY MAKE YOU A BAD PERSON.
I KNOW, DOUG, I...I DIDN'T MEAN YOU.
I JUST WANT TO KNOW WHAT SHE'S DOING. ARE THERE ANY OTHER PATTERNS?
OF COURSE. EVERYTHING'S LINKED.
CONNECTORS INCLUDE WILDLIFE MIGRATIONS, EIGHTEEN SEPARATE REGIONAL ADVERTISING CAMPAIGNS, CELL PHONE COVERAGE AREAS...
OKAY.
...FOUR OF THE DISASTERS BEGAN AT THE SAME TIME OF DAY. SIX OF THEM HAPPENED IN PLACES THAT HAD BEEN VISITED BY THE SAME TOURING COMPANY OF SHAKESPEAREAN PLAYERS...
OKAY.
...NINE SITES ARE SERVED BY THE SAME AIR CARRIERS. ALL HAVE BRANCHES OF STARBUCKS. SIX HAVE RECENT REPORTS OF BALL LIGHTNING. THREE HAD HOSTED CONCERTS BY THE BAND DISKHORD. FIVE HAVE STATISTICALLY HIGH NUMBERS OF ROAD TRAFFIC ACCIDENTS. SEVEN HAVE BRANCHES OF THE SO-CALLED CHURCH OF THE HIGHER VISITORS--
OKAY. OKAY.
PATTERNS. THAT'S WHAT I'M SAYING. I'M LOOKING AT ALL OF THEM.
THAT'S THE THING WITH A TELEPORTER. THERE'S NO POINT WORKING OUT WHERE SHE'S BEEN.
IF YOU WANT TO FIND HER, YOU'VE GOT TO WORK OUT WHERE SHE'S GOING.

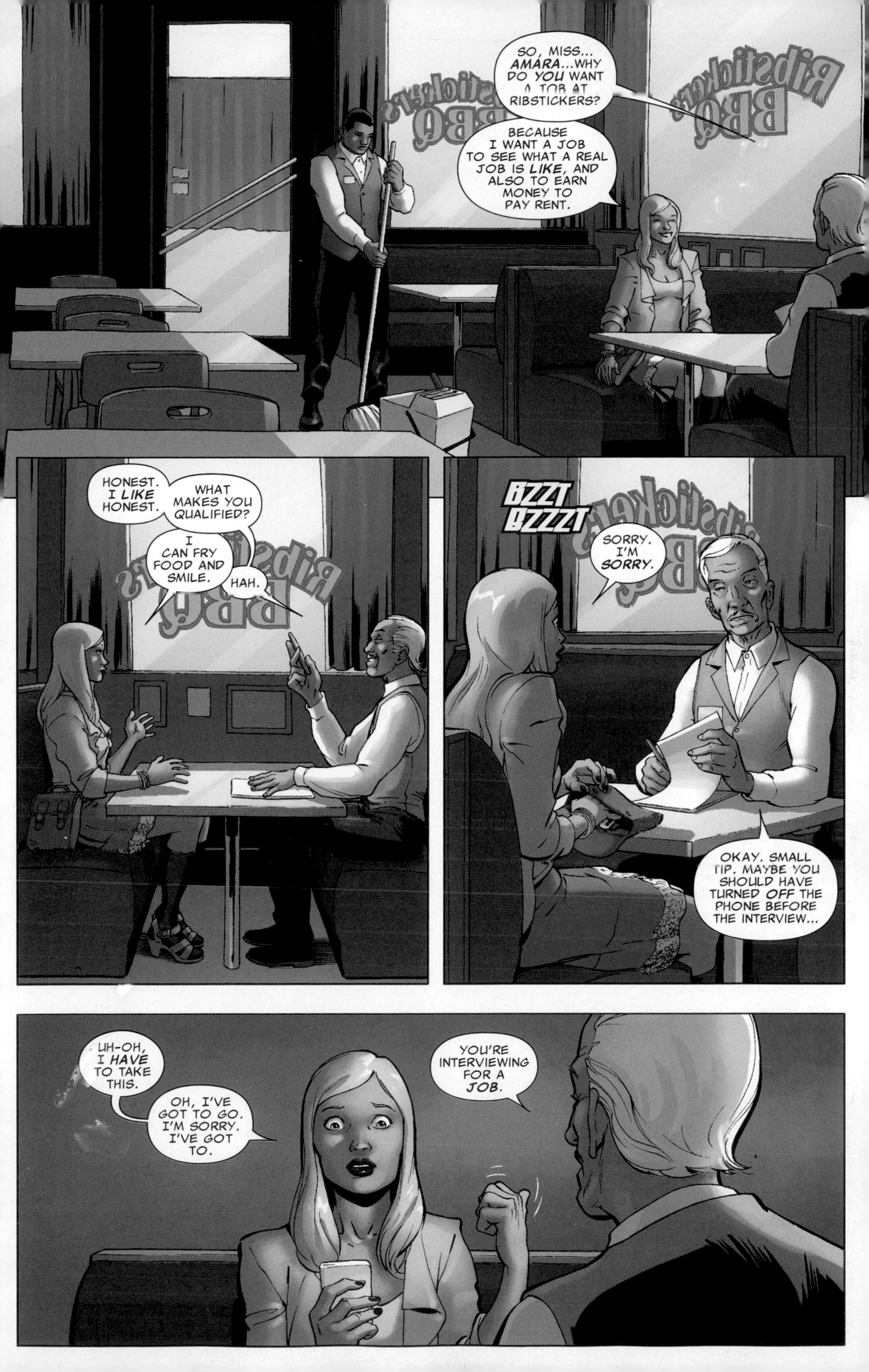
SO, MISS... AMARA...WHY DO YOU WANT A JOB AT RIBSTICKERS?
BECAUSE I WANT A JOB TO SEE WHAT A REAL JOB IS LIKE, AND ALSO TO EARN MONEY TO PAY RENT.
RIBSTICKERS BBQ
HONEST. I LIKE HONEST.
WHAT MAKES YOU QUALIFIED?
I CAN FRY FOOD AND SMILE.
HAH.
BZZT BZZZT
SORRY. I'M SORRY.
OKAY. SMALL TIP. MAYBE YOU SHOULD HAVE TURNED OFF THE PHONE BEFORE THE INTERVIEW...
UH-OH, I HAVE TO TAKE THIS.
OH, I'VE GOT TO GO. I'M SORRY. I'VE GOT TO.
YOU'RE INTERVIEWING FOR A JOB.

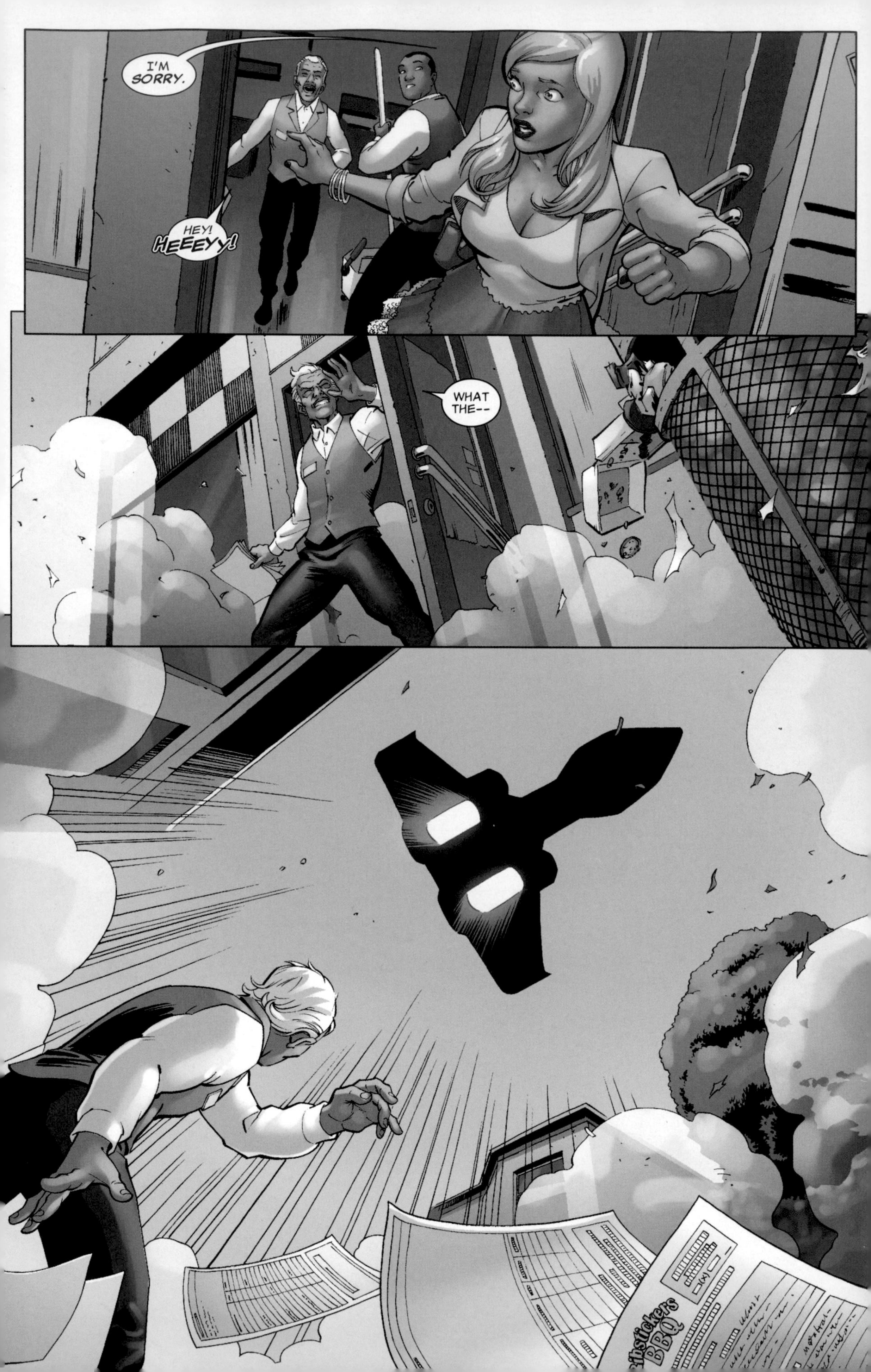
I'M SORRY.
HEY! HEEEYY!
WHAT THE--

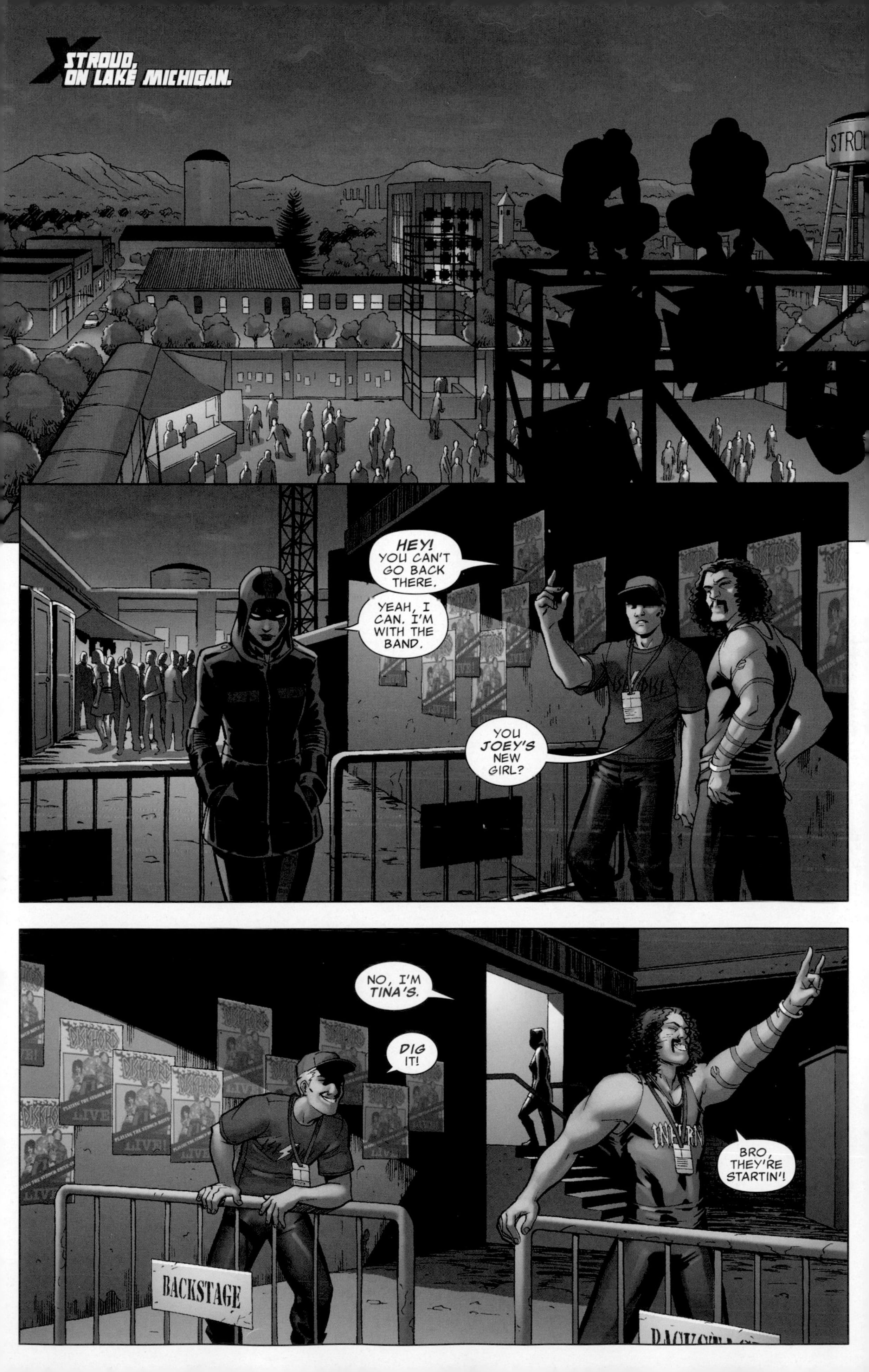
STROUD, ON LAKE MICHIGAN.
STROU
HEY! YOU CAN'T GO BACK THERE.
YEAH, I CAN. I'M WITH THE BAND.
YOU JOEY'S NEW GIRL?
NO, I'M TINA'S.
DIG IT!
BRO, THEY'RE STARTIN'!
BACKSTAGE

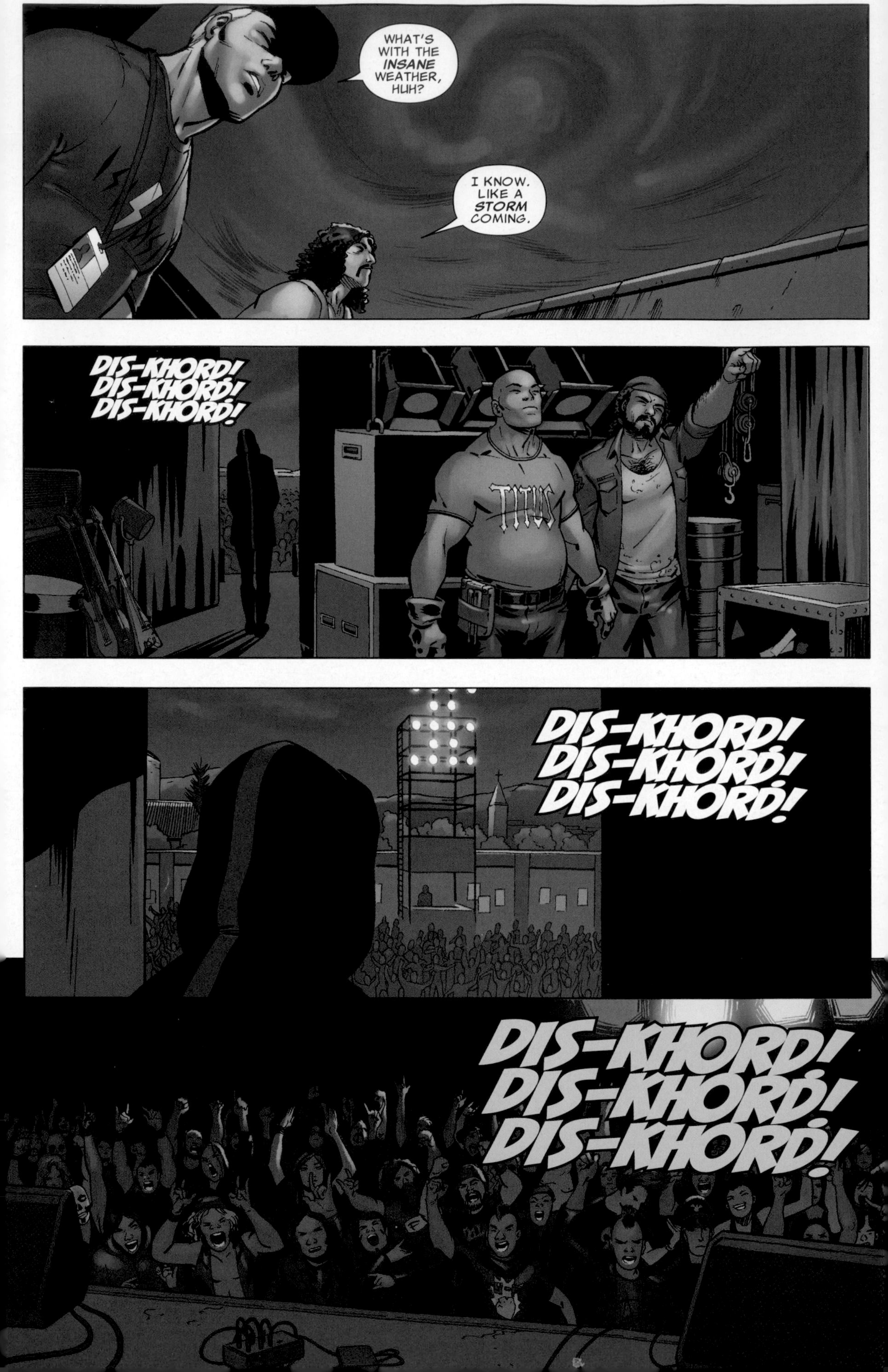
WHAT'S WITH THE INSANE WEATHER, HUH?
I KNOW. LIKE A STORM COMING.
DIS-KHORD! DIS-KHORD! DIS-KHORD!
TITUS
DIS-KHORD! DIS-KHORD! DIS-KHORD!
DIS-KHORD! DIS-KHORD! DIS-KHORD!

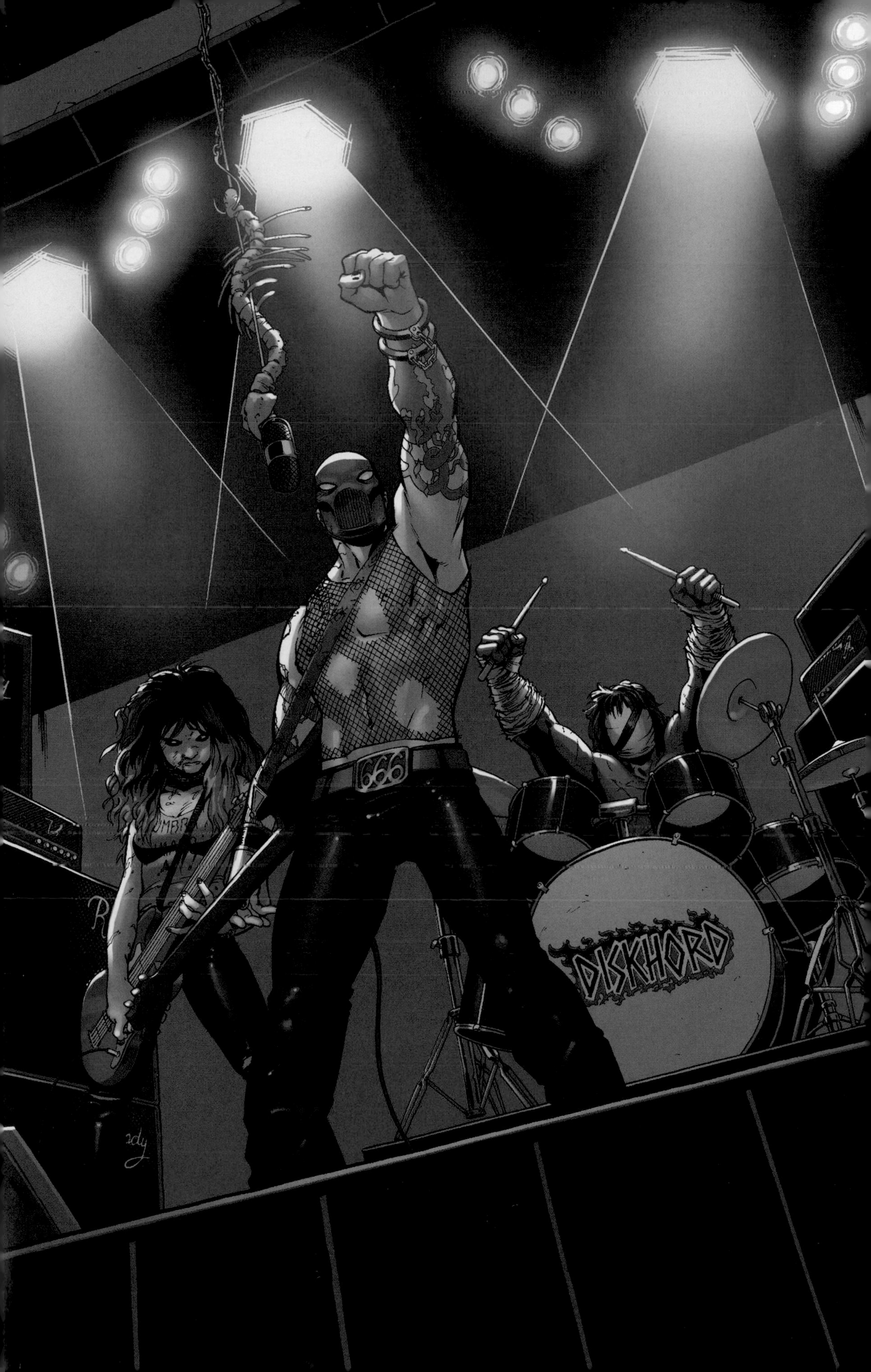
666
DISKHORD

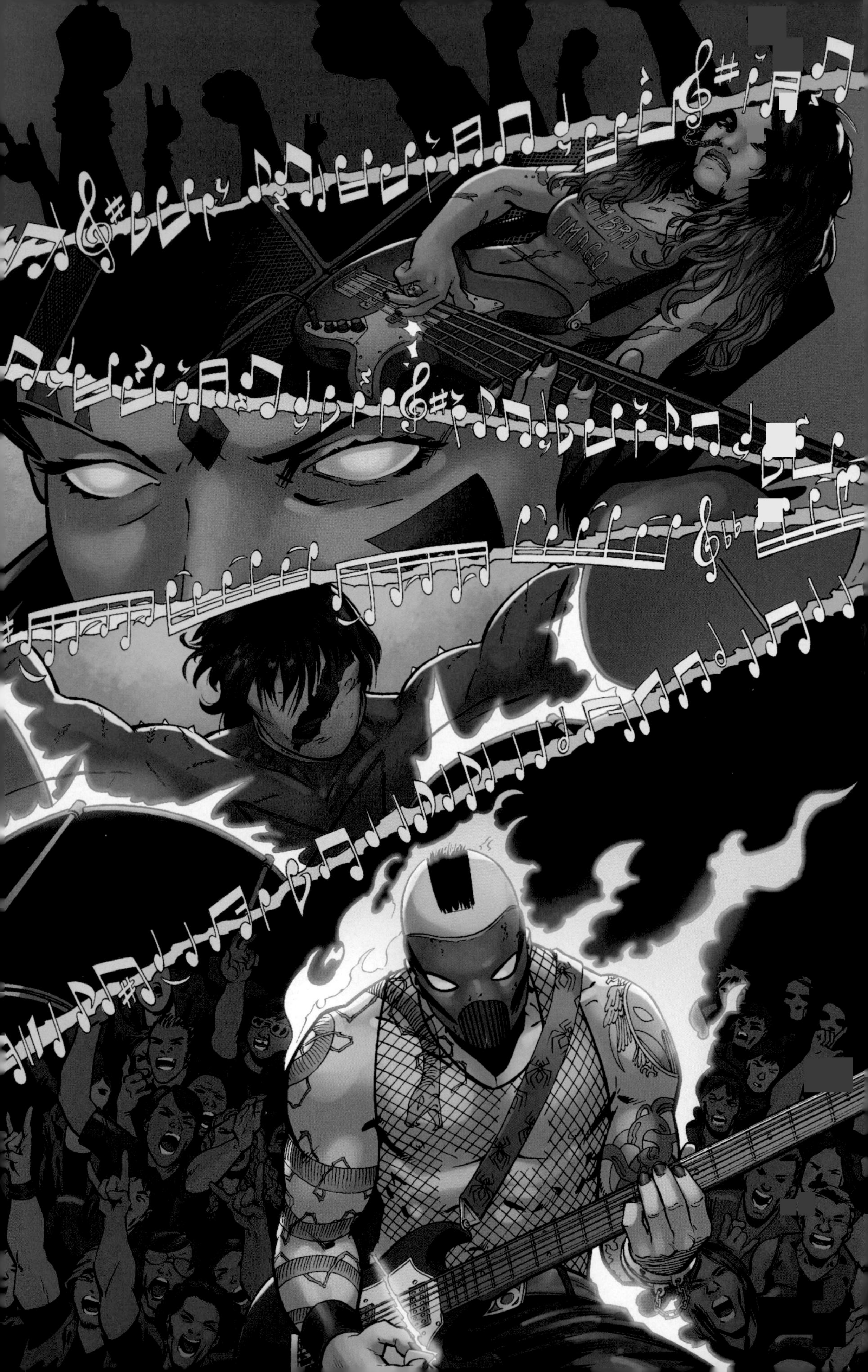
UMBRA
IMAGO

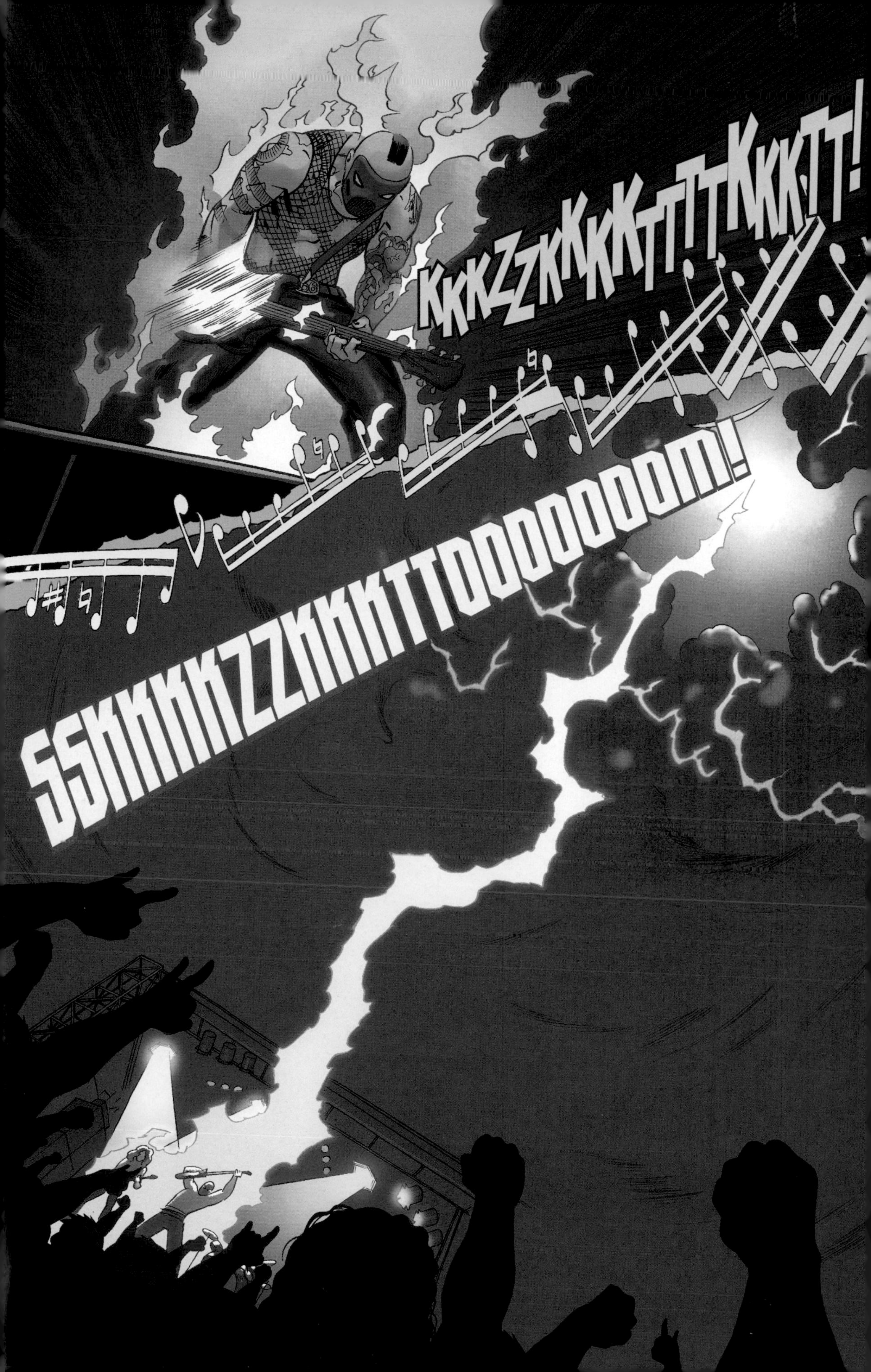
KKKZZKKKKTTTTTKKKTT!
SSHKKKKZZKKKKTTOOOOOOOOOM!

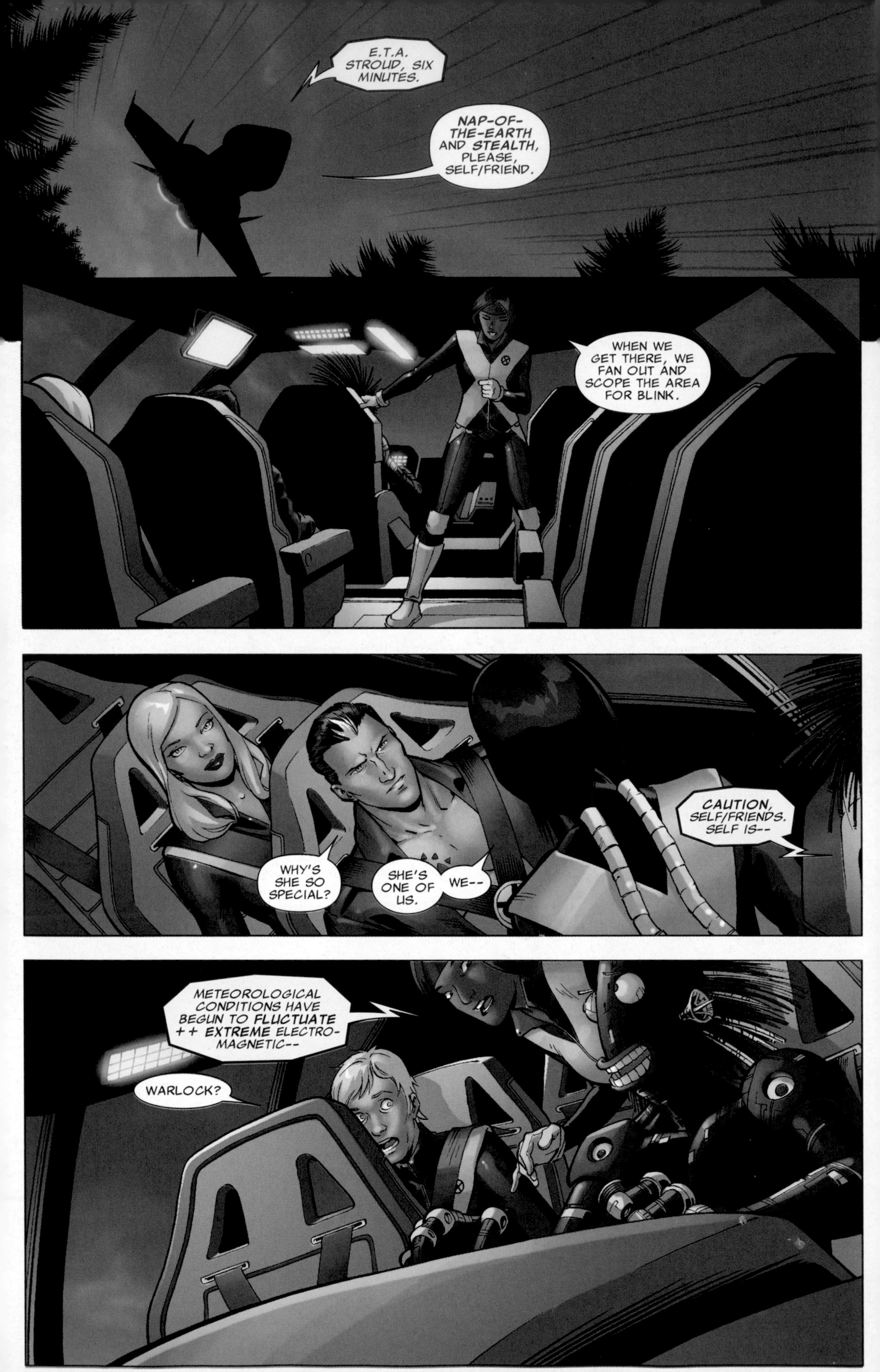
E.T.A. STROUD, SIX MINUTES.
NAP-OF-THE-EARTH AND STEALTH, PLEASE, SELF/FRIEND.
WHEN WE GET THERE, WE FAN OUT AND SCOPE THE AREA FOR BLINK.
WHY'S SHE SO SPECIAL?
SHE'S ONE OF US.
WE--
CAUTION, SELF/FRIENDS. SELF IS--
METEOROLOGICAL CONDITIONS HAVE BEGUN TO FLUCTUATE ++ EXTREME ELECTRO-MAGNETIC--
WARLOCK?

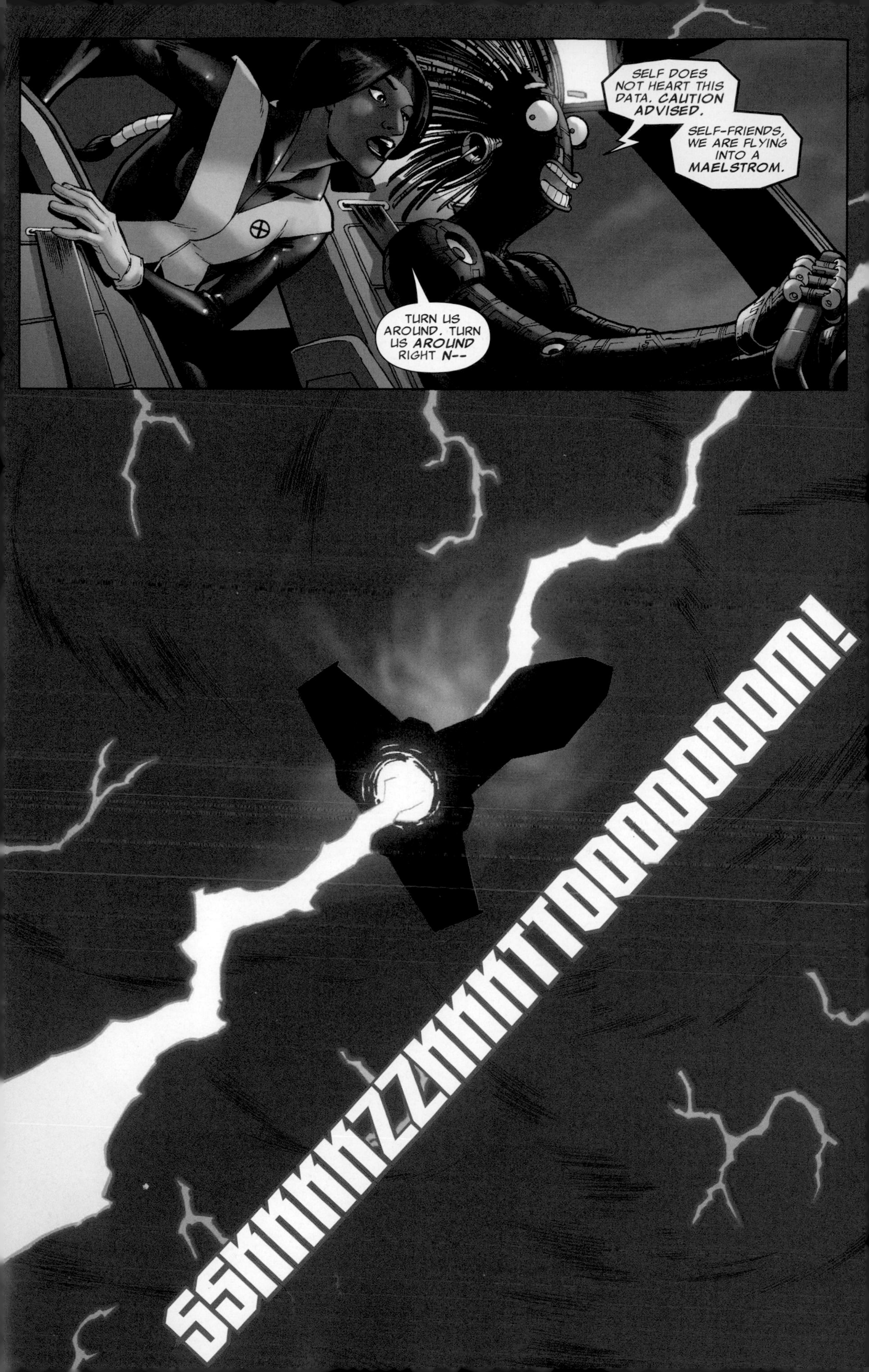
SELF DOES NOT HEART THIS DATA. CAUTION ADVISED.
SELF-FRIENDS, WE ARE FLYING INTO A MAELSTROM.
TURN US AROUND. TURN US AROUND RIGHT N--
SSKKKKZZKKKTOOOOOOOOOM!

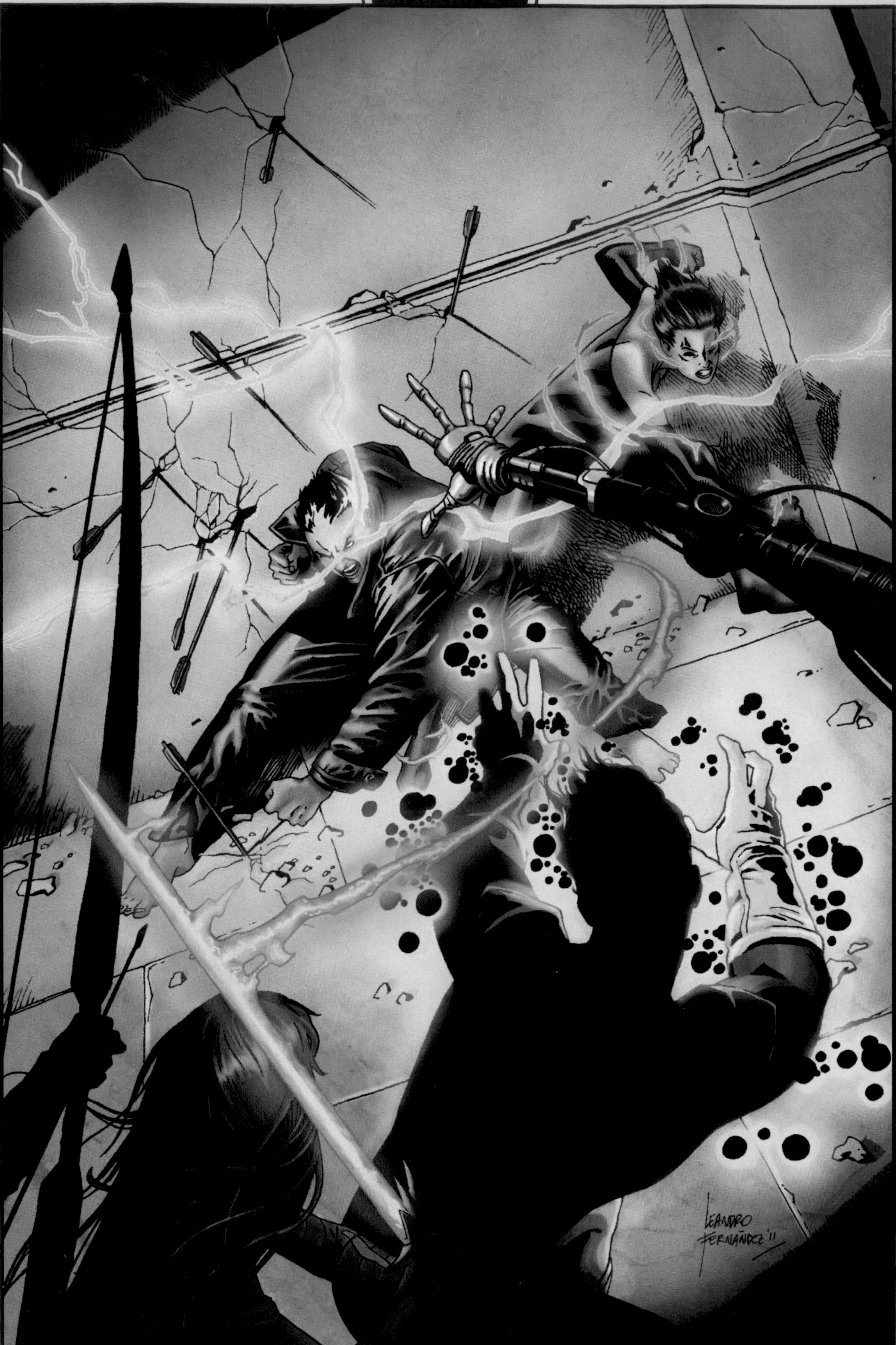
LEANDRO FERNANDEZ '11

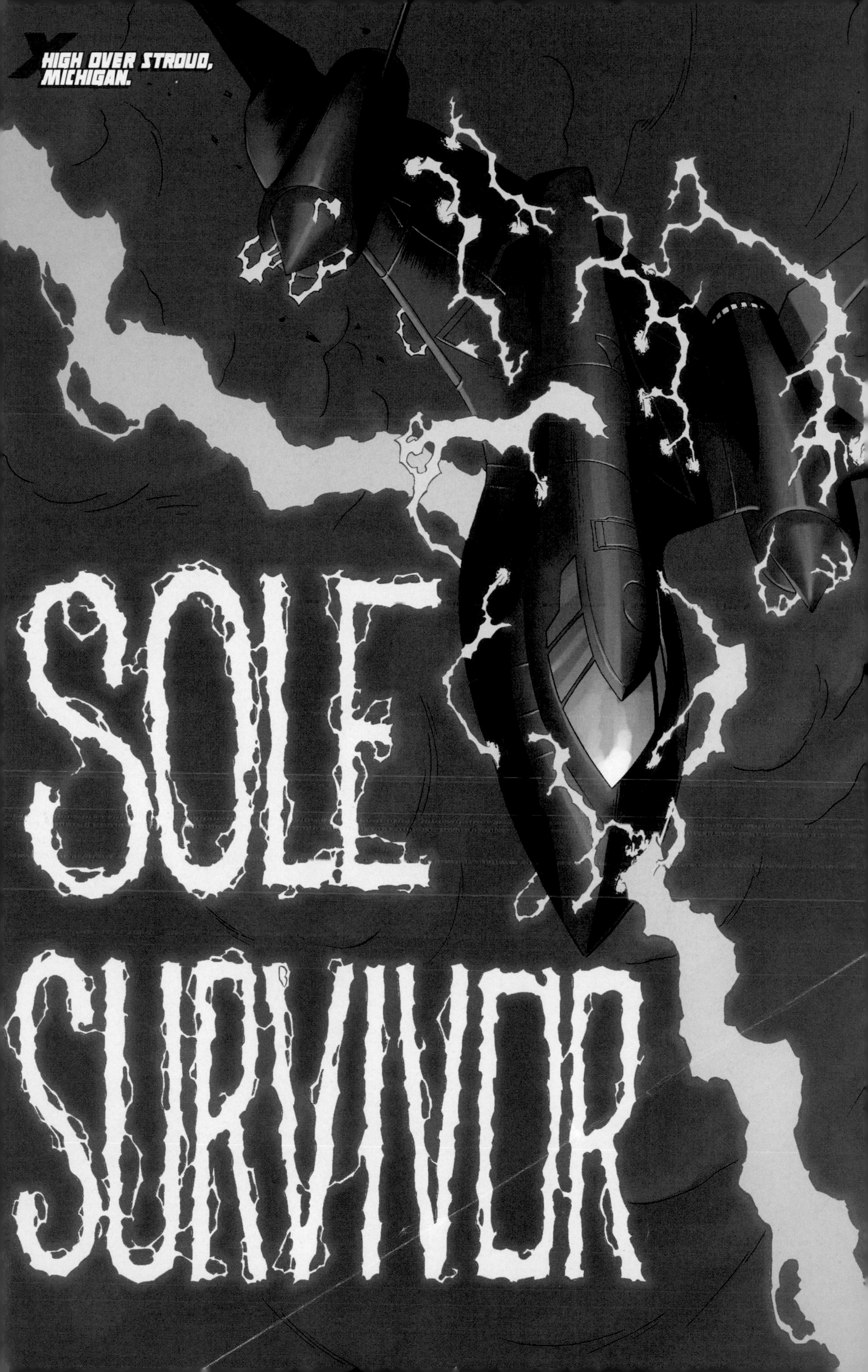
HIGH OVER STROUD, MICHIGAN.
SOLE SURVIVOR

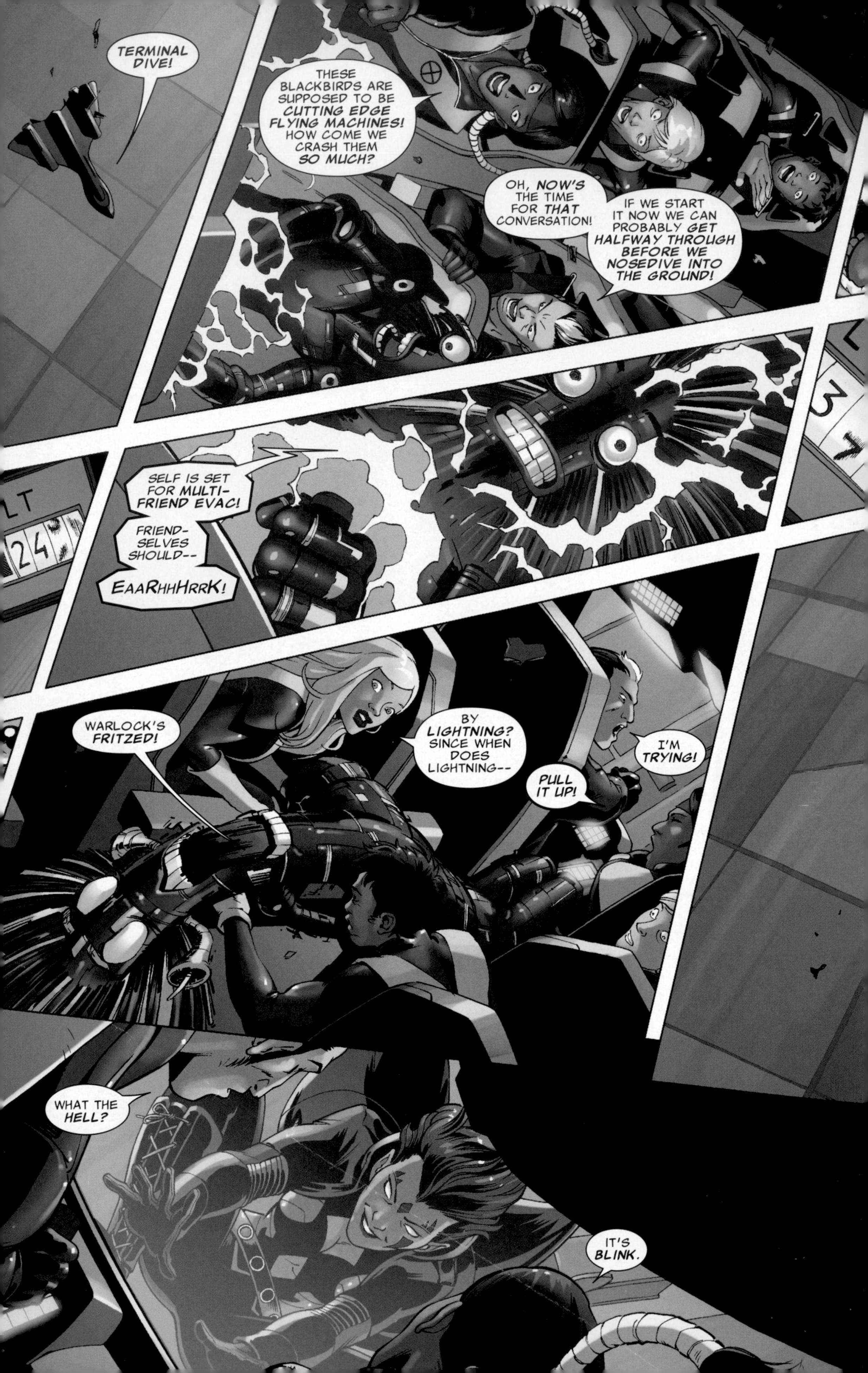
TERMINAL DIVE!
THESE BLACKBIRDS ARE SUPPOSED TO BE CUTTING EDGE FLYING MACHINES! HOW COME WE CRASH THEM SO MUCH?
OH, NOW'S THE TIME FOR THAT CONVERSATION!
IF WE START IT NOW WE CAN PROBABLY GET HALFWAY THROUGH BEFORE WE NOSEDIVE INTO THE GROUND!
SELF IS SET FOR MULTI-FRIEND EVAC!
FRIEND-SELVES SHOULD--
EAARHHHRRK!
WARLOCK'S FRITZED!
BY LIGHTNING? SINCE WHEN DOES LIGHTNING--
I'M TRYING!
PULL IT UP!
WHAT THE HELL?
IT'S BLINK.

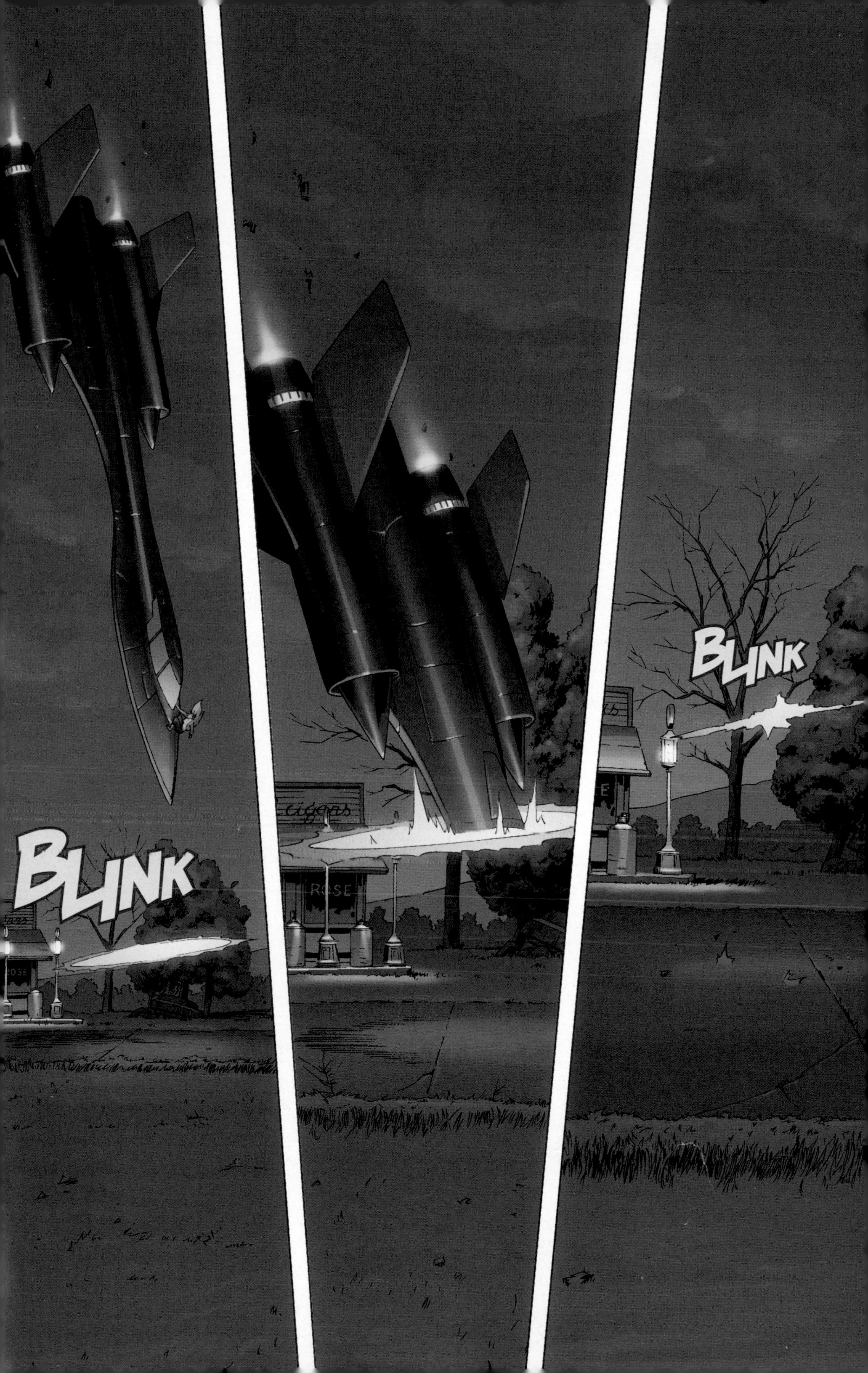
BLINK
ROSE
cigars
ROSE
BLINK

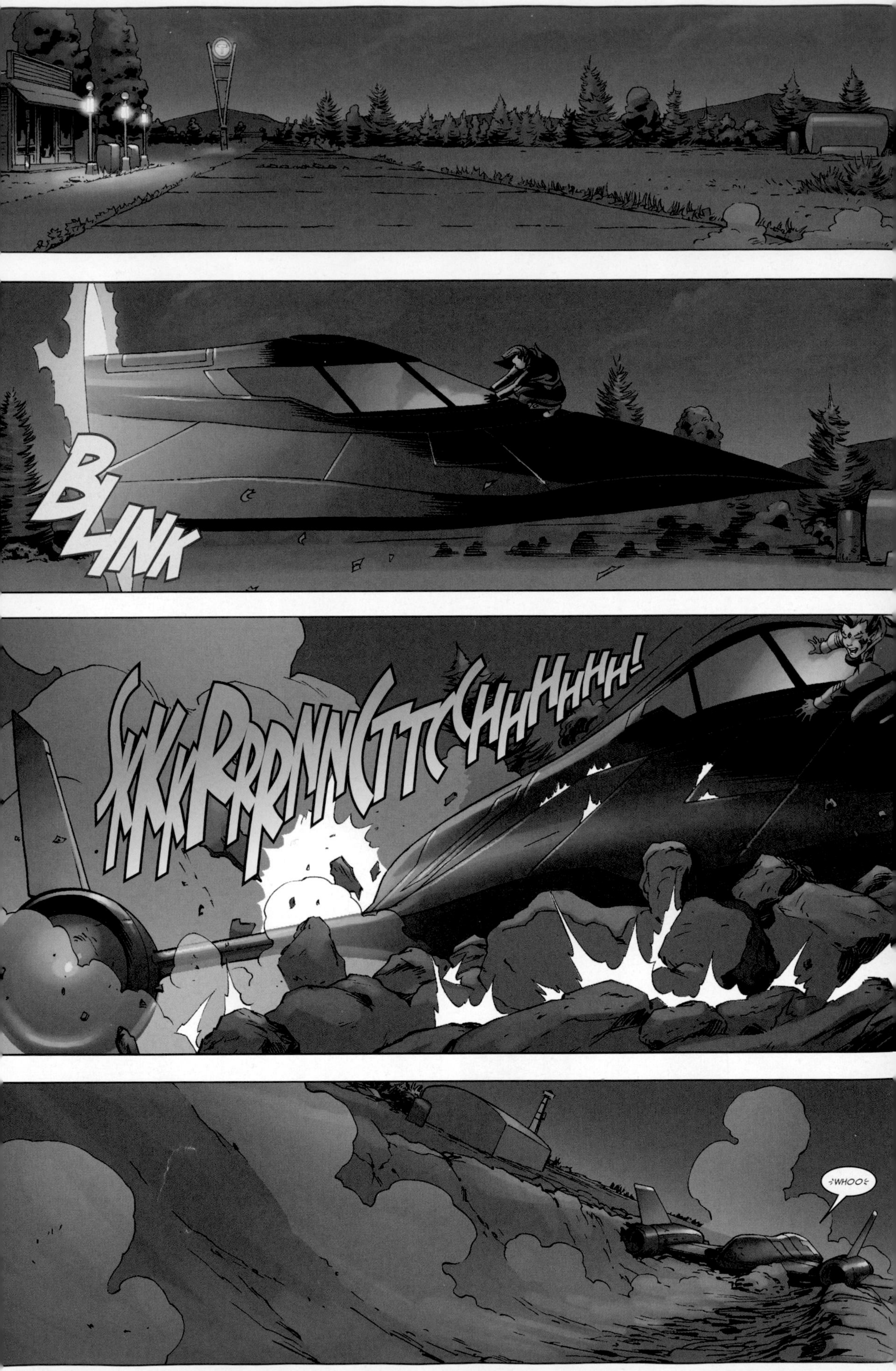
BLINK
SKKKRRRNNGTTTCHHHHHH!
WHOO

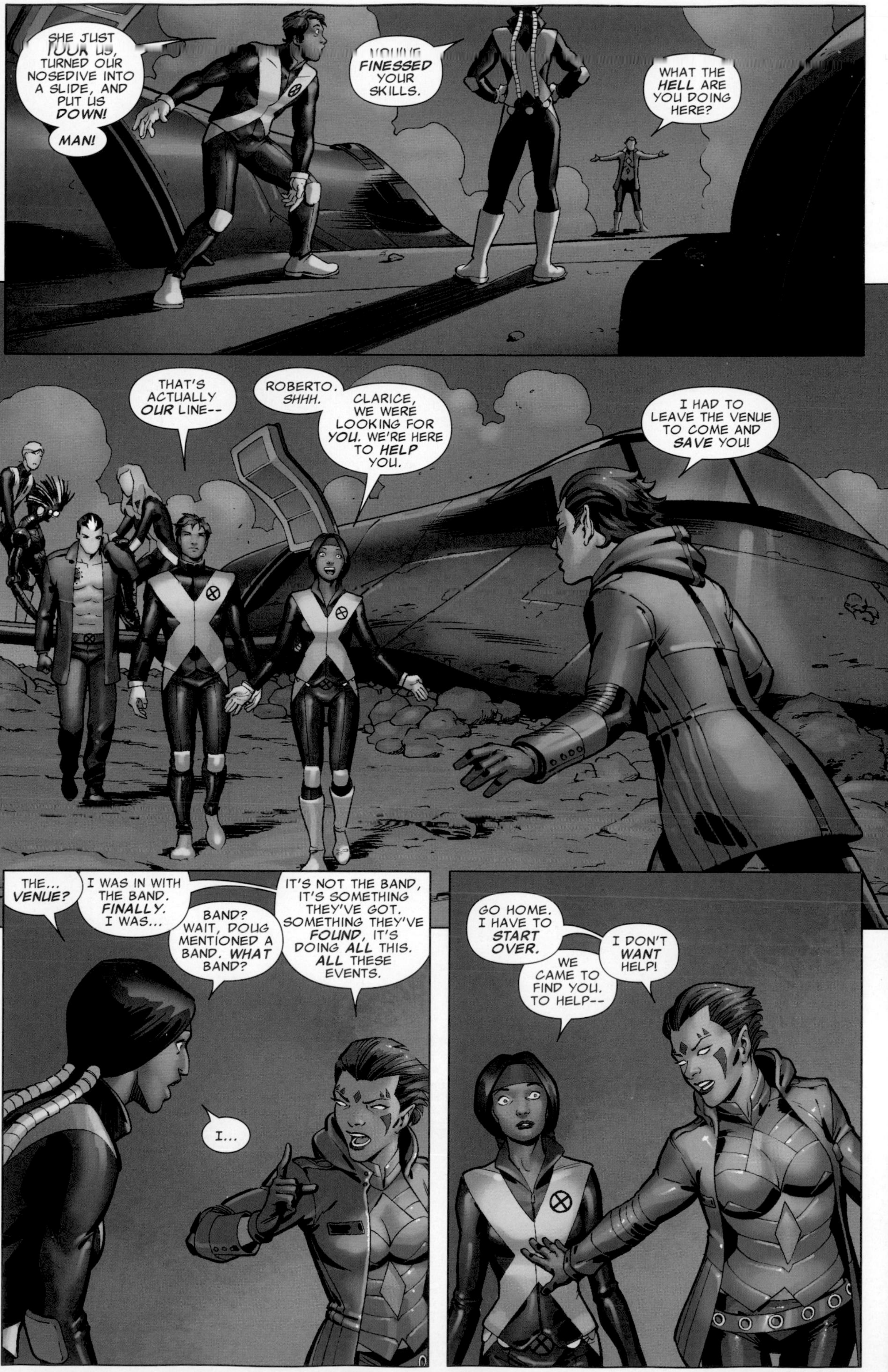
SHE JUST TOOK US, TURNED OUR NOSEDIVE INTO A SLIDE, AND PUT US DOWN!
MAN!
FINESSED YOUR SKILLS.
WHAT THE HELL ARE YOU DOING HERE?
THAT'S ACTUALLY OUR LINE--
ROBERTO. SHHH.
CLARICE, WE WERE LOOKING FOR YOU. WE'RE HERE TO HELP YOU.
I HAD TO LEAVE THE VENUE TO COME AND SAVE YOU!
THE... VENUE?
I WAS IN WITH THE BAND. FINALLY. I WAS...
BAND? WAIT, DOUG MENTIONED A BAND. WHAT BAND?
IT'S NOT THE BAND, IT'S SOMETHING THEY'VE GOT. SOMETHING THEY'VE FOUND, IT'S DOING ALL THIS. ALL THESE EVENTS.
I...
GO HOME. I HAVE TO START OVER.
WE CAME TO FIND YOU. TO HELP--
I DON'T WANT HELP!

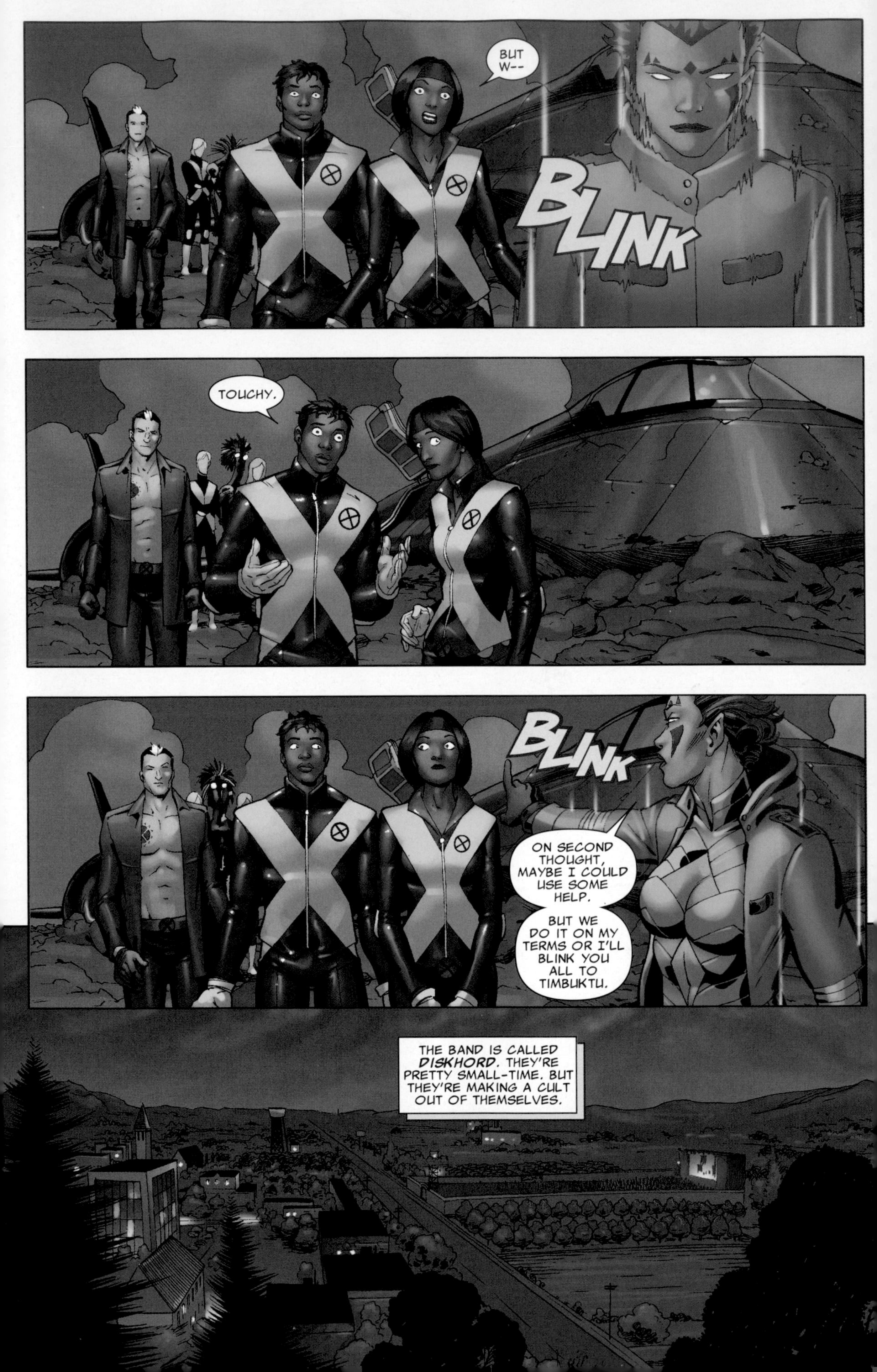
BUT W--
BLINK
TOUCHY.
BLINK
ON SECOND THOUGHT, MAYBE I COULD USE SOME HELP.
BUT WE DO IT ON MY TERMS OR I'LL BLINK YOU ALL TO TIMBUKTU.
THE BAND IS CALLED DISKHORD. THEY'RE PRETTY SMALL-TIME. BUT THEY'RE MAKING A CULT OUT OF THEMSELVES.

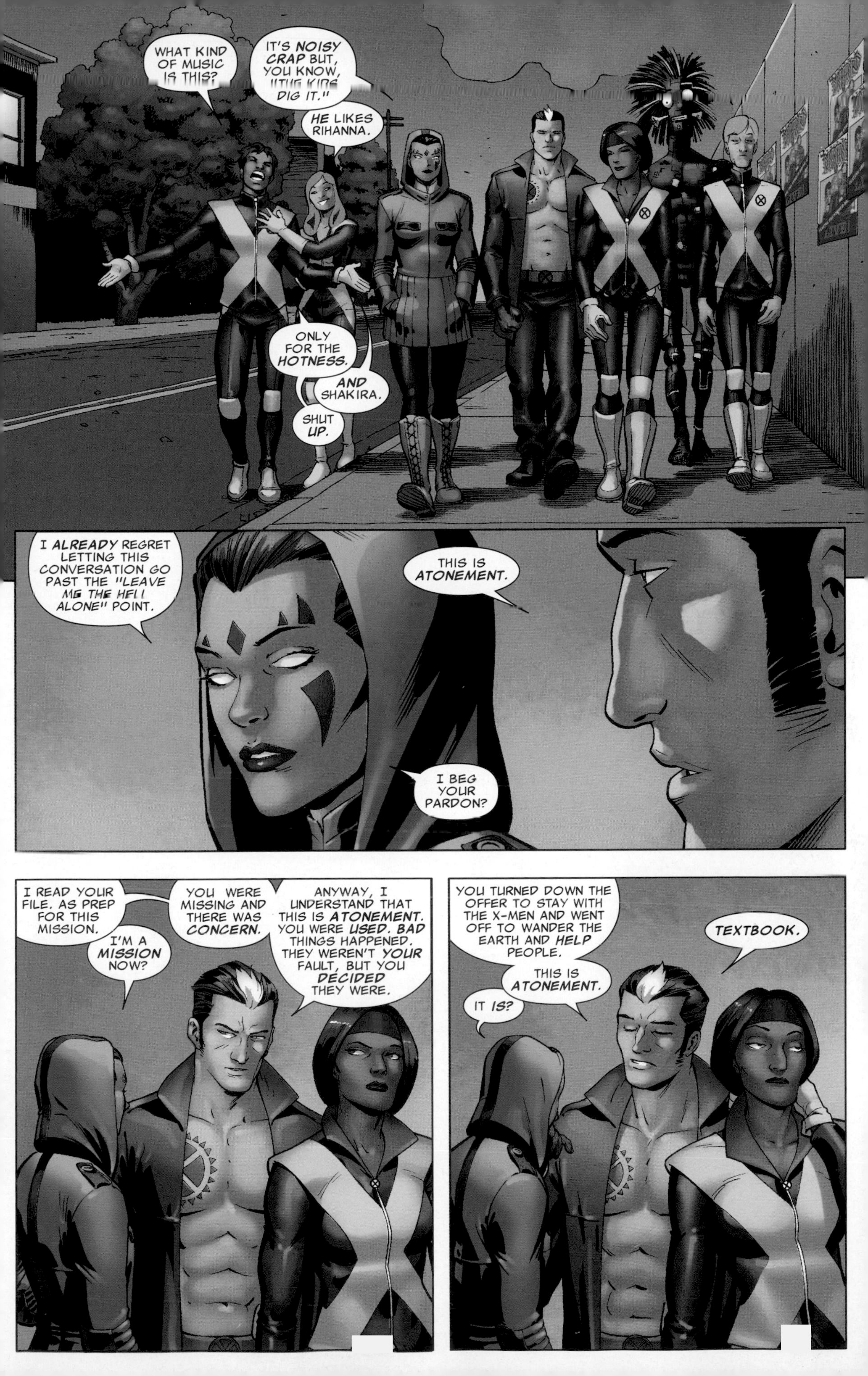
WHAT KIND OF MUSIC IS THIS?
IT'S NOISY CRAP BUT, YOU KNOW, "THE KIDS DIG IT."
HE LIKES RIHANNA.
ONLY FOR THE HOTNESS.
AND SHAKIRA.
SHUT UP.
I ALREADY REGRET LETTING THIS CONVERSATION GO PAST THE "LEAVE ME THE HELL ALONE" POINT.
THIS IS ATONEMENT.
I BEG YOUR PARDON?
I READ YOUR FILE. AS PREP FOR THIS MISSION.
YOU WERE MISSING AND THERE WAS CONCERN.
I'M A MISSION NOW?
ANYWAY, I UNDERSTAND THAT THIS IS ATONEMENT. YOU WERE USED. BAD THINGS HAPPENED. THEY WEREN'T YOUR FAULT, BUT YOU DECIDED THEY WERE.
YOU TURNED DOWN THE OFFER TO STAY WITH THE X-MEN AND WENT OFF TO WANDER THE EARTH AND HELP PEOPLE.
THIS IS ATONEMENT.
IT IS?
TEXTBOOK.

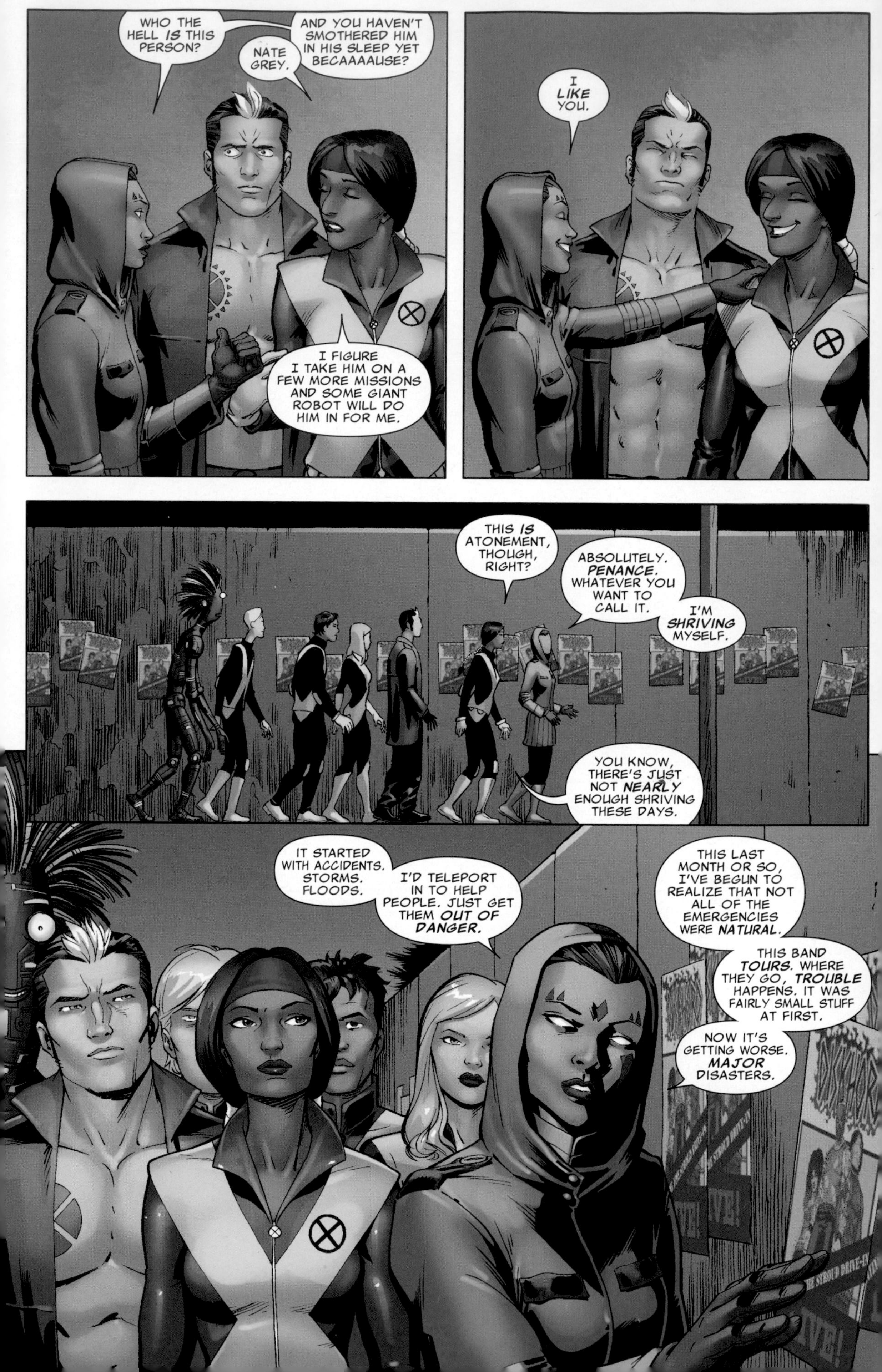
WHO THE HELL *IS* THIS PERSON?
NATE GREY.
AND YOU HAVEN'T SMOTHERED HIM IN HIS SLEEP YET BECAAAAAUSE?
I FIGURE I TAKE HIM ON A FEW MORE MISSIONS AND SOME GIANT ROBOT WILL DO HIM IN FOR ME.
I *LIKE* YOU.
THIS *IS* ATONEMENT, THOUGH, RIGHT?
ABSOLUTELY. *PENANCE.* WHATEVER YOU WANT TO CALL IT.
I'M *SHRIVING* MYSELF.
YOU KNOW, THERE'S JUST NOT *NEARLY* ENOUGH SHRIVING THESE DAYS.
IT STARTED WITH ACCIDENTS. STORMS. FLOODS.
I'D TELEPORT IN TO HELP PEOPLE. JUST GET THEM *OUT OF DANGER.*
THIS LAST MONTH OR SO, I'VE BEGUN TO REALIZE THAT NOT ALL OF THE EMERGENCIES WERE *NATURAL.*
THIS BAND *TOURS.* WHERE THEY GO, *TROUBLE* HAPPENS. IT WAS FAIRLY SMALL STUFF AT FIRST.
NOW IT'S GETTING WORSE. *MAJOR* DISASTERS.

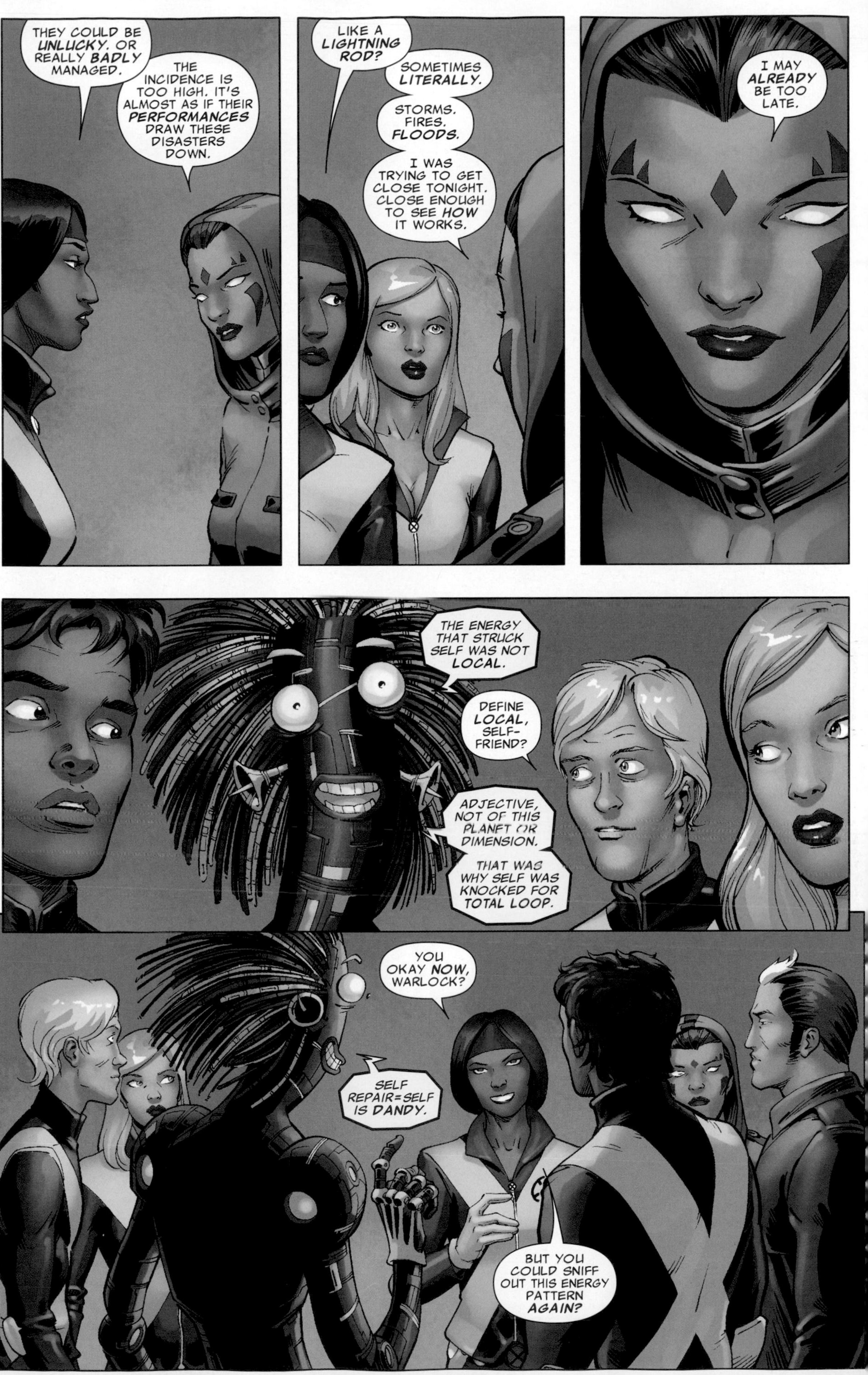
THEY COULD BE UNLUCKY. OR REALLY BADLY MANAGED.
THE INCIDENCE IS TOO HIGH. IT'S ALMOST AS IF THEIR PERFORMANCES DRAW THESE DISASTERS DOWN.
LIKE A LIGHTNING ROD?
SOMETIMES LITERALLY.
STORMS. FIRES. FLOODS.
I WAS TRYING TO GET CLOSE TONIGHT. CLOSE ENOUGH TO SEE HOW IT WORKS.
I MAY ALREADY BE TOO LATE.
THE ENERGY THAT STRUCK SELF WAS NOT LOCAL.
DEFINE LOCAL, SELF-FRIEND?
ADJECTIVE, NOT OF THIS PLANET OR DIMENSION.
THAT WAS WHY SELF WAS KNOCKED FOR TOTAL LOOP.
YOU OKAY NOW, WARLOCK?
SELF REPAIR=SELF IS DANDY.
BUT YOU COULD SNIFF OUT THIS ENERGY PATTERN AGAIN?

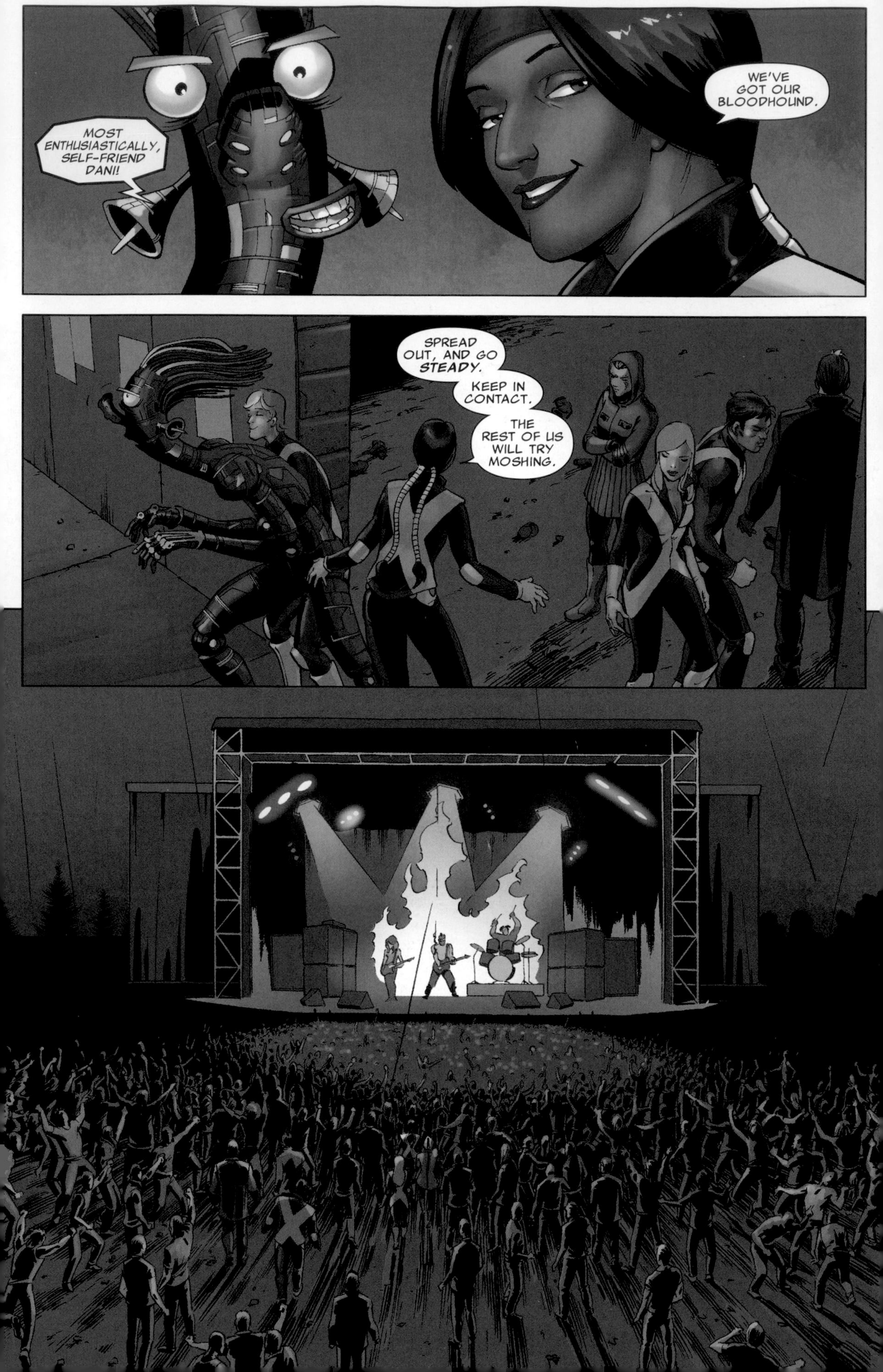
WE'VE GOT OUR BLOODHOUND.
MOST ENTHUSIASTICALLY, SELF-FRIEND DANI!
SPREAD OUT, AND GO STEADY.
KEEP IN CONTACT.
THE REST OF US WILL TRY MOSHING.

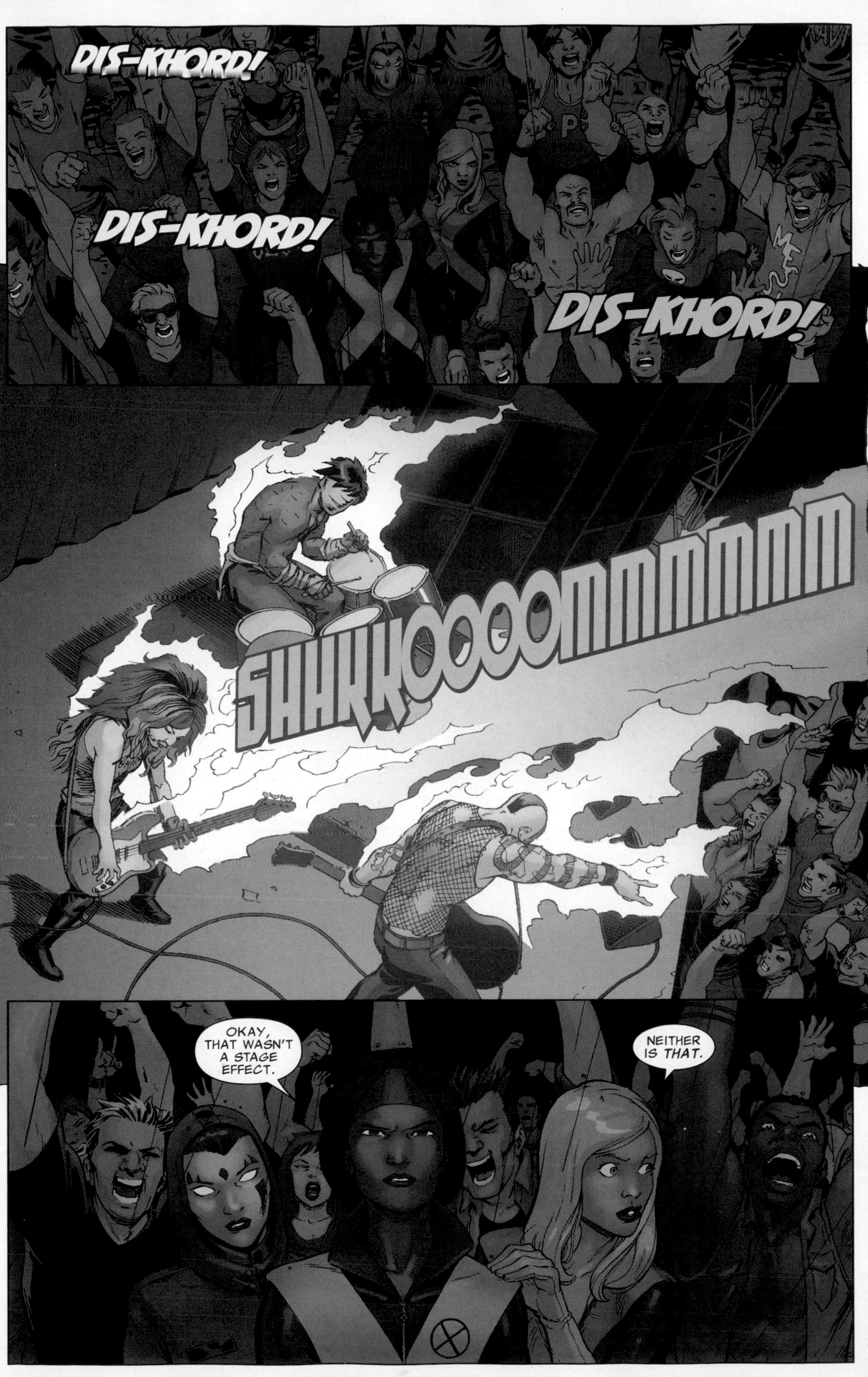
DIS-KHORD!
DIS-KHORD!
DIS-KHORD!
SHHKKOOOOOMMMMMMMM
OKAY, THAT WASN'T A STAGE EFFECT.
NEITHER IS THAT.

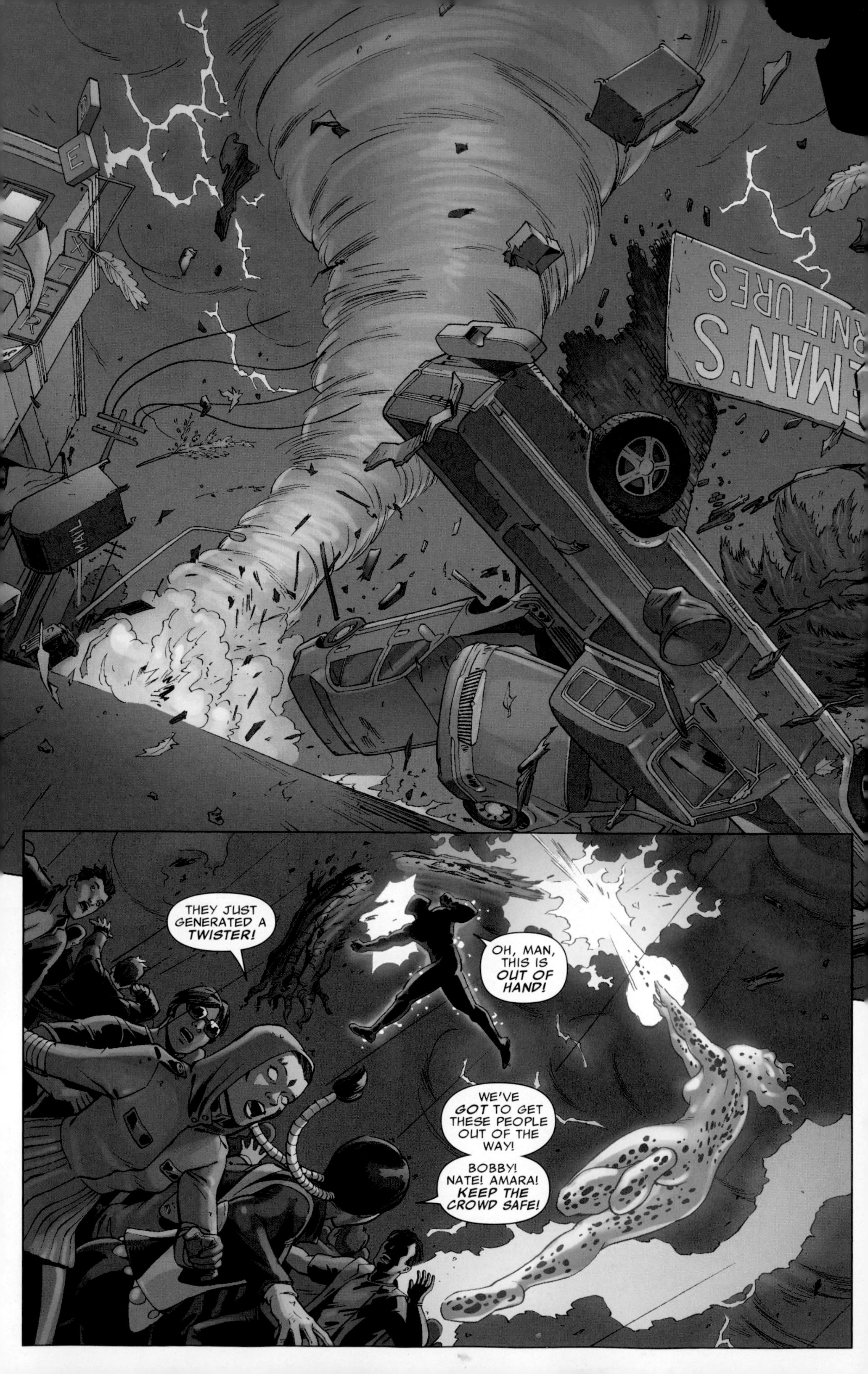
THEY JUST GENERATED A TWISTER!
OH, MAN, THIS IS OUT OF HAND!
WE'VE GOT TO GET THESE PEOPLE OUT OF THE WAY!
BOBBY! NATE! AMARA! KEEP THE CROWD SAFE!

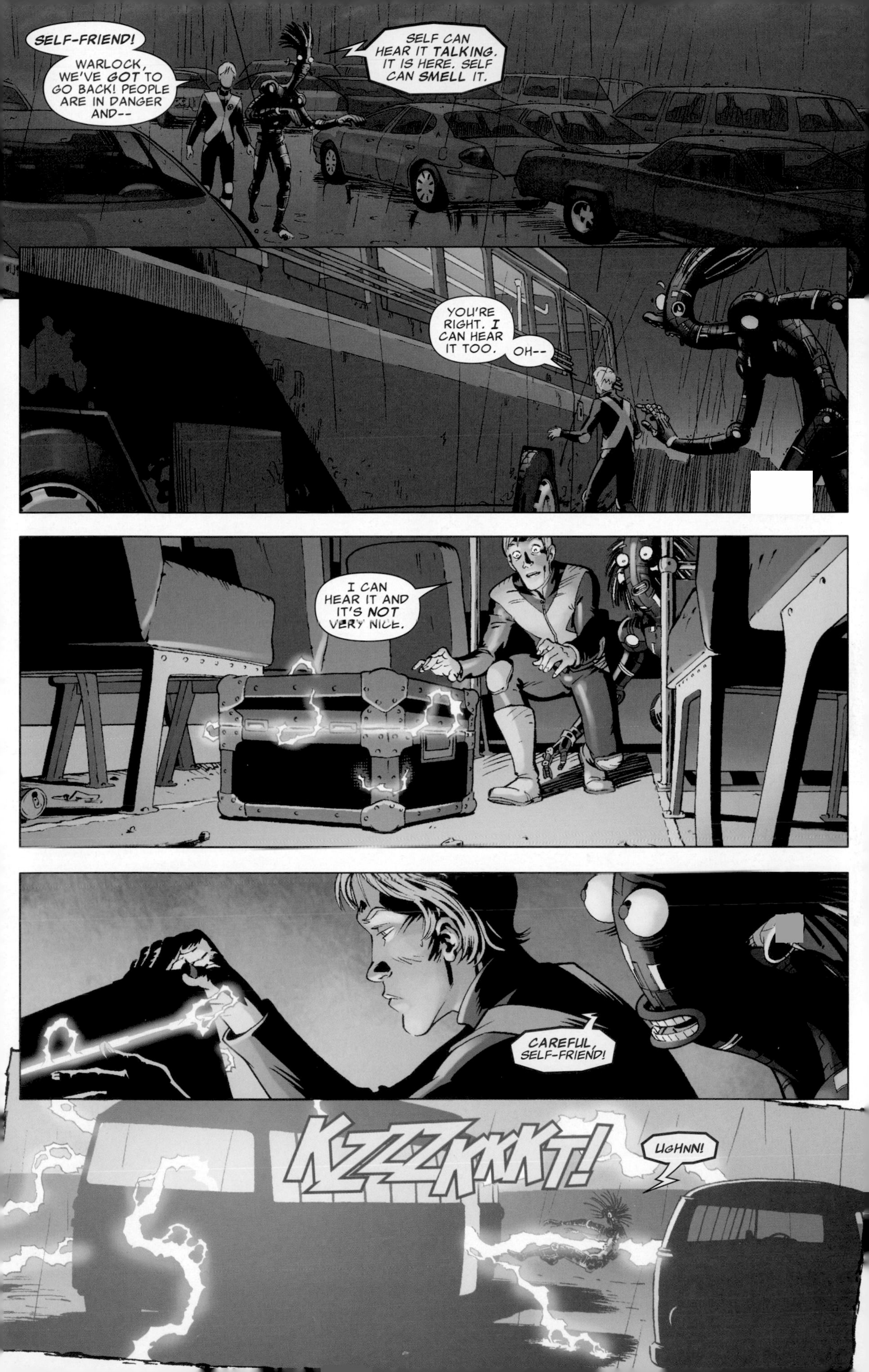
SELF-FRIEND!
WARLOCK, WE'VE GOT TO GO BACK! PEOPLE ARE IN DANGER AND--
SELF CAN HEAR IT TALKING. IT IS HERE. SELF CAN SMELL IT.
YOU'RE RIGHT. I CAN HEAR IT TOO.
OH--
I CAN HEAR IT AND IT'S NOT VERY NICE.
CAREFUL, SELF-FRIEND!
KZZZKKKKT!
UGHNN!

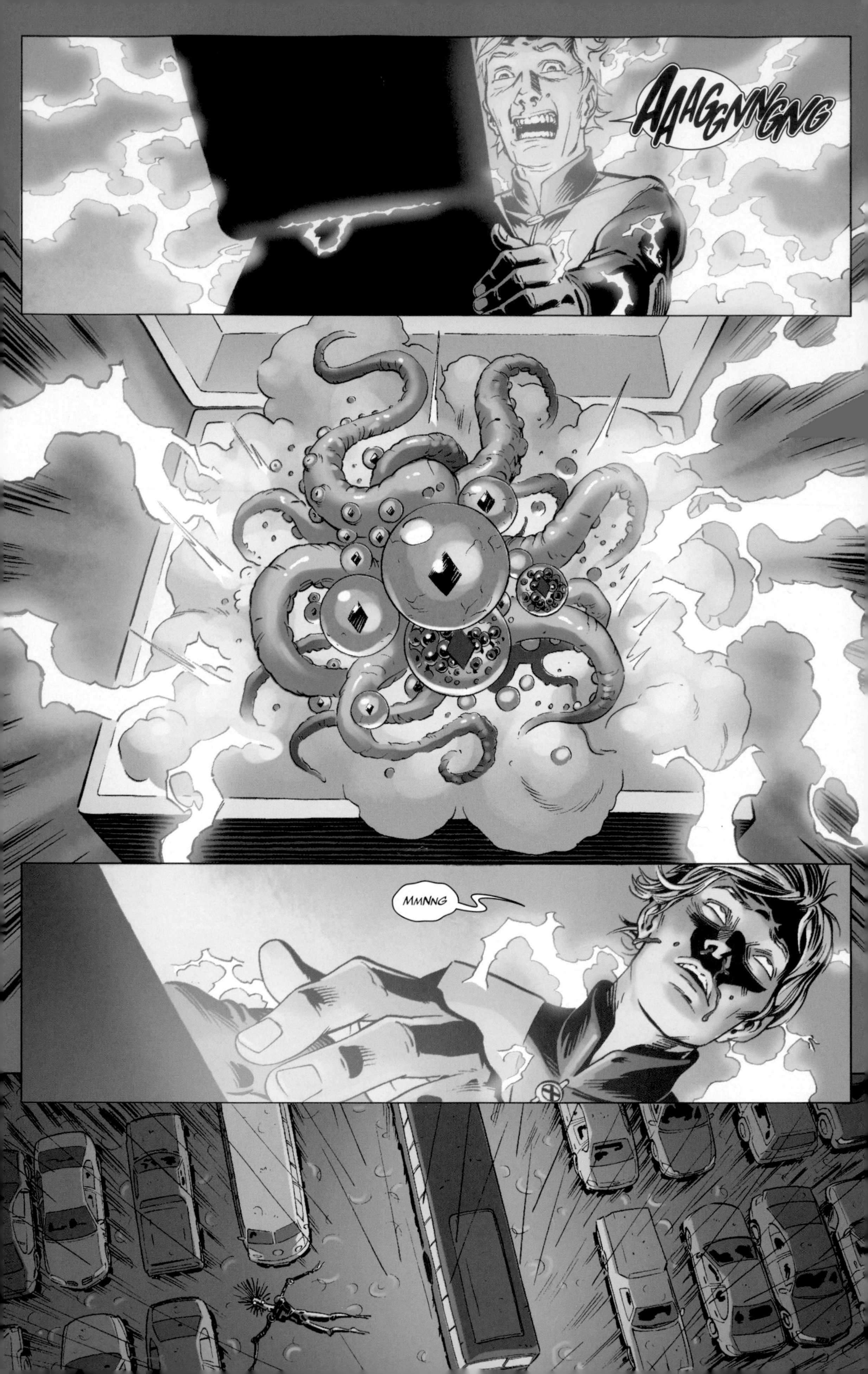
AAAAGGNNNGNG
MMNNG

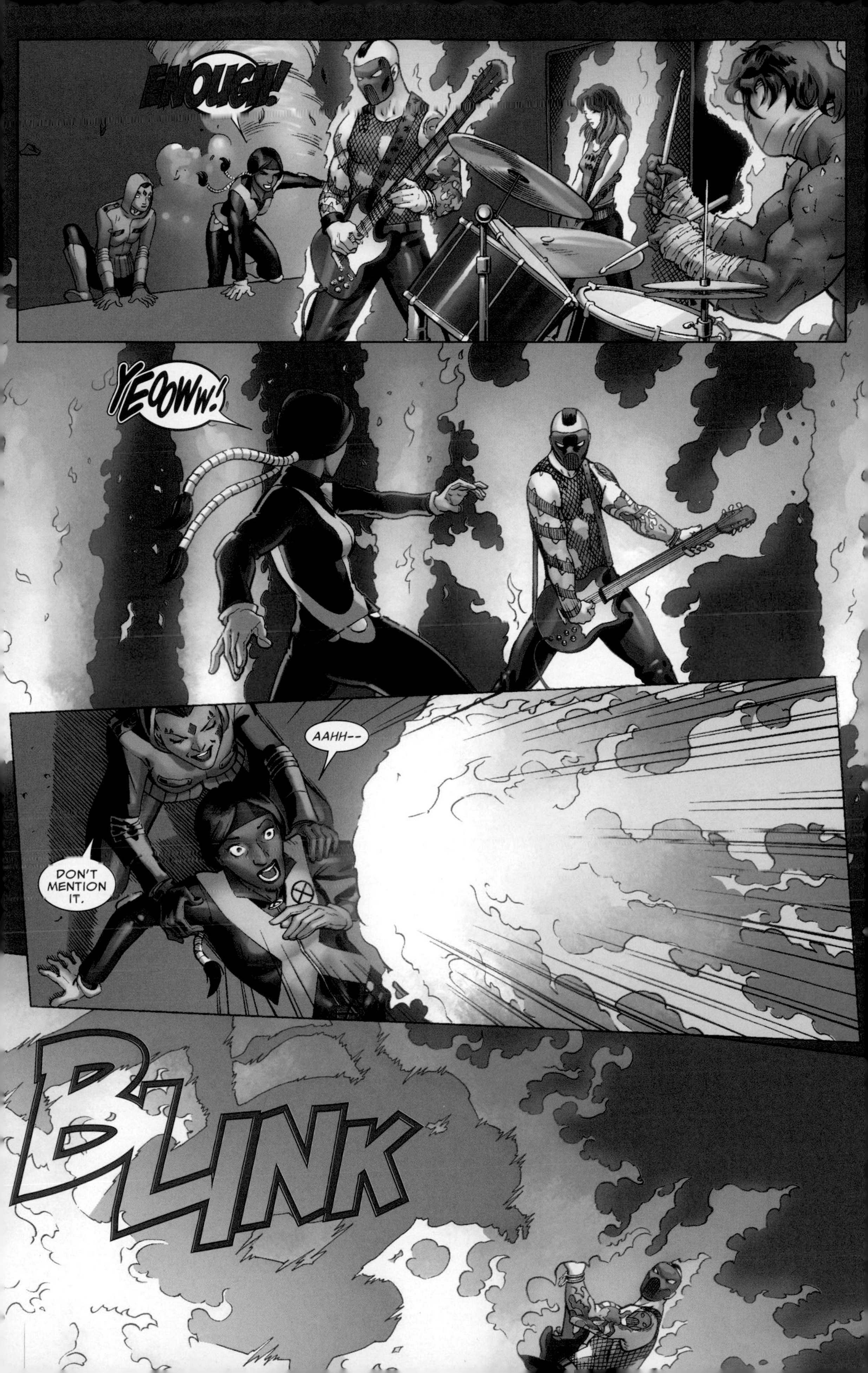
ENOUGH!
YEOOWW!
AAHH--
DON'T MENTION IT.
BLINK

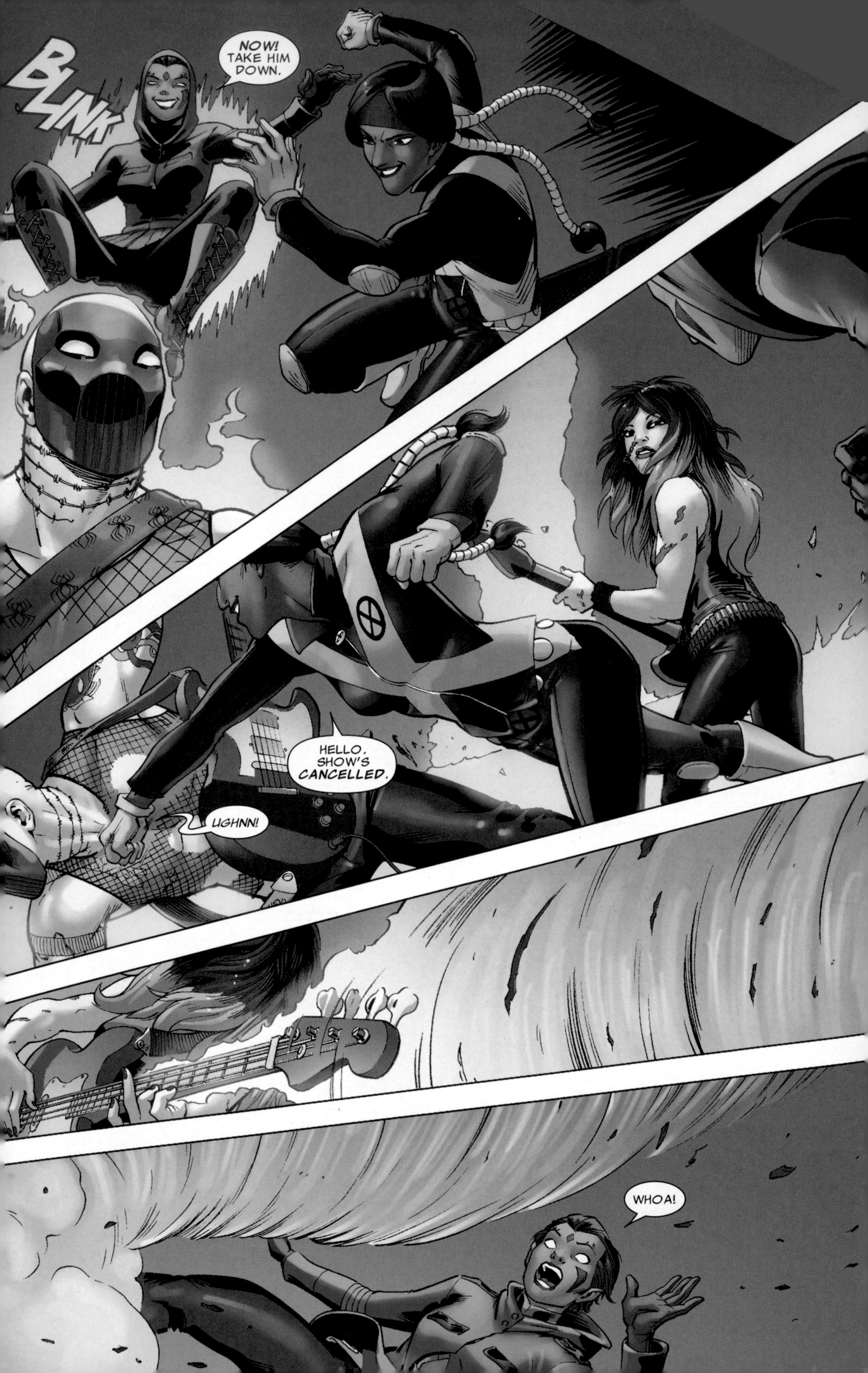
BLINK
NOW! TAKE HIM DOWN.
HELLO. SHOW'S CANCELLED.
UGHNN!
WHOA!

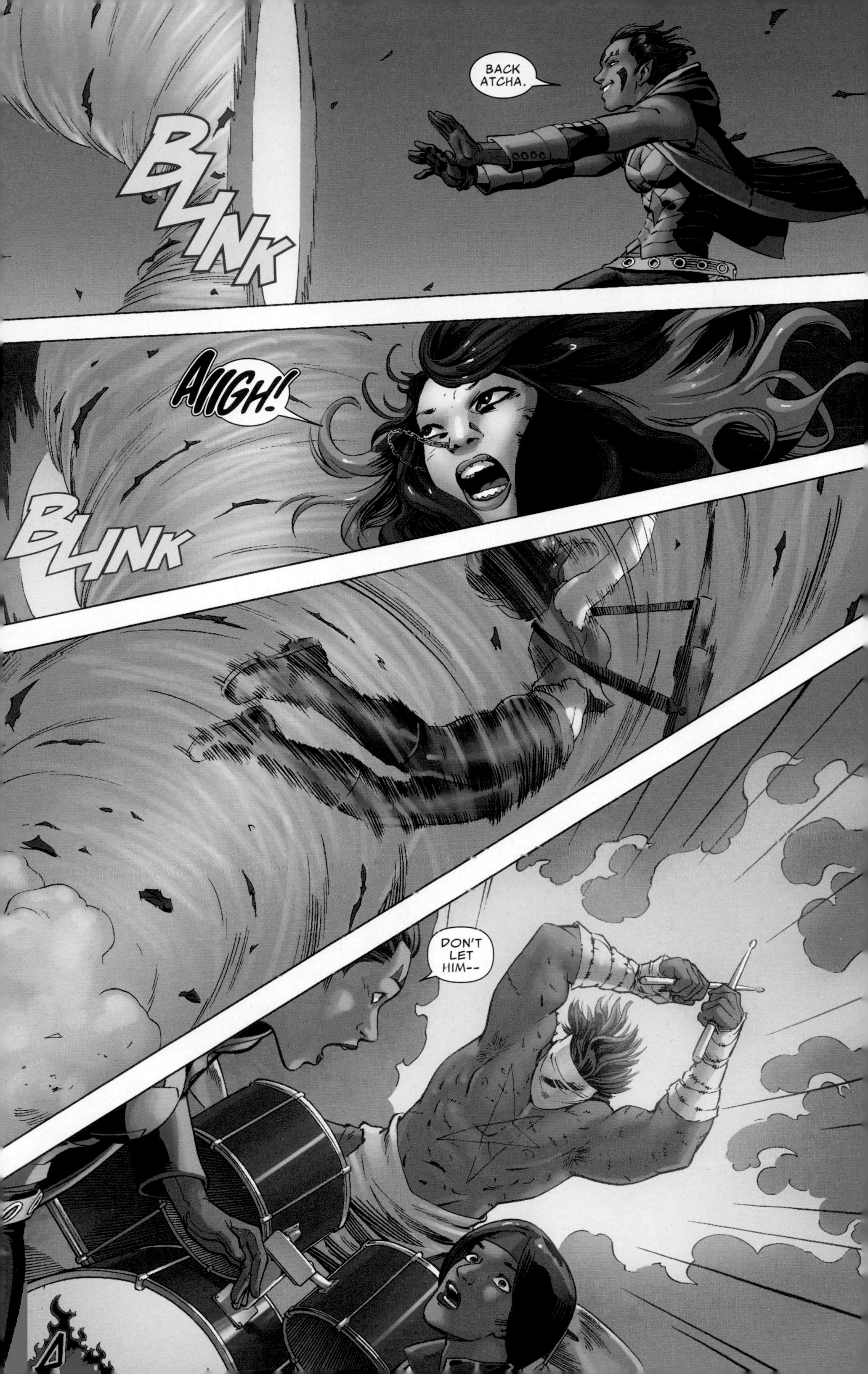
BACK ATCHA.
BLINK
AIIGH!
BLINK
DON'T LET HIM--

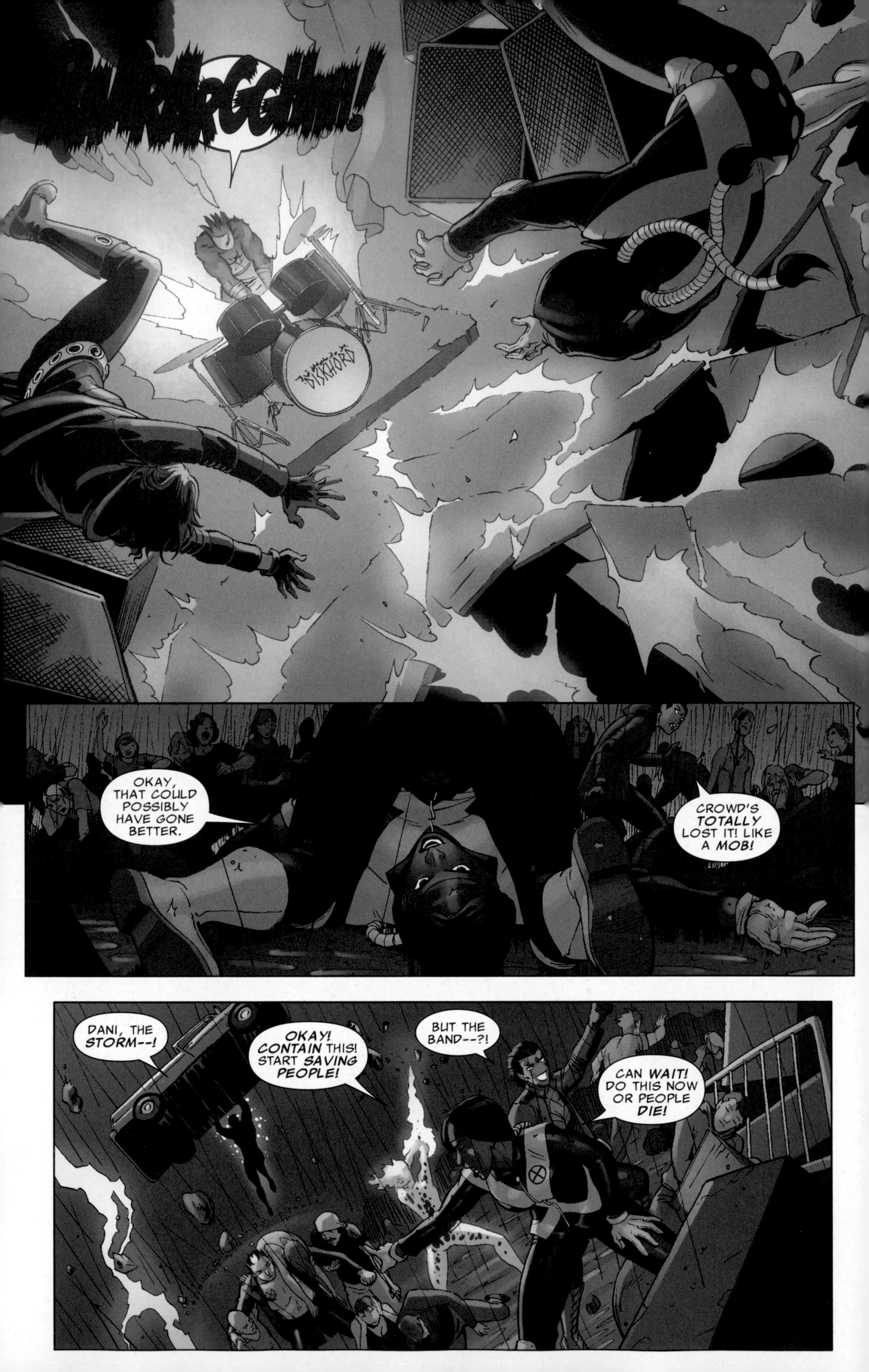
BWRRRGGHHH!
DISKHORD
OKAY, THAT COULD POSSIBLY HAVE GONE BETTER.
CROWD'S TOTALLY LOST IT! LIKE A MOB!
DANI, THE STORM--!
OKAY! CONTAIN THIS! START SAVING PEOPLE!
BUT THE BAND--?!
CAN WAIT! DO THIS NOW OR PEOPLE DIE!

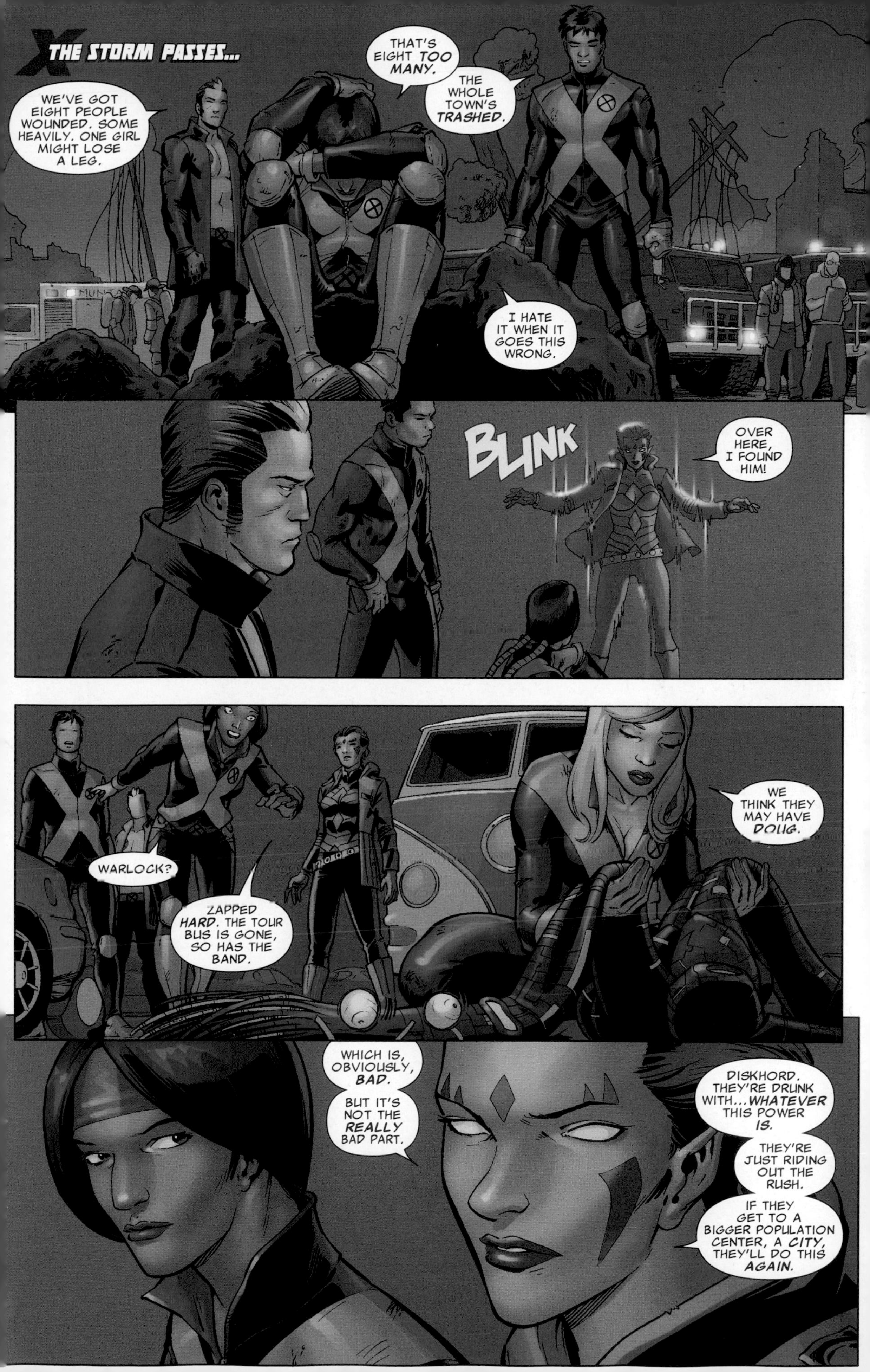
THE STORM PASSES...
WE'VE GOT EIGHT PEOPLE WOUNDED. SOME HEAVILY. ONE GIRL MIGHT LOSE A LEG.
THAT'S EIGHT TOO MANY.
THE WHOLE TOWN'S TRASHED.
I HATE IT WHEN IT GOES THIS WRONG.
BLINK
OVER HERE, I FOUND HIM!
WE THINK THEY MAY HAVE DOUG.
WARLOCK?
ZAPPED HARD. THE TOUR BUS IS GONE, SO HAS THE BAND.
WHICH IS, OBVIOUSLY, BAD.
BUT IT'S NOT THE REALLY BAD PART.
DISKHORD. THEY'RE DRUNK WITH...WHATEVER THIS POWER IS.
THEY'RE JUST RIDING OUT THE RUSH.
IF THEY GET TO A BIGGER POPULATION CENTER, A CITY, THEY'LL DO THIS AGAIN.

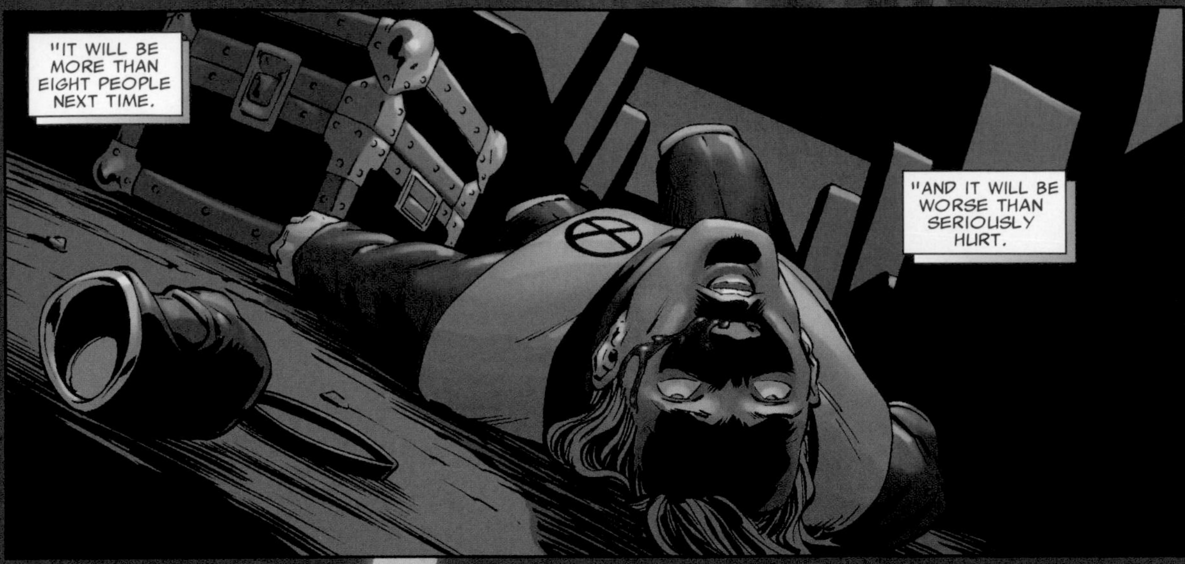
"IT WILL BE MORE THAN EIGHT PEOPLE NEXT TIME.
"AND IT WILL BE WORSE THAN SERIOUSLY HURT.
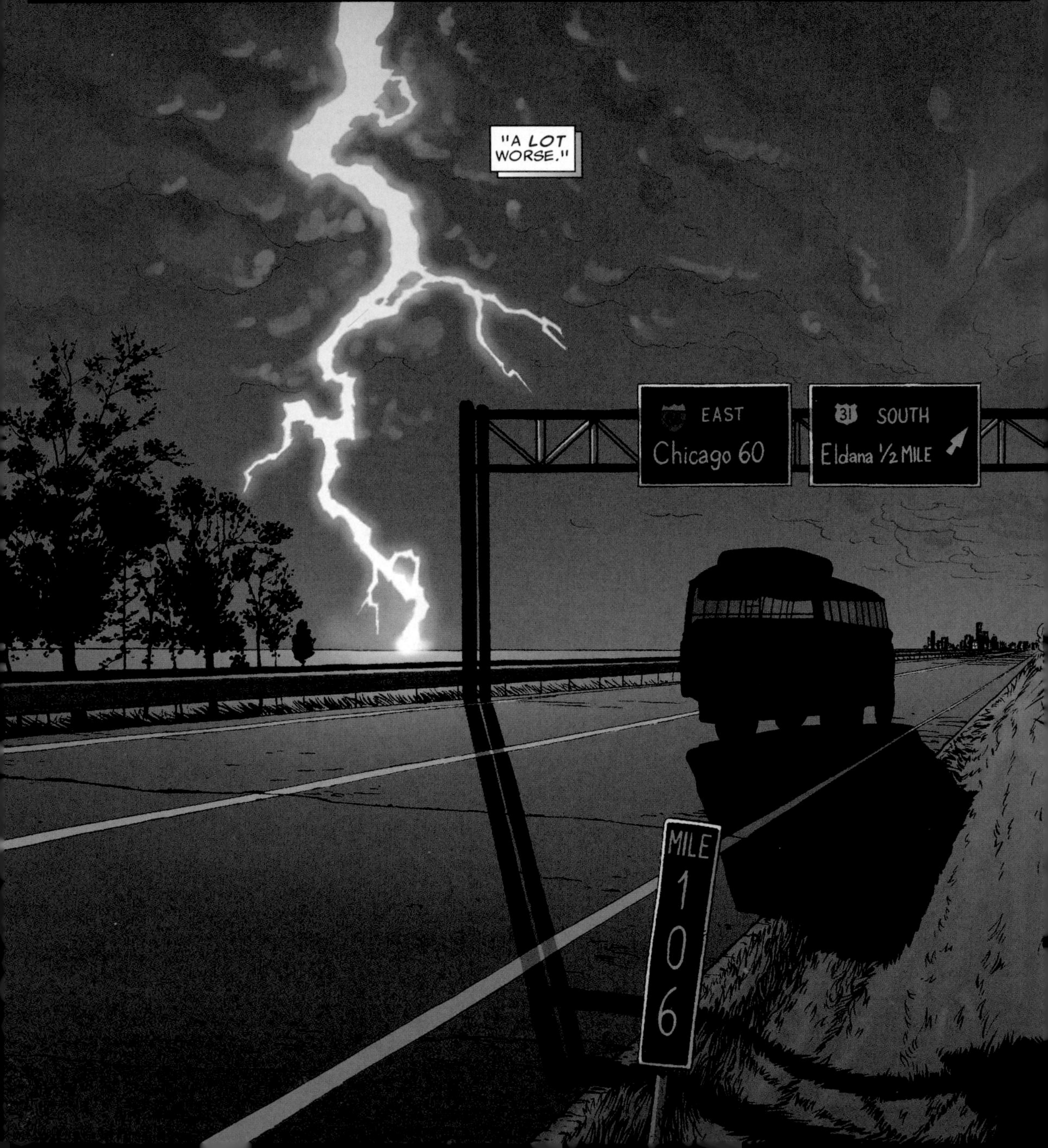
"A LOT WORSE."
EAST
Chicago 60
31 SOUTH
Eldana 1/2 MILE
MILE
106

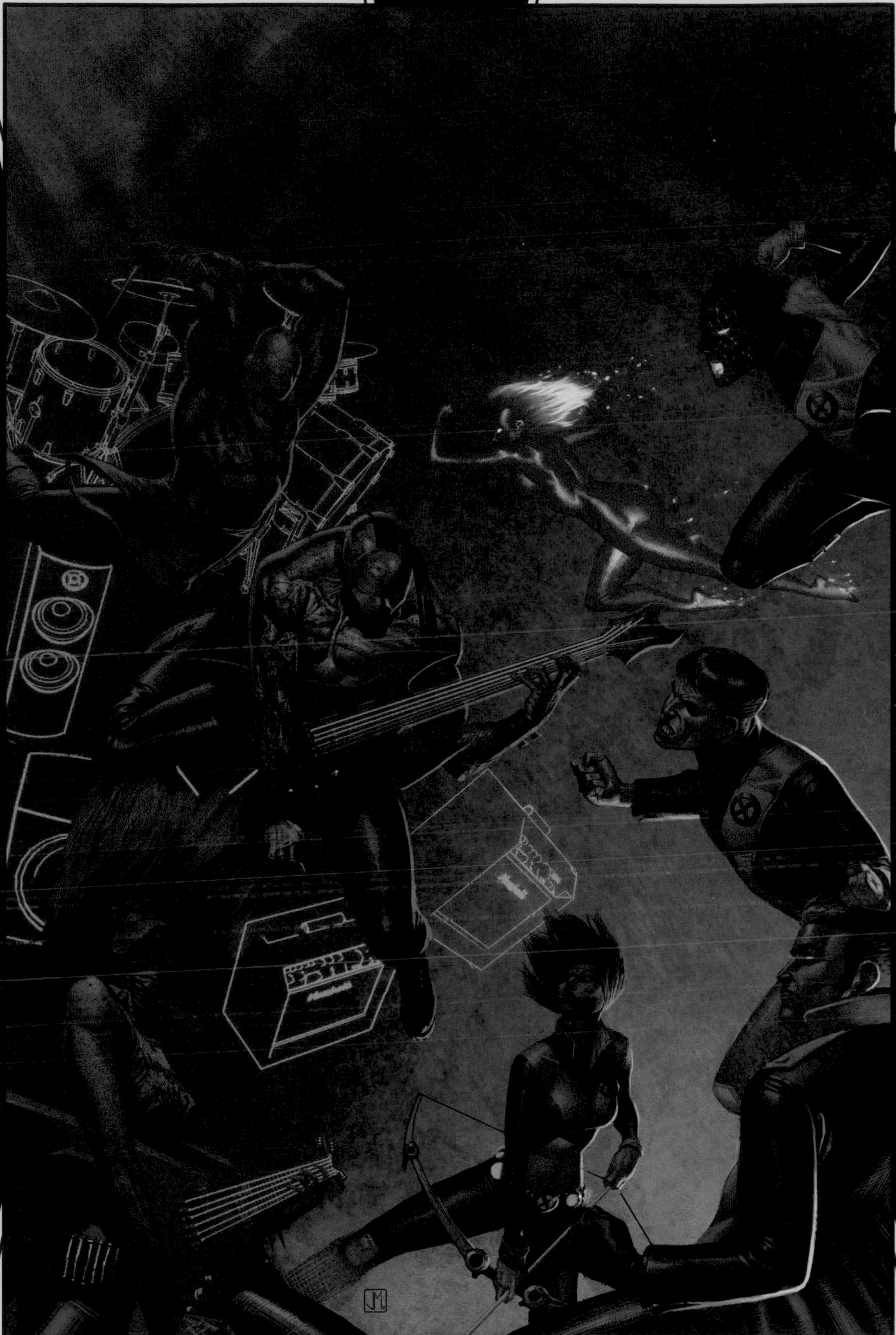

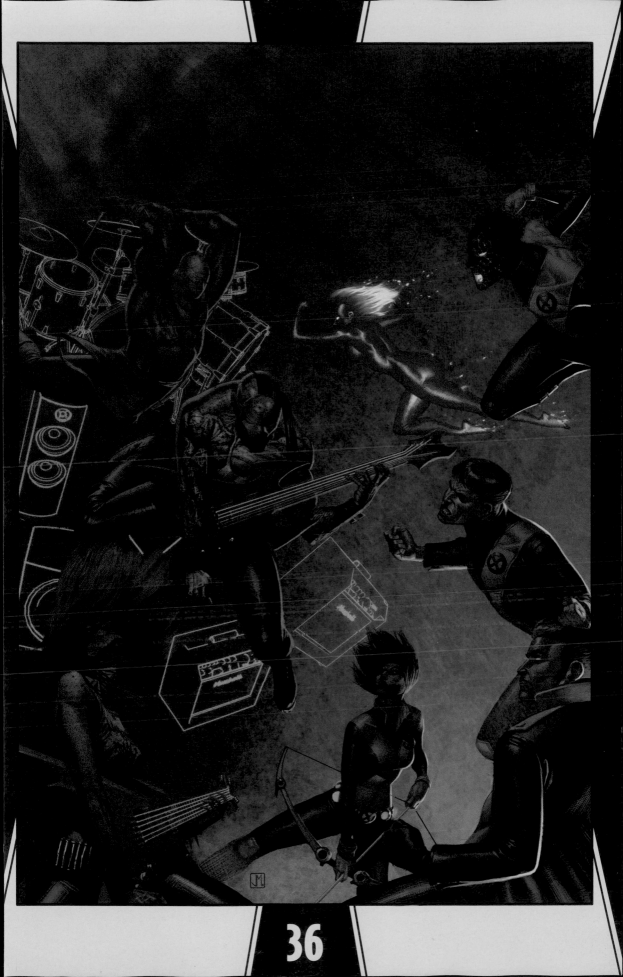

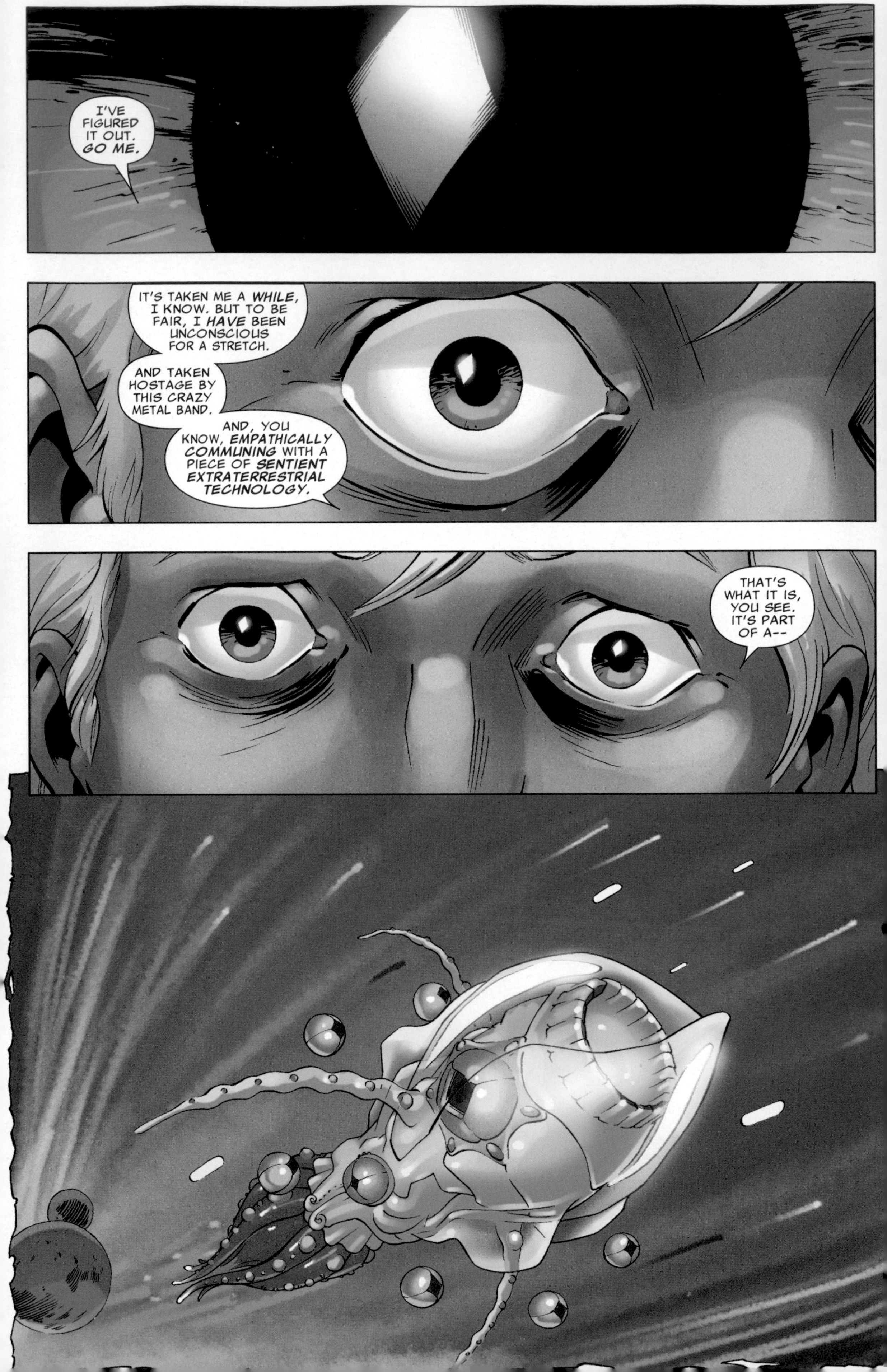
I'VE FIGURED IT OUT. GO ME.
IT'S TAKEN ME A WHILE, I KNOW. BUT TO BE FAIR, I HAVE BEEN UNCONSCIOUS FOR A STRETCH.
AND TAKEN HOSTAGE BY THIS CRAZY METAL BAND.
AND, YOU KNOW, EMPATHICALLY COMMUNING WITH A PIECE OF SENTIENT EXTRATERRESTRIAL TECHNOLOGY.
THAT'S WHAT IT IS, YOU SEE. IT'S PART OF A--

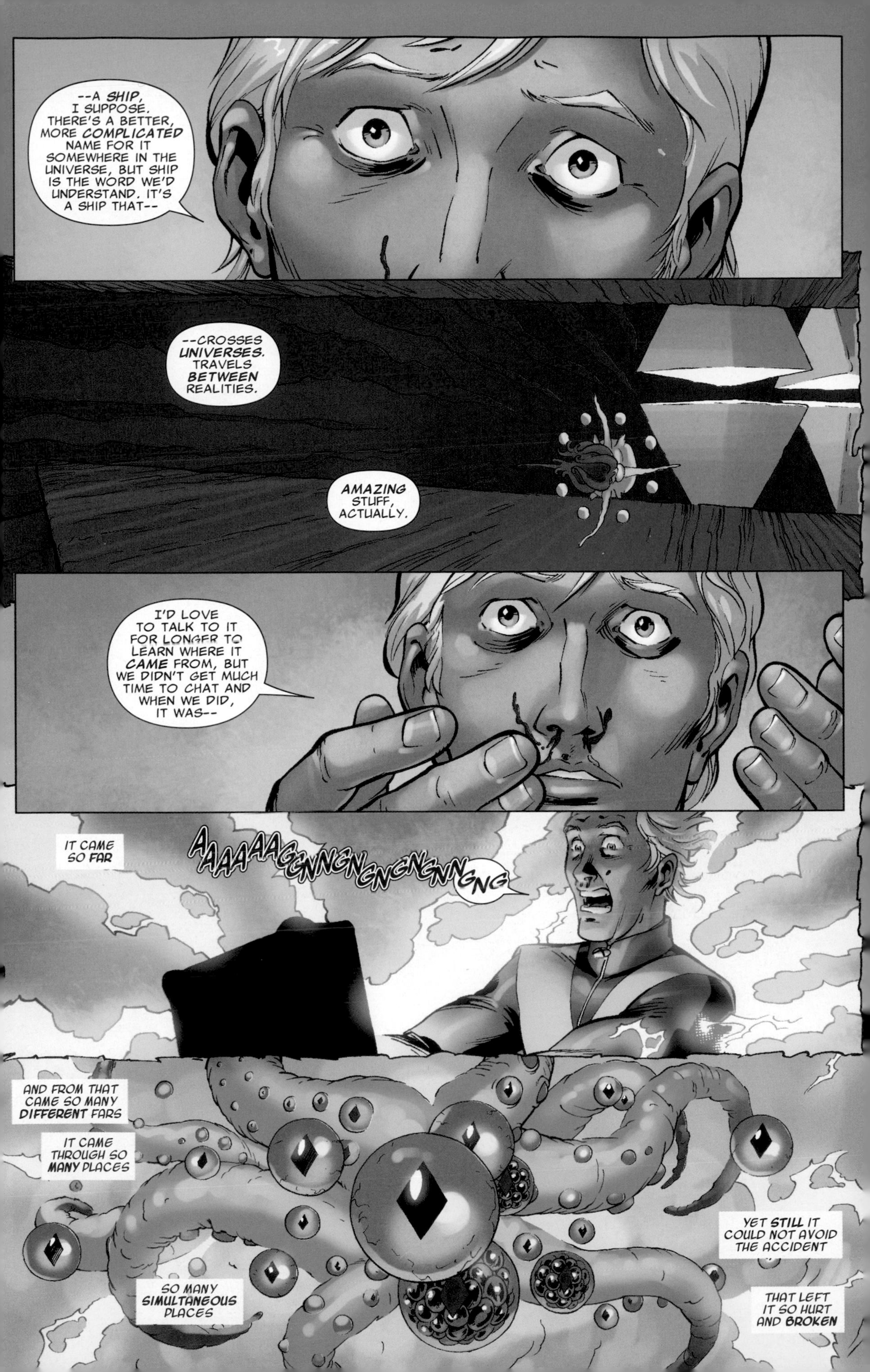
--A SHIP, I SUPPOSE. THERE'S A BETTER, MORE COMPLICATED NAME FOR IT SOMEWHERE IN THE UNIVERSE, BUT SHIP IS THE WORD WE'D UNDERSTAND. IT'S A SHIP THAT--
--CROSSES UNIVERSES. TRAVELS BETWEEN REALITIES.
AMAZING STUFF, ACTUALLY.
I'D LOVE TO TALK TO IT FOR LONGER TO LEARN WHERE IT CAME FROM, BUT WE DIDN'T GET MUCH TIME TO CHAT AND WHEN WE DID, IT WAS--
IT CAME SO FAR
AAAAAAGGNNGNGNGNGNNNGNG
AND FROM THAT CAME SO MANY DIFFERENT FARS
IT CAME THROUGH SO MANY PLACES
SO MANY SIMULTANEOUS PLACES
YET STILL IT COULD NOT AVOID THE ACCIDENT
THAT LEFT IT SO HURT AND BROKEN

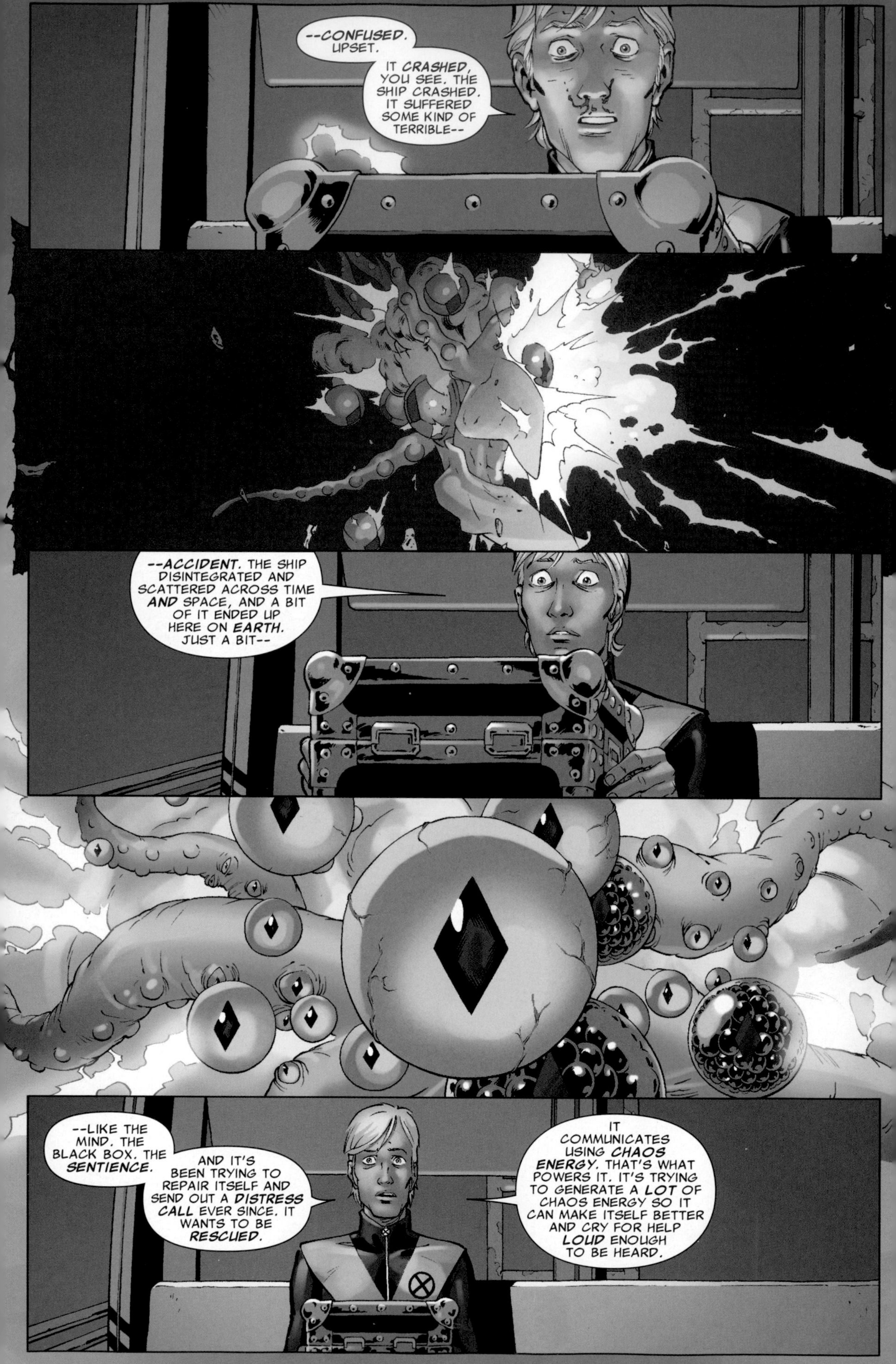
--CONFUSED. UPSET.
IT CRASHED, YOU SEE. THE SHIP CRASHED. IT SUFFERED SOME KIND OF TERRIBLE--
--ACCIDENT. THE SHIP DISINTEGRATED AND SCATTERED ACROSS TIME AND SPACE, AND A BIT OF IT ENDED UP HERE ON EARTH. JUST A BIT--
--LIKE THE MIND. THE BLACK BOX. THE SENTIENCE.
AND IT'S BEEN TRYING TO REPAIR ITSELF AND SEND OUT A DISTRESS CALL EVER SINCE. IT WANTS TO BE RESCUED.
IT COMMUNICATES USING CHAOS ENERGY. THAT'S WHAT POWERS IT. IT'S TRYING TO GENERATE A LOT OF CHAOS ENERGY SO IT CAN MAKE ITSELF BETTER AND CRY FOR HELP LOUD ENOUGH TO BE HEARD.

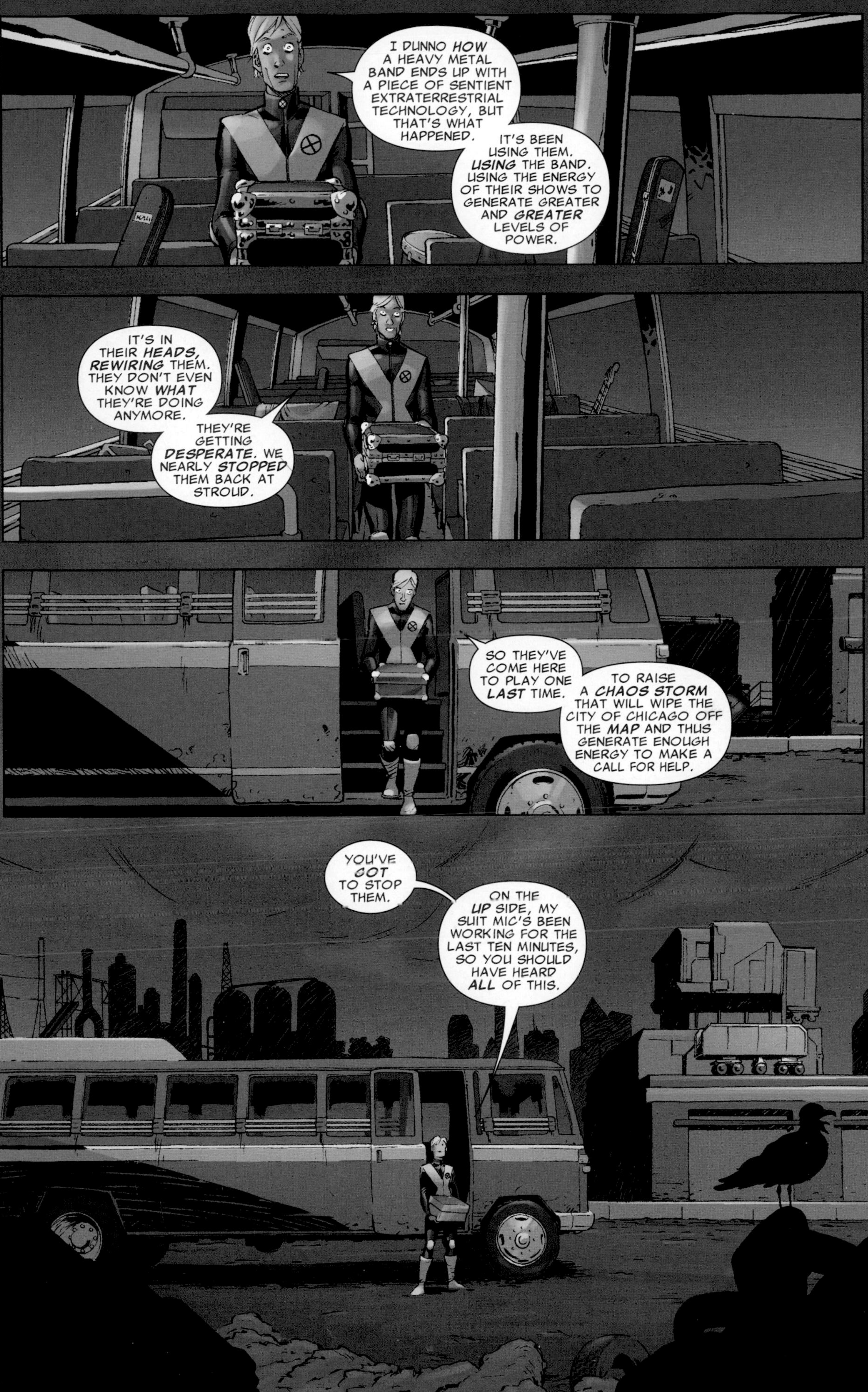

I DUNNO HOW A HEAVY METAL BAND ENDS UP WITH A PIECE OF SENTIENT EXTRATERRESTRIAL TECHNOLOGY, BUT THAT'S WHAT HAPPENED.
IT'S BEEN USING THEM. USING THE BAND. USING THE ENERGY OF THEIR SHOWS TO GENERATE GREATER AND GREATER LEVELS OF POWER.
IT'S IN THEIR HEADS, REWIRING THEM. THEY DON'T EVEN KNOW WHAT THEY'RE DOING ANYMORE.
THEY'RE GETTING DESPERATE. WE NEARLY STOPPED THEM BACK AT STROUD.
SO THEY'VE COME HERE TO PLAY ONE LAST TIME.
TO RAISE A CHAOS STORM THAT WILL WIPE THE CITY OF CHICAGO OFF THE MAP AND THUS GENERATE ENOUGH ENERGY TO MAKE A CALL FOR HELP.
YOU'VE GOT TO STOP THEM.
ON THE UP SIDE, MY SUIT MIC'S BEEN WORKING FOR THE LAST TEN MINUTES, SO YOU SHOULD HAVE HEARD ALL OF THIS.

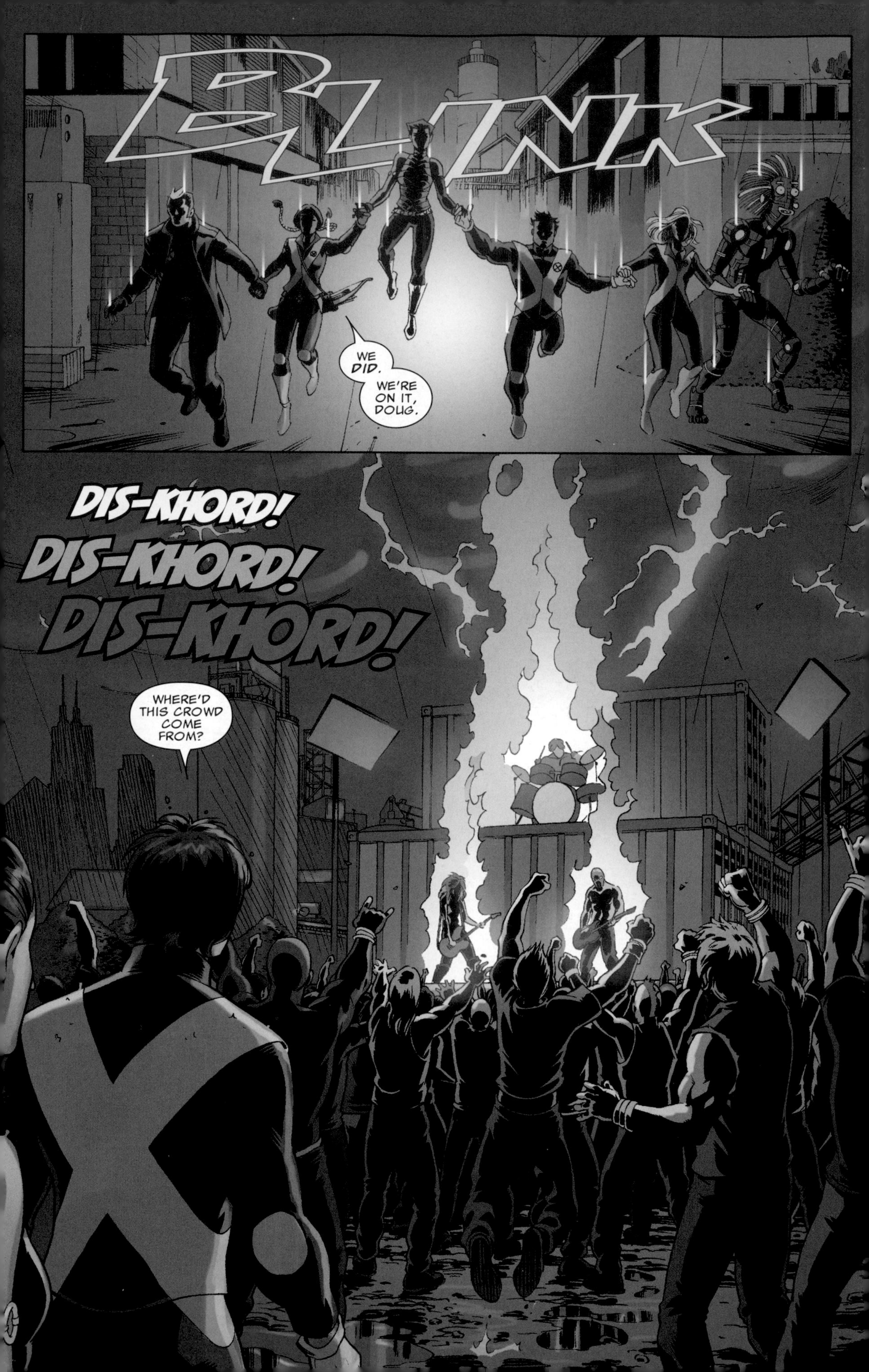
BLINK
WE DID.
WE'RE ON IT, DOUG.
DIS-KHORD!
DIS-KHORD!
DIS-KHORD!
WHERE'D THIS CROWD COME FROM?

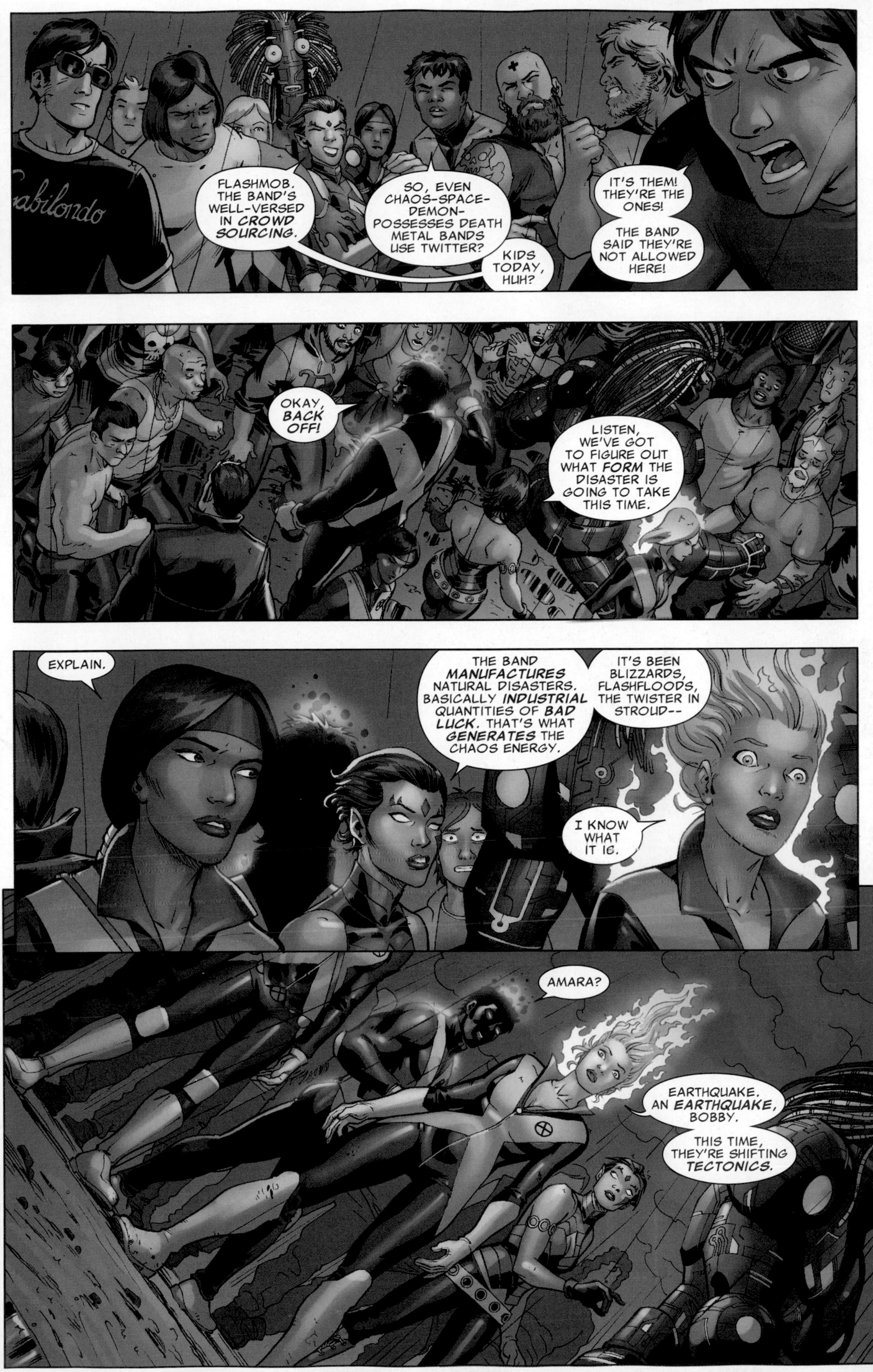

Gabilondo
FLASHMOB. THE BAND'S WELL-VERSED IN CROWD SOURCING.
SO, EVEN CHAOS-SPACE-DEMON-POSSESSES DEATH METAL BANDS USE TWITTER?
KIDS TODAY, HUH?
IT'S THEM! THEY'RE THE ONES!
THE BAND SAID THEY'RE NOT ALLOWED HERE!
OKAY, BACK OFF!
LISTEN, WE'VE GOT TO FIGURE OUT WHAT FORM THE DISASTER IS GOING TO TAKE THIS TIME.
EXPLAIN.
THE BAND MANUFACTURES NATURAL DISASTERS. BASICALLY INDUSTRIAL QUANTITIES OF BAD LUCK. THAT'S WHAT GENERATES THE CHAOS ENERGY.
IT'S BEEN BLIZZARDS, FLASHFLOODS, THE TWISTER IN STROUD--
I KNOW WHAT IT IS.
AMARA?
EARTHQUAKE. AN EARTHQUAKE, BOBBY.
THIS TIME, THEY'RE SHIFTING TECTONICS.

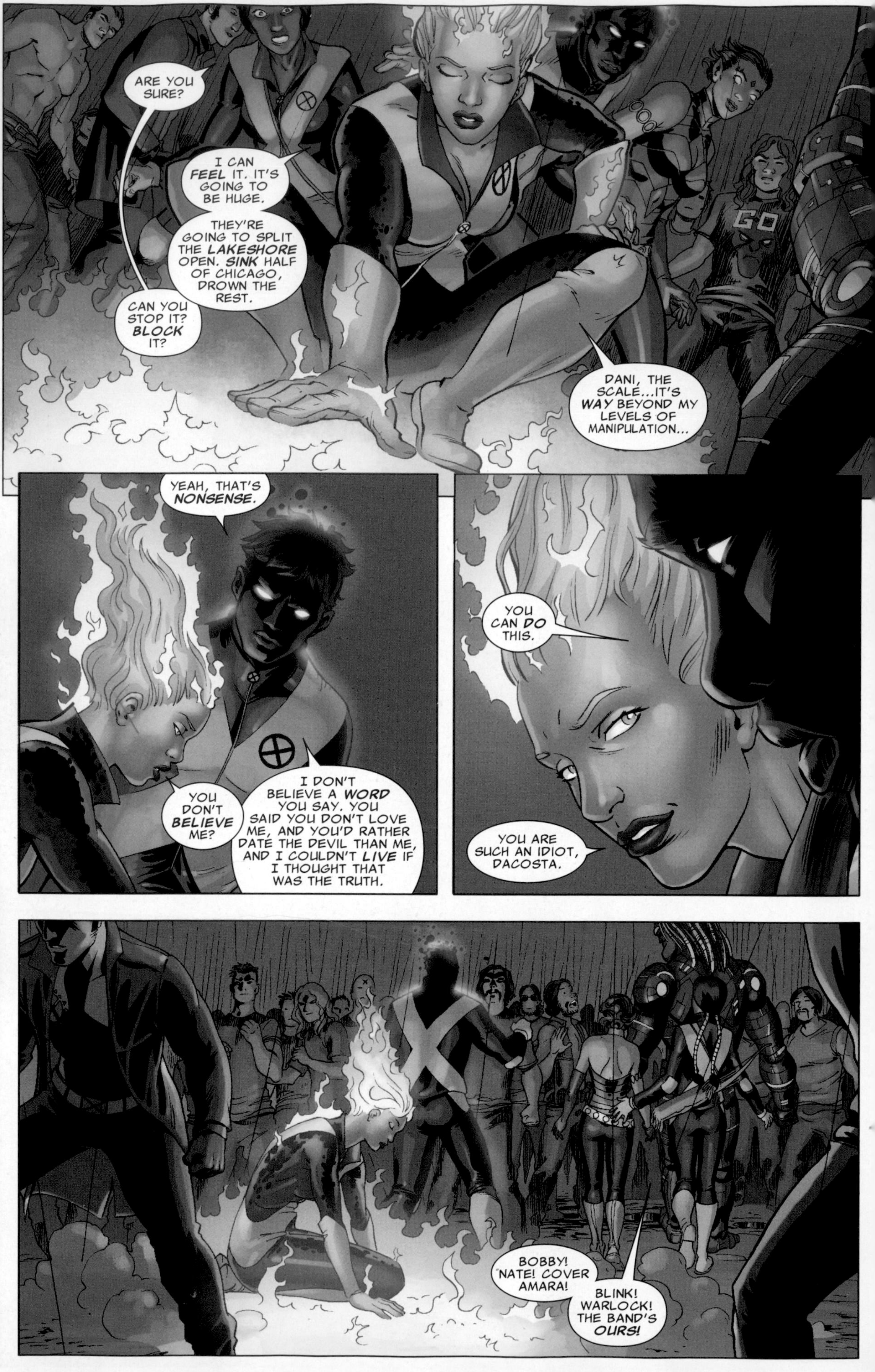
ARE YOU SURE?
I CAN FEEL IT. IT'S GOING TO BE HUGE.
THEY'RE GOING TO SPLIT THE LAKESHORE OPEN. SINK HALF OF CHICAGO, DROWN THE REST.
CAN YOU STOP IT? BLOCK IT?
DANI, THE SCALE...IT'S WAY BEYOND MY LEVELS OF MANIPULATION...
YEAH, THAT'S NONSENSE.
YOU DON'T BELIEVE ME?
I DON'T BELIEVE A WORD YOU SAY. YOU SAID YOU DON'T LOVE ME, AND YOU'D RATHER DATE THE DEVIL THAN ME, AND I COULDN'T LIVE IF I THOUGHT THAT WAS THE TRUTH.
YOU CAN DO THIS.
YOU ARE SUCH AN IDIOT, DACOSTA.
BOBBY! NATE! COVER AMARA!
BLINK! WARLOCK! THE BAND'S OURS!

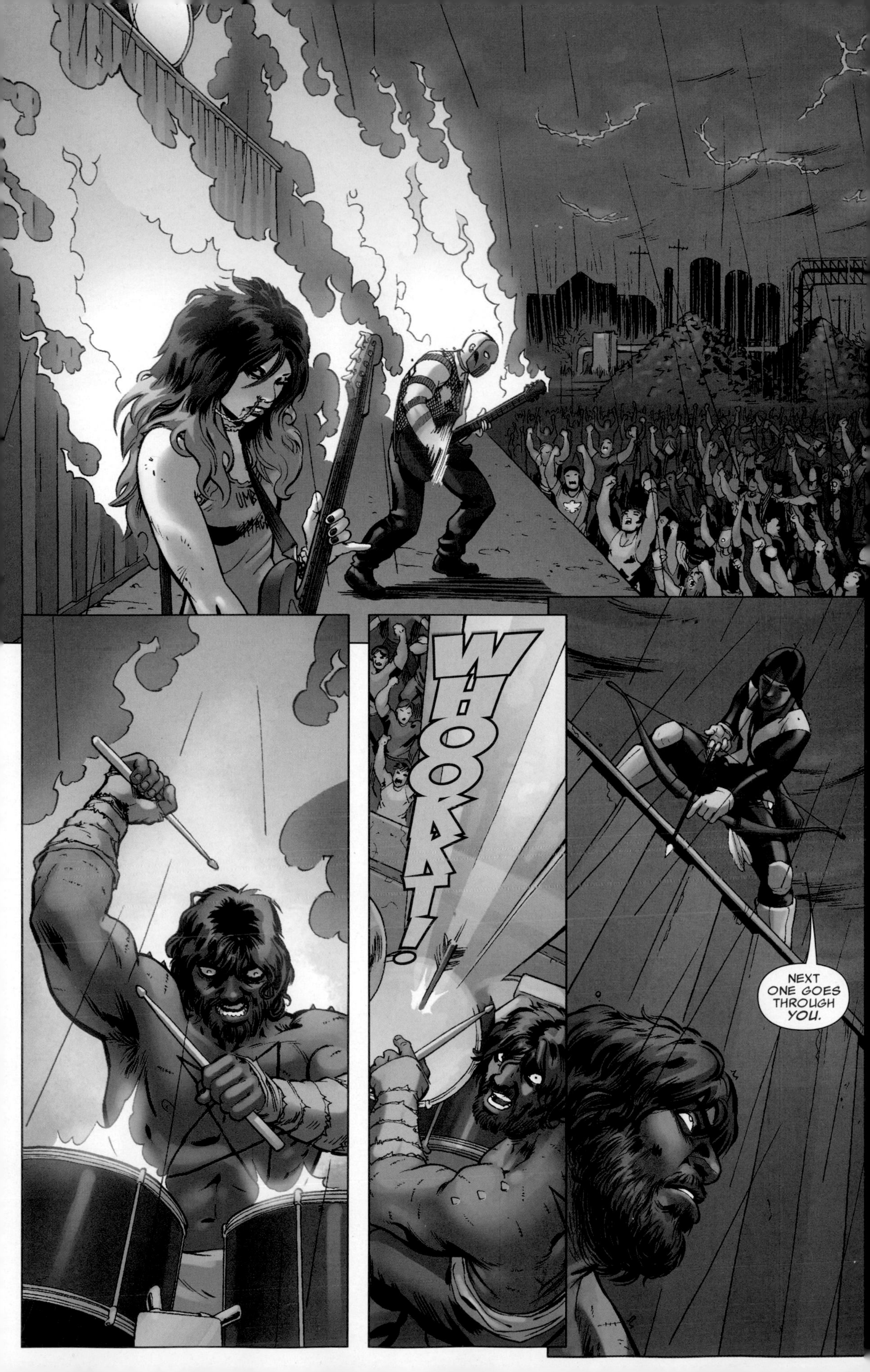
WHOOKAT!
NEXT ONE GOES THROUGH YOU.

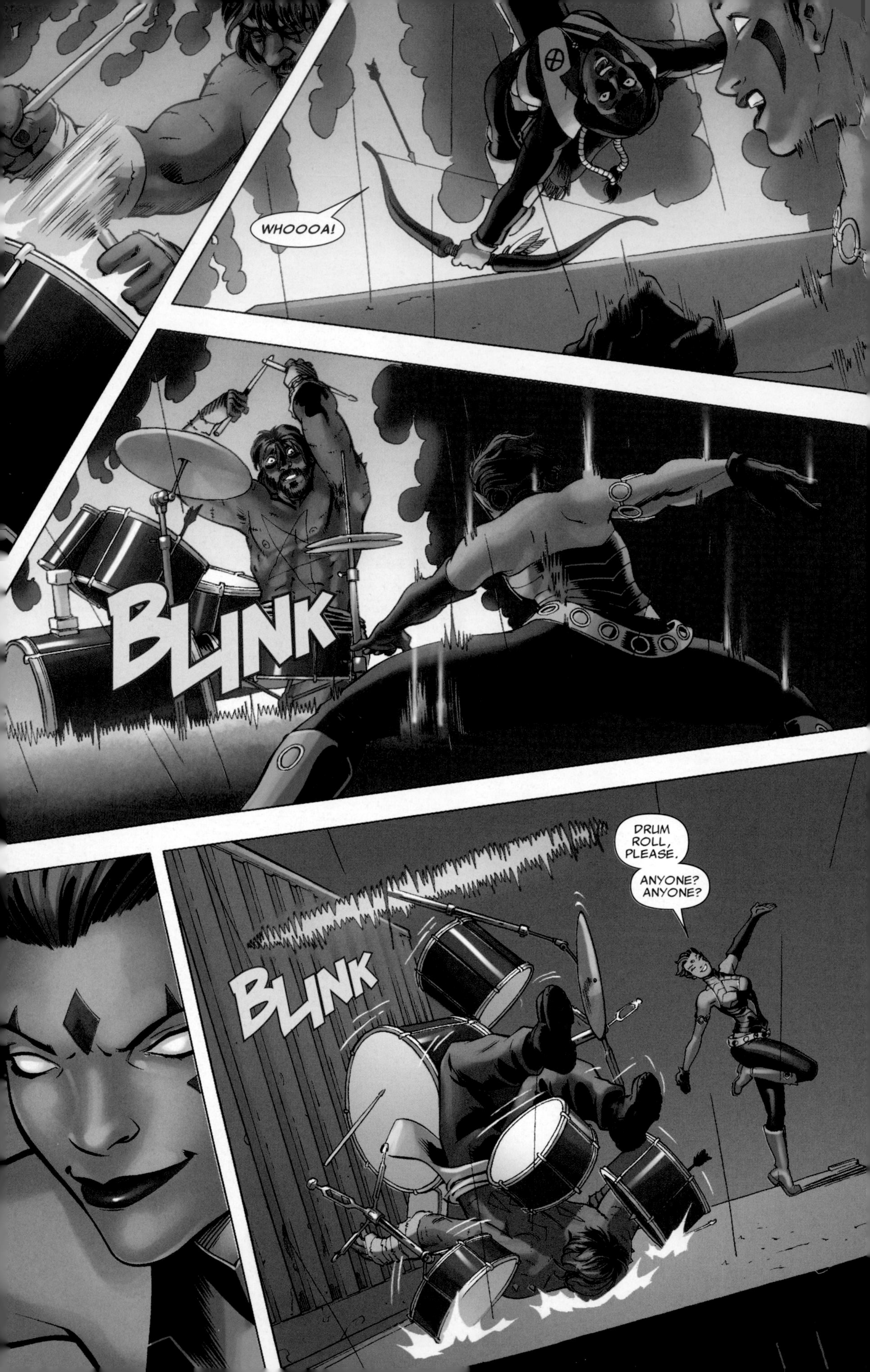
WHOOOA!
BLINK
BLINK
DRUM ROLL, PLEASE.
ANYONE? ANYONE?

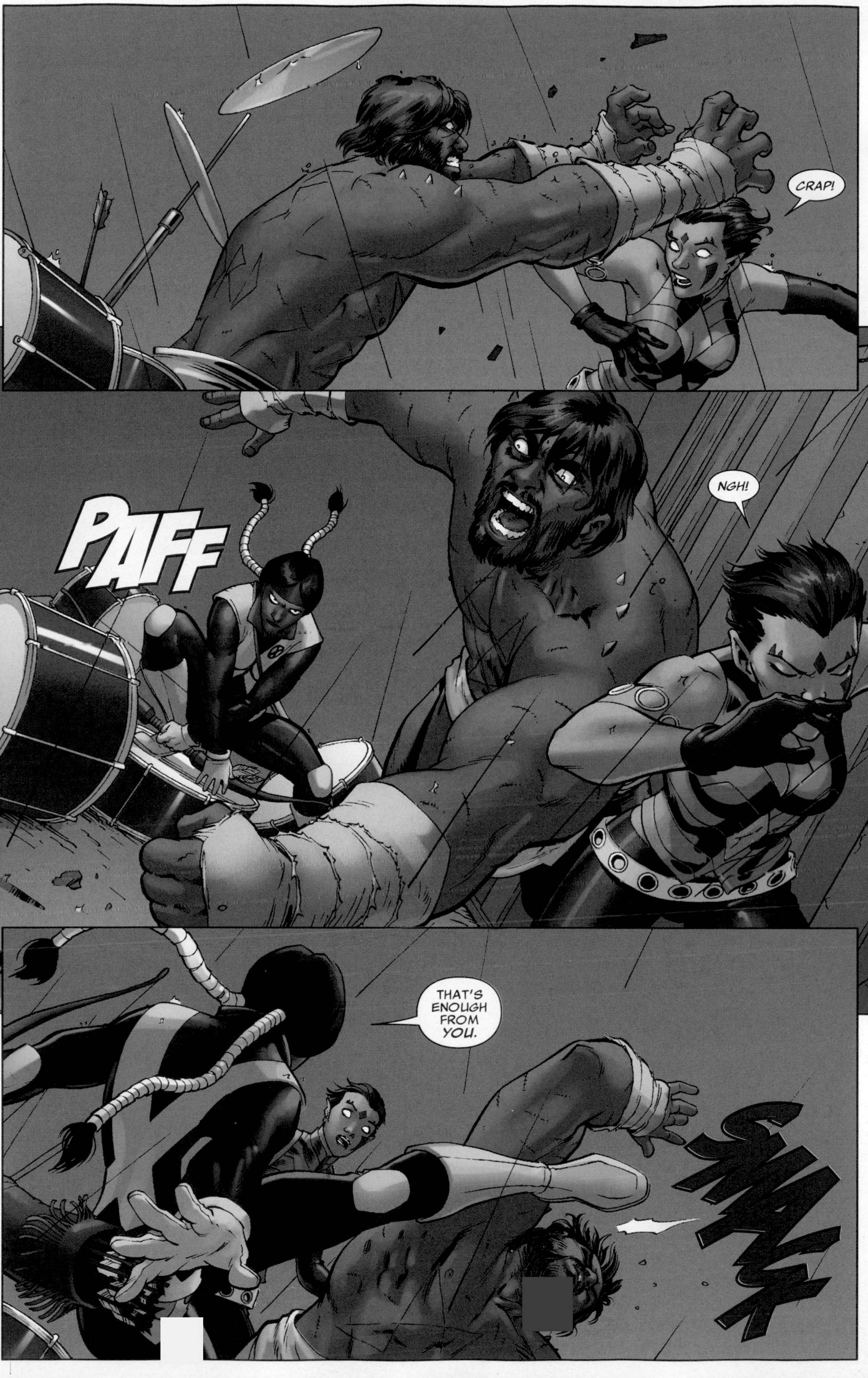
CRAP!
PAFF
NGH!
THAT'S ENOUGH FROM YOU.
SMAK

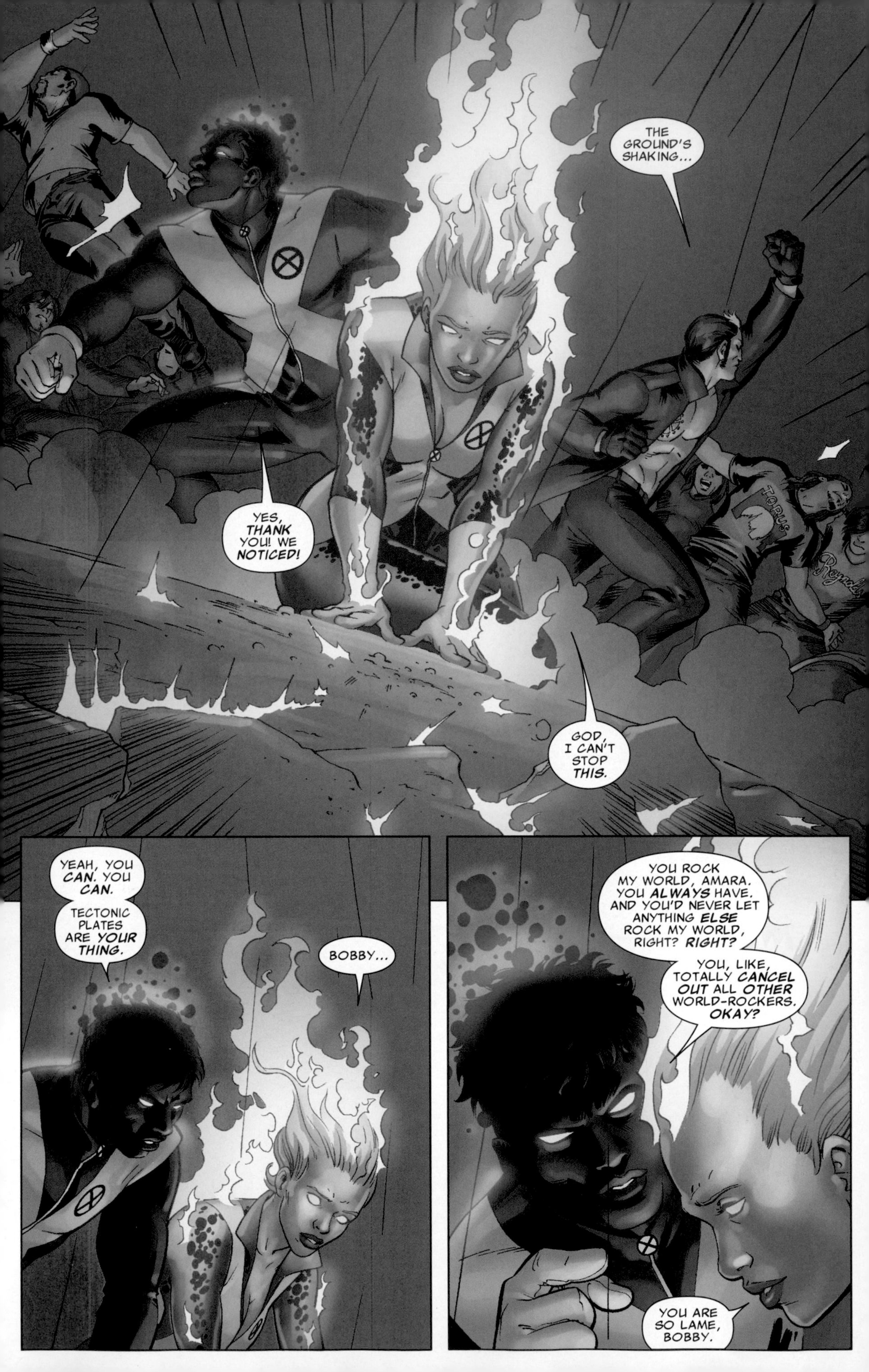
THE GROUND'S SHAKING...
YES, THANK YOU! WE NOTICED!
GOD, I CAN'T STOP THIS.
YEAH, YOU CAN. YOU CAN.
TECTONIC PLATES ARE YOUR THING.
BOBBY...
YOU ROCK MY WORLD, AMARA. YOU ALWAYS HAVE. AND YOU'D NEVER LET ANYTHING ELSE ROCK MY WORLD, RIGHT? RIGHT?
YOU, LIKE, TOTALLY CANCEL OUT ALL OTHER WORLD-ROCKERS. OKAY?
YOU ARE SO LAME, BOBBY.

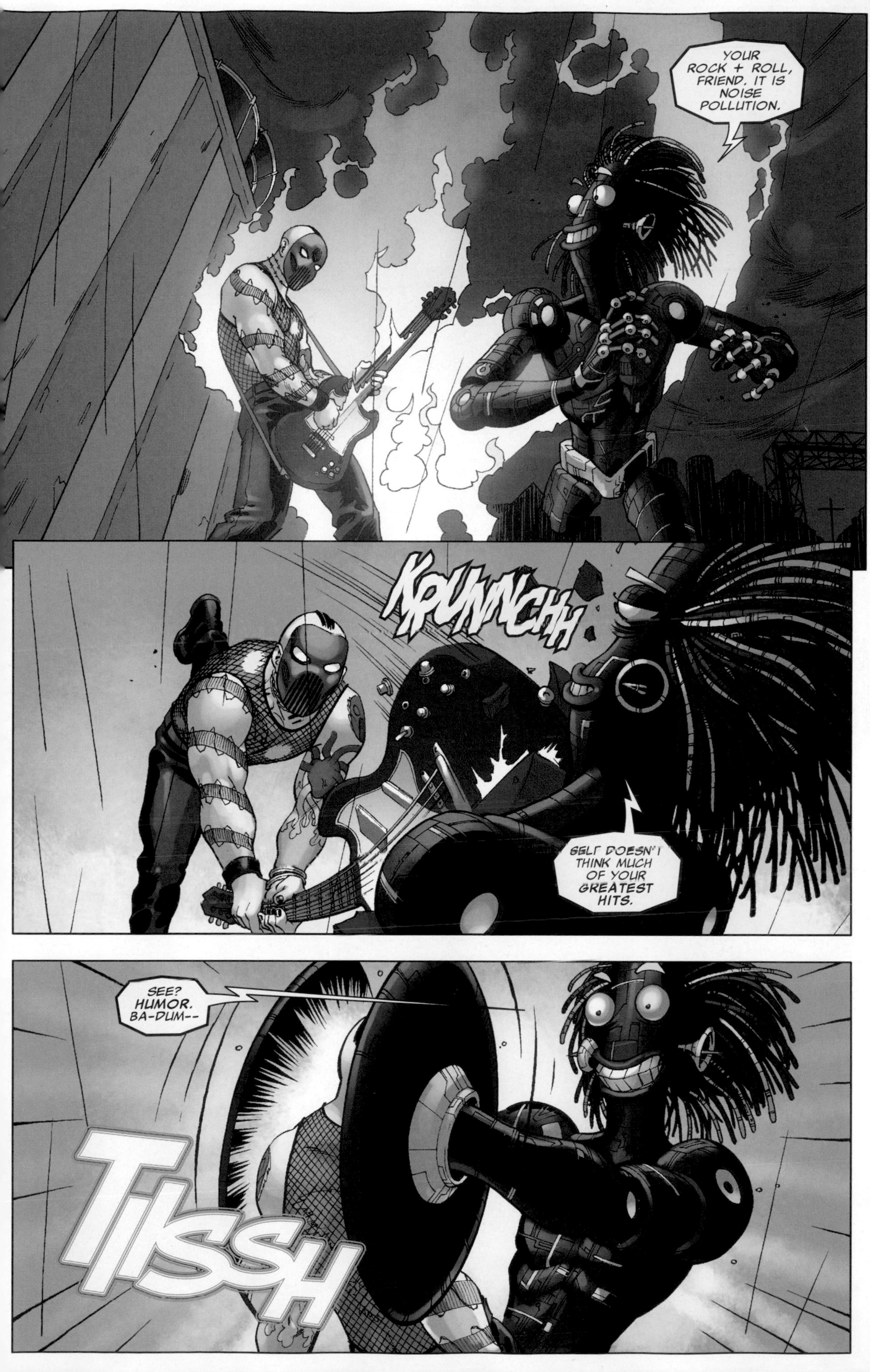
YOUR ROCK + ROLL, FRIEND. IT IS NOISE POLLUTION.
KRUNNCHH
SELF DOESN'T THINK MUCH OF YOUR GREATEST HITS.
SEE? HUMOR. BA-DUM--
TISSH

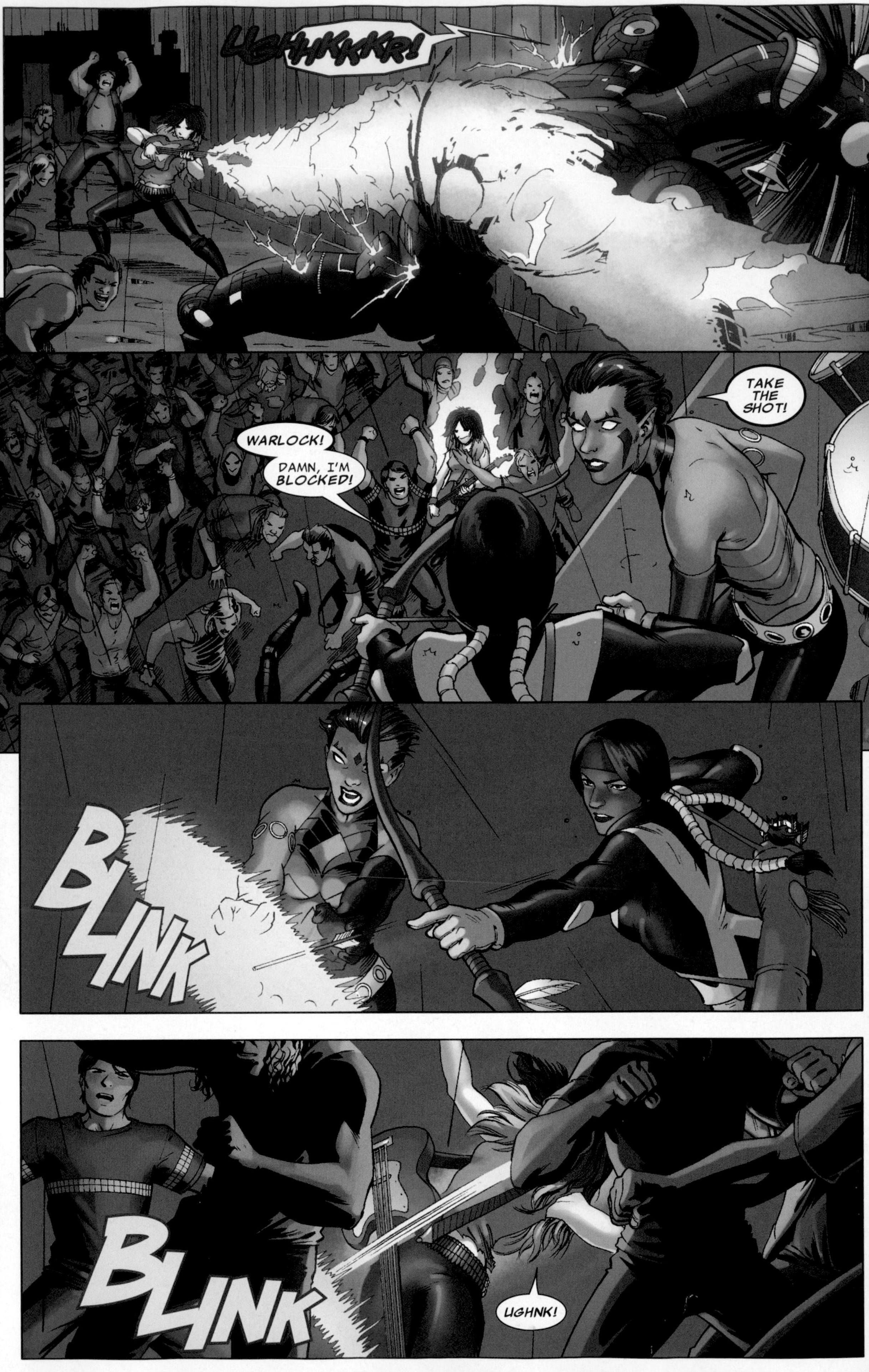
UGHHKKKR!
TAKE THE SHOT!
WARLOCK!
DAMN, I'M BLOCKED!
BLINK
BLINK
UGHNK!

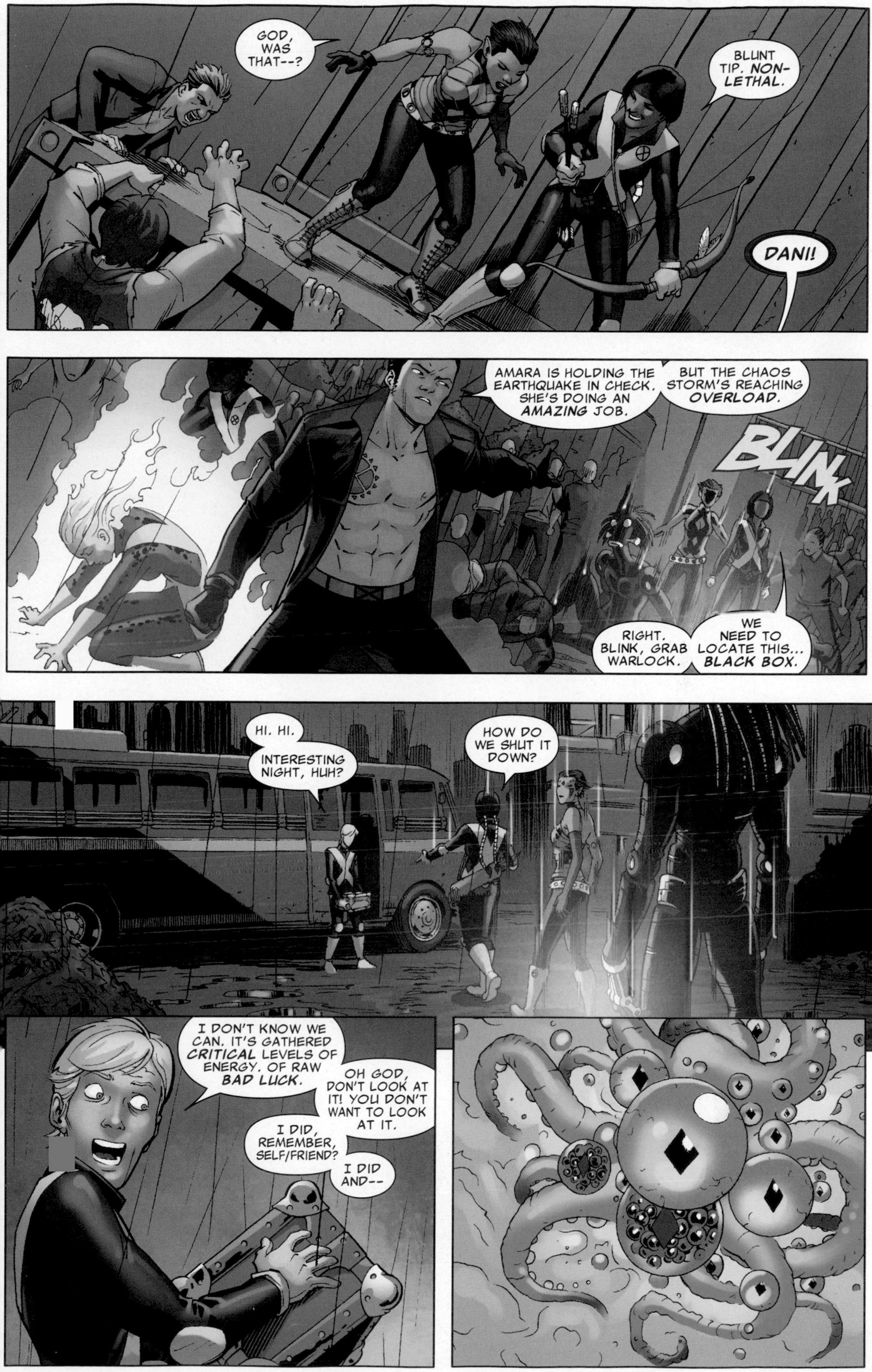
GOD, WAS THAT--?
BLUNT TIP. NON-LETHAL.
DANI!
AMARA IS HOLDING THE EARTHQUAKE IN CHECK. SHE'S DOING AN AMAZING JOB.
BUT THE CHAOS STORM'S REACHING OVERLOAD.
BLINK
RIGHT. BLINK, GRAB WARLOCK.
WE NEED TO LOCATE THIS... BLACK BOX.
HI. HI.
INTERESTING NIGHT, HUH?
HOW DO WE SHUT IT DOWN?
I DON'T KNOW WE CAN. IT'S GATHERED CRITICAL LEVELS OF ENERGY. OF RAW BAD LUCK.
OH GOD, DON'T LOOK AT IT! YOU DON'T WANT TO LOOK AT IT.
I DID, REMEMBER, SELF/FRIEND?
I DID AND--

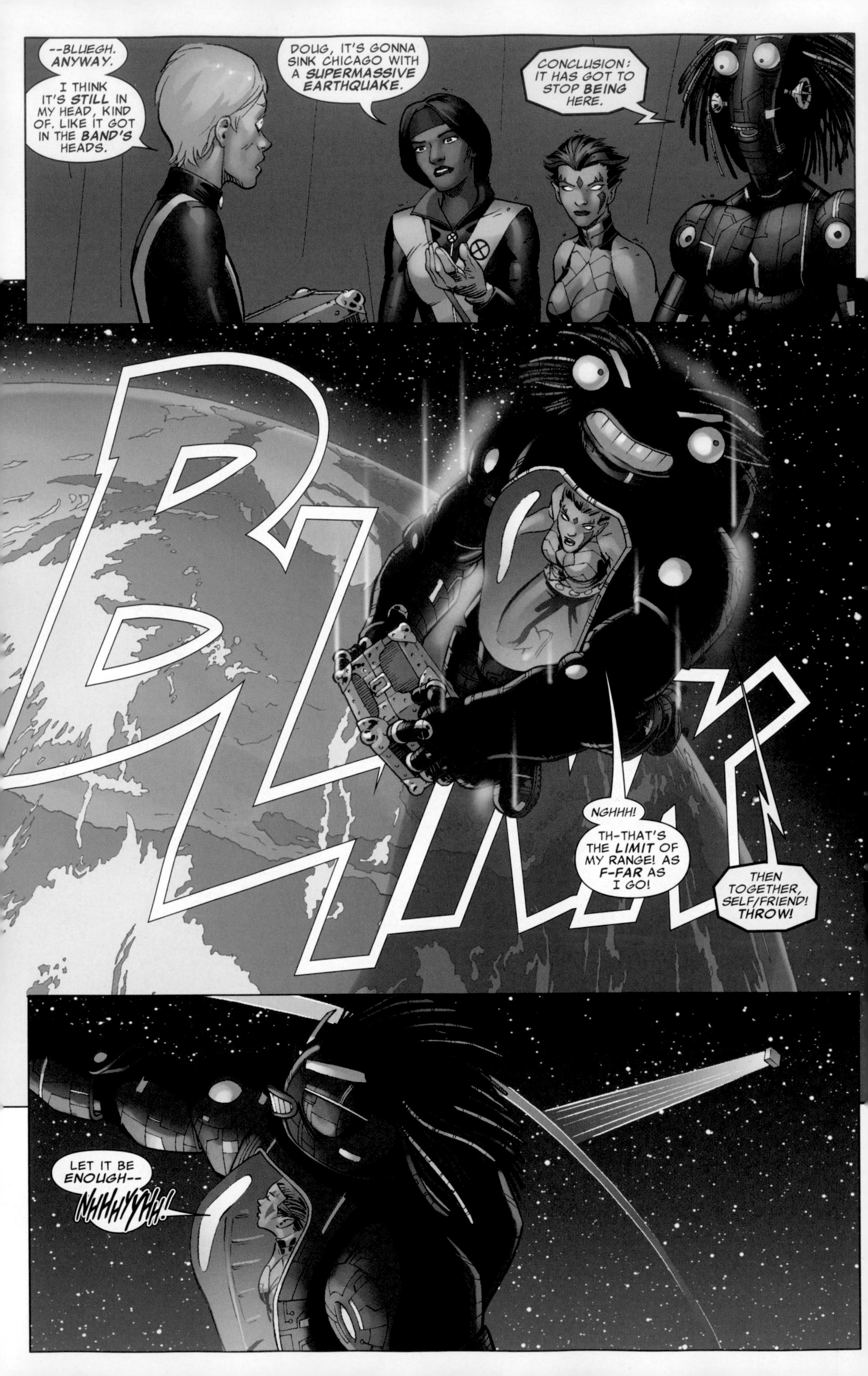
--BLUEGH. ANYWAY.
I THINK IT'S STILL IN MY HEAD, KIND OF. LIKE IT GOT IN THE BAND'S HEADS.
DOUG, IT'S GONNA SINK CHICAGO WITH A SUPERMASSIVE EARTHQUAKE.
CONCLUSION: IT HAS GOT TO STOP BEING HERE.
BLINK
NGHHH!
TH-THAT'S THE LIMIT OF MY RANGE! AS F-FAR AS I GO!
THEN TOGETHER, SELF/FRIEND! THROW!
LET IT BE ENOUGH--
NHHHYHH!

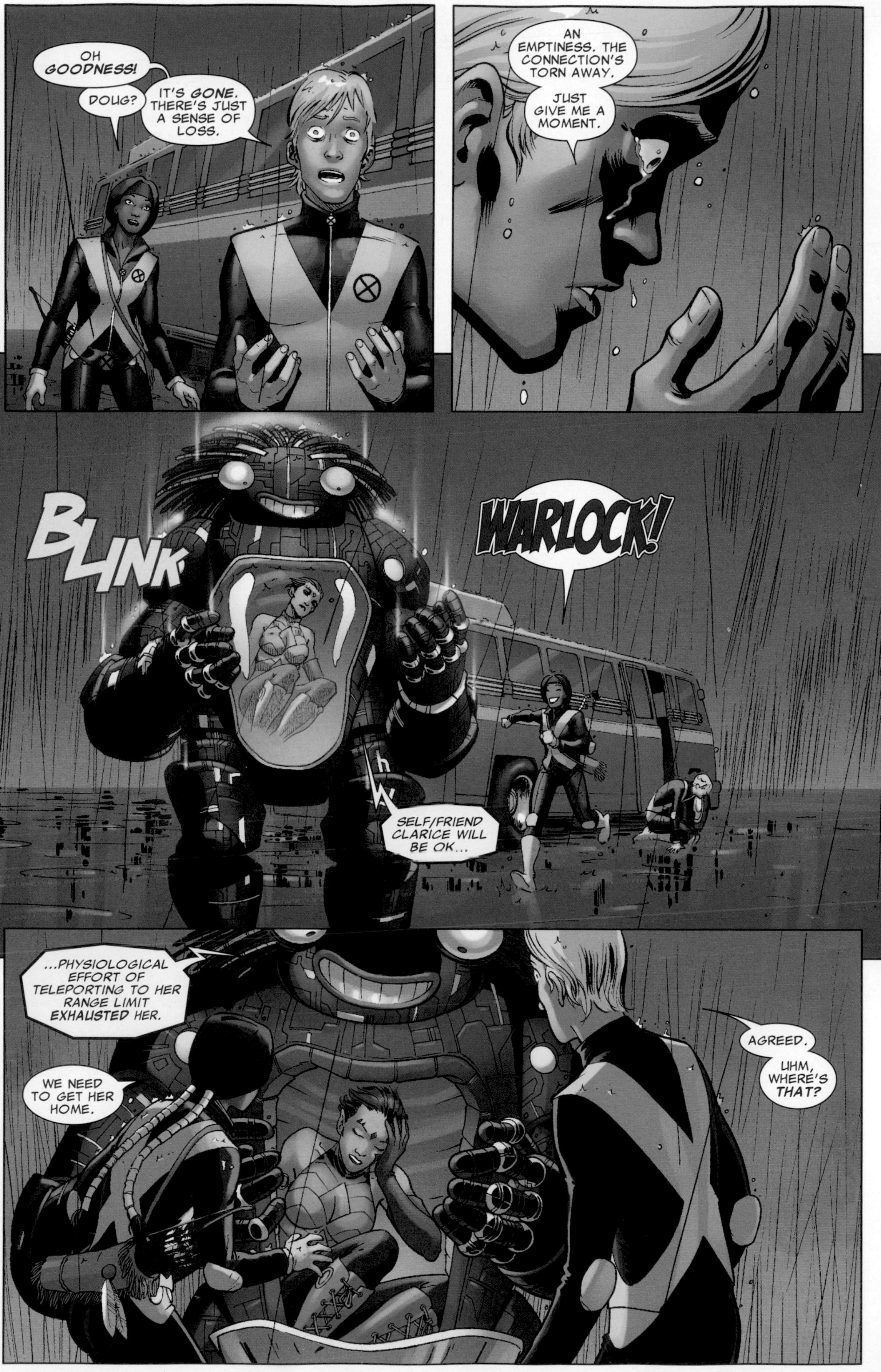
OH GOODNESS!
DOUG?
IT'S GONE. THERE'S JUST A SENSE OF LOSS.
AN EMPTINESS. THE CONNECTION'S TORN AWAY.
JUST GIVE ME A MOMENT.
BLINK
WARLOCK!
SELF/FRIEND CLARICE WILL BE OK...
...PHYSIOLOGICAL EFFORT OF TELEPORTING TO HER RANGE LIMIT EXHAUSTED HER.
WE NEED TO GET HER HOME.
AGREED.
UHM, WHERE'S THAT?

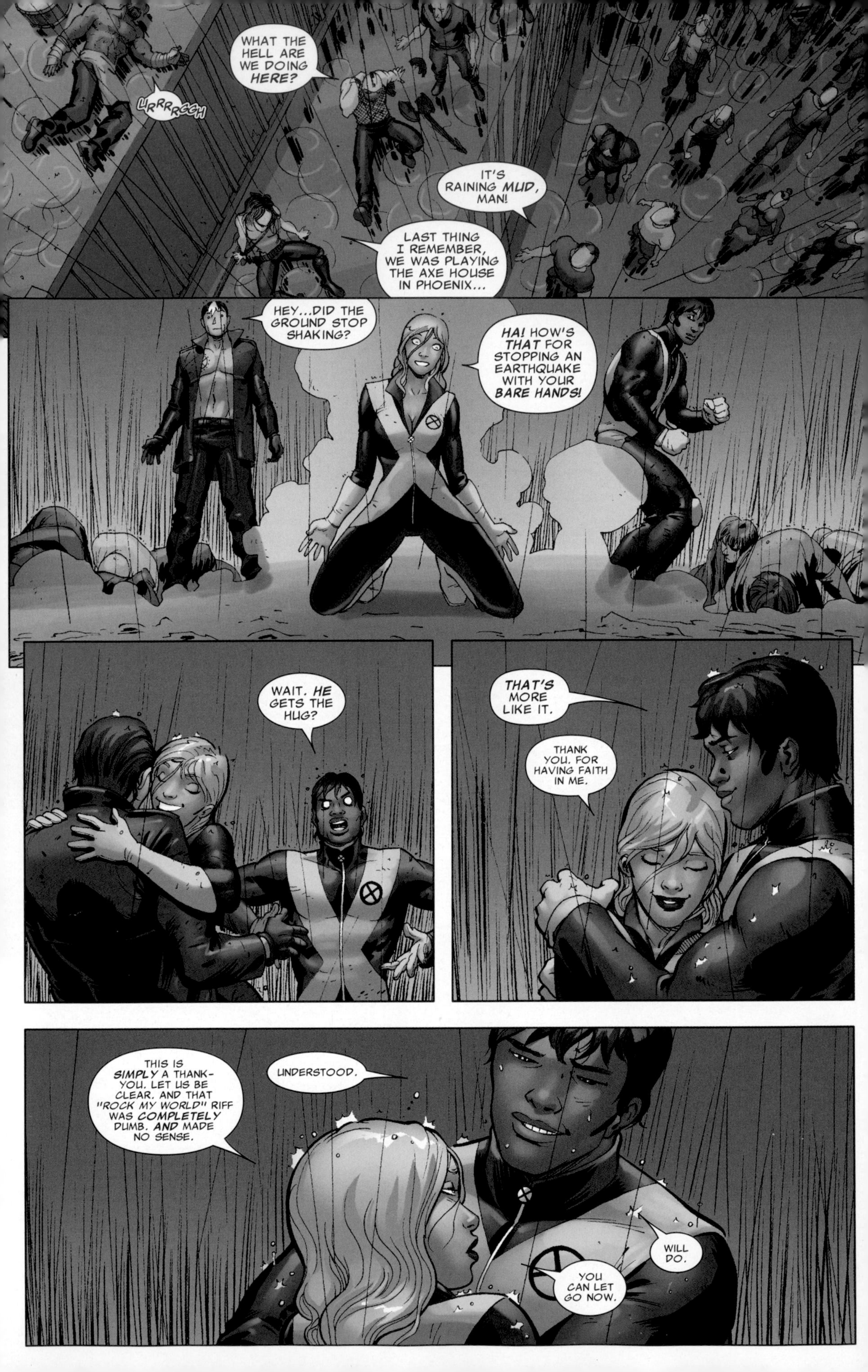
WHAT THE HELL ARE WE DOING HERE?
URRRRGGH
IT'S RAINING MUD, MAN!
LAST THING I REMEMBER, WE WAS PLAYING THE AXE HOUSE IN PHOENIX...
HEY...DID THE GROUND STOP SHAKING?
HA! HOW'S THAT FOR STOPPING AN EARTHQUAKE WITH YOUR BARE HANDS!
WAIT. HE GETS THE HUG?
THAT'S MORE LIKE IT.
THANK YOU. FOR HAVING FAITH IN ME.
THIS IS SIMPLY A THANK-YOU. LET US BE CLEAR. AND THAT "ROCK MY WORLD" RIFF WAS COMPLETELY DUMB. AND MADE NO SENSE.
UNDERSTOOD.
YOU CAN LET GO NOW.
WILL DO.

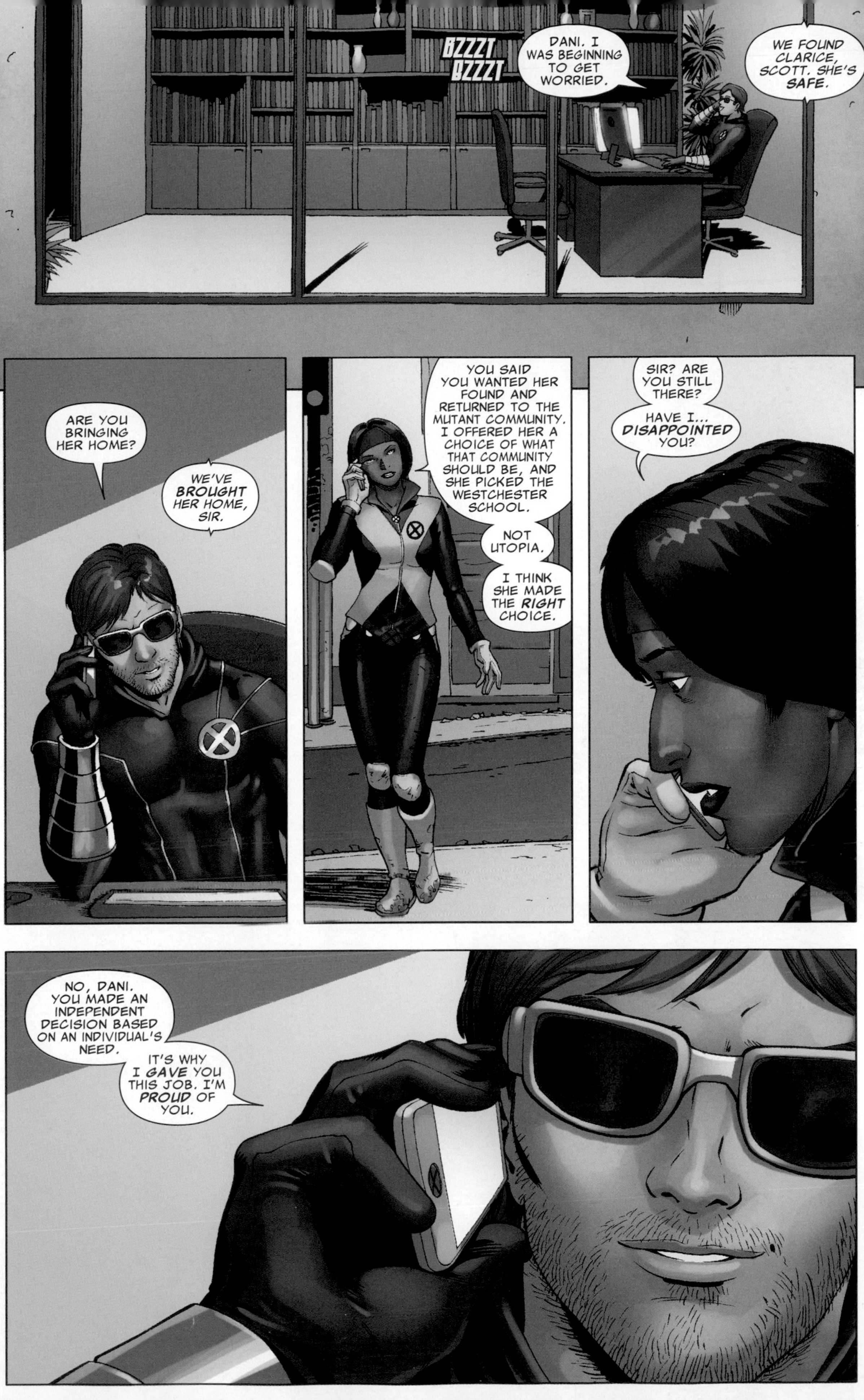
BZZZT BZZZT
DANI. I WAS BEGINNING TO GET WORRIED.
WE FOUND CLARICE, SCOTT. SHE'S SAFE.
ARE YOU BRINGING HER HOME?
WE'VE BROUGHT HER HOME, SIR.
YOU SAID YOU WANTED HER FOUND AND RETURNED TO THE MUTANT COMMUNITY. I OFFERED HER A CHOICE OF WHAT THAT COMMUNITY SHOULD BE, AND SHE PICKED THE WESTCHESTER SCHOOL.
NOT UTOPIA.
I THINK SHE MADE THE RIGHT CHOICE.
SIR? ARE YOU STILL THERE?
HAVE I... DISAPPOINTED YOU?
NO, DANI. YOU MADE AN INDEPENDENT DECISION BASED ON AN INDIVIDUAL'S NEED.
IT'S WHY I GAVE YOU THIS JOB. I'M PROUD OF YOU.

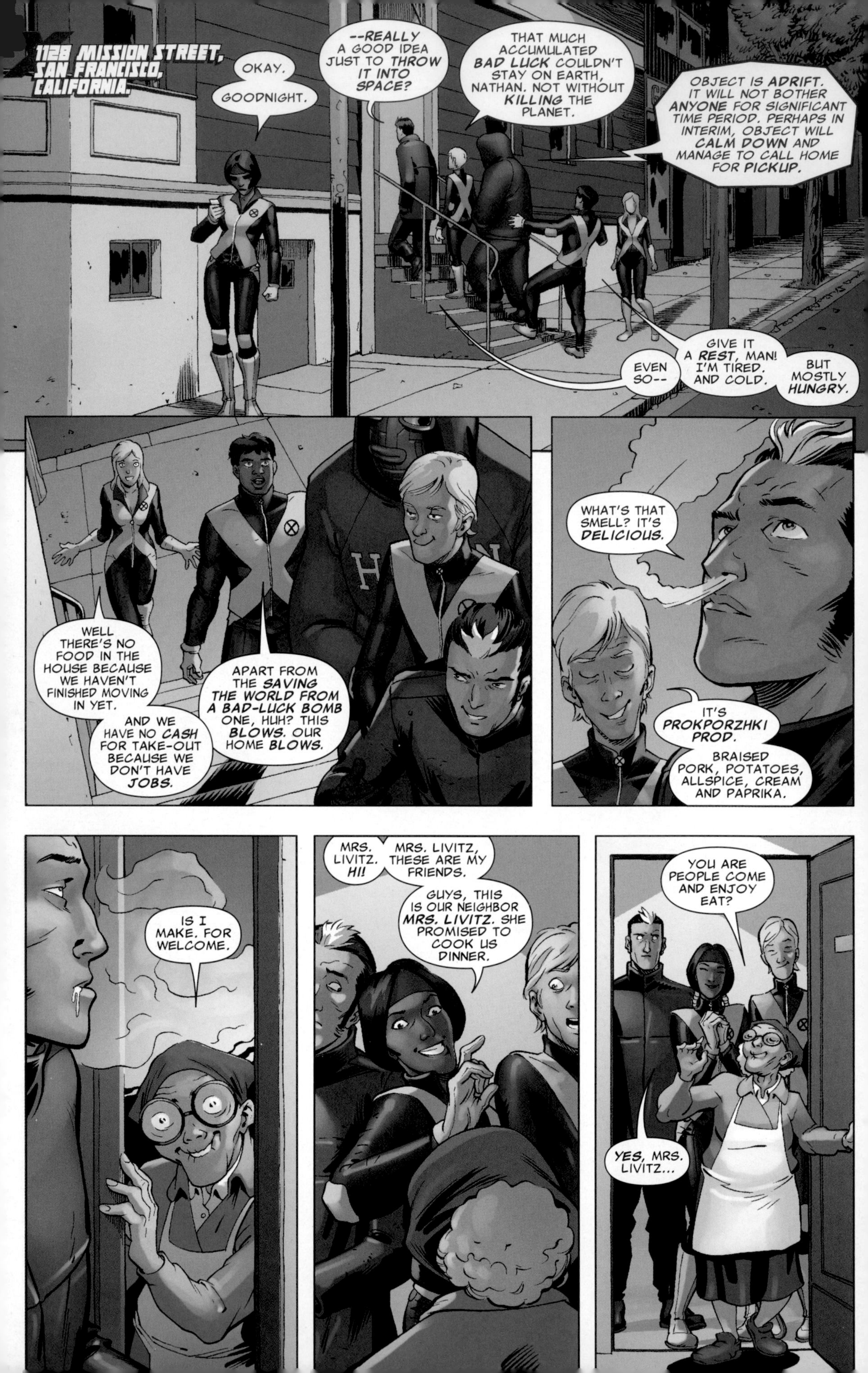
1128 MISSION STREET, SAN FRANCISCO, CALIFORNIA.
OKAY.
GOODNIGHT.
--REALLY A GOOD IDEA JUST TO THROW IT INTO SPACE?
THAT MUCH ACCUMULATED BAD LUCK COULDN'T STAY ON EARTH, NATHAN. NOT WITHOUT KILLING THE PLANET.
OBJECT IS ADRIFT. IT WILL NOT BOTHER ANYONE FOR SIGNIFICANT TIME PERIOD. PERHAPS IN INTERIM, OBJECT WILL CALM DOWN AND MANAGE TO CALL HOME FOR PICKUP.
EVEN SO--
GIVE IT A REST, MAN! I'M TIRED. AND COLD.
BUT MOSTLY HUNGRY.
WELL THERE'S NO FOOD IN THE HOUSE BECAUSE WE HAVEN'T FINISHED MOVING IN YET.
AND WE HAVE NO CASH FOR TAKE-OUT BECAUSE WE DON'T HAVE JOBS.
APART FROM THE SAVING THE WORLD FROM A BAD-LUCK BOMB ONE, HUH? THIS BLOWS. OUR HOME BLOWS.
WHAT'S THAT SMELL? IT'S DELICIOUS.
IT'S PROKPORZHKI PROD.
BRAISED PORK, POTATOES, ALLSPICE, CREAM AND PAPRIKA.
IS I MAKE. FOR WELCOME.
MRS. LIVITZ. HI!
MRS. LIVITZ, THESE ARE MY FRIENDS.
GUYS, THIS IS OUR NEIGHBOR MRS. LIVITZ. SHE PROMISED TO COOK US DINNER.
YOU ARE PEOPLE COME AND ENJOY EAT?
YES, MRS. LIVITZ...

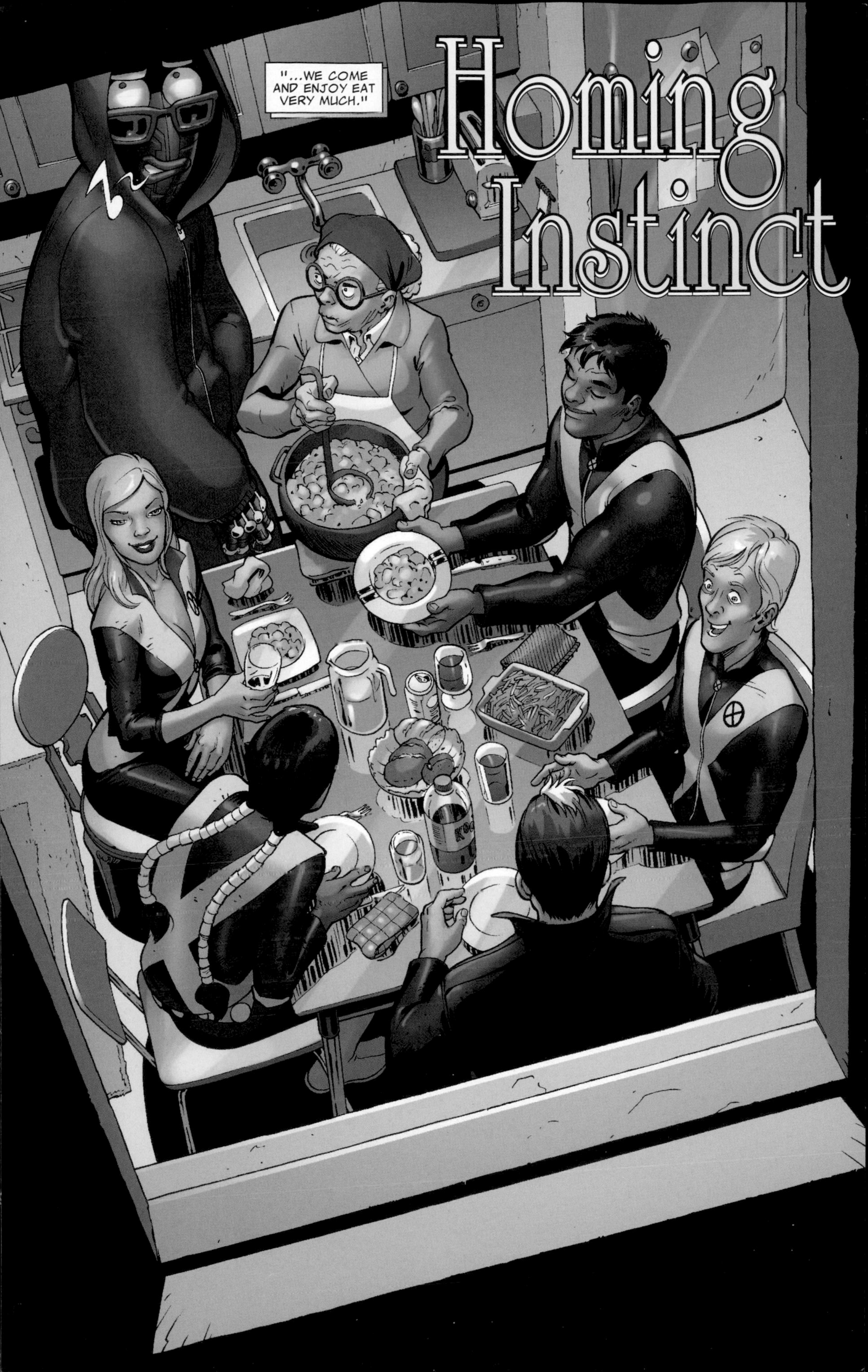
"...WE COME AND ENJOY EAT VERY MUCH."
Homing Instinct

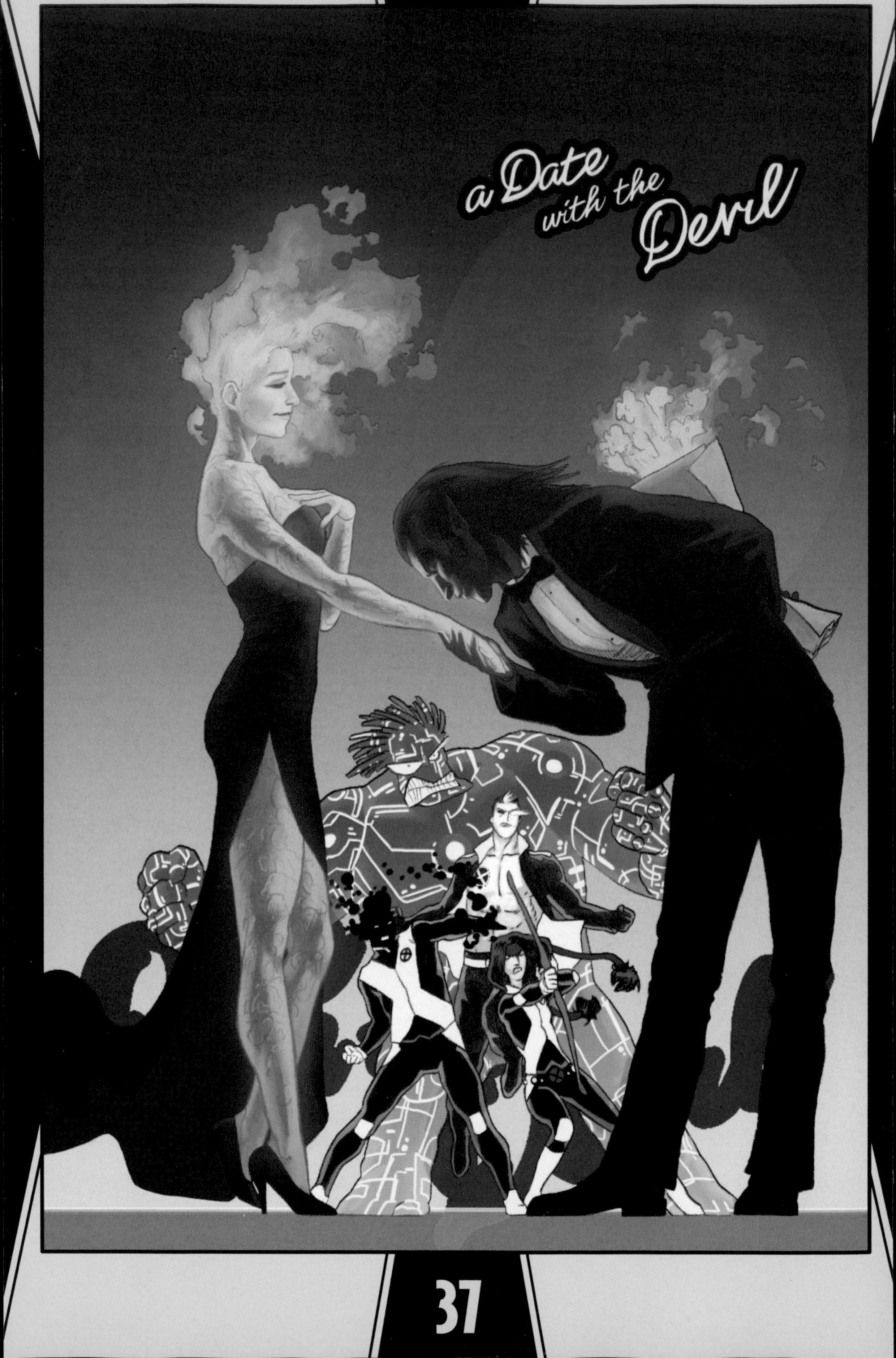
a Date with the Devil

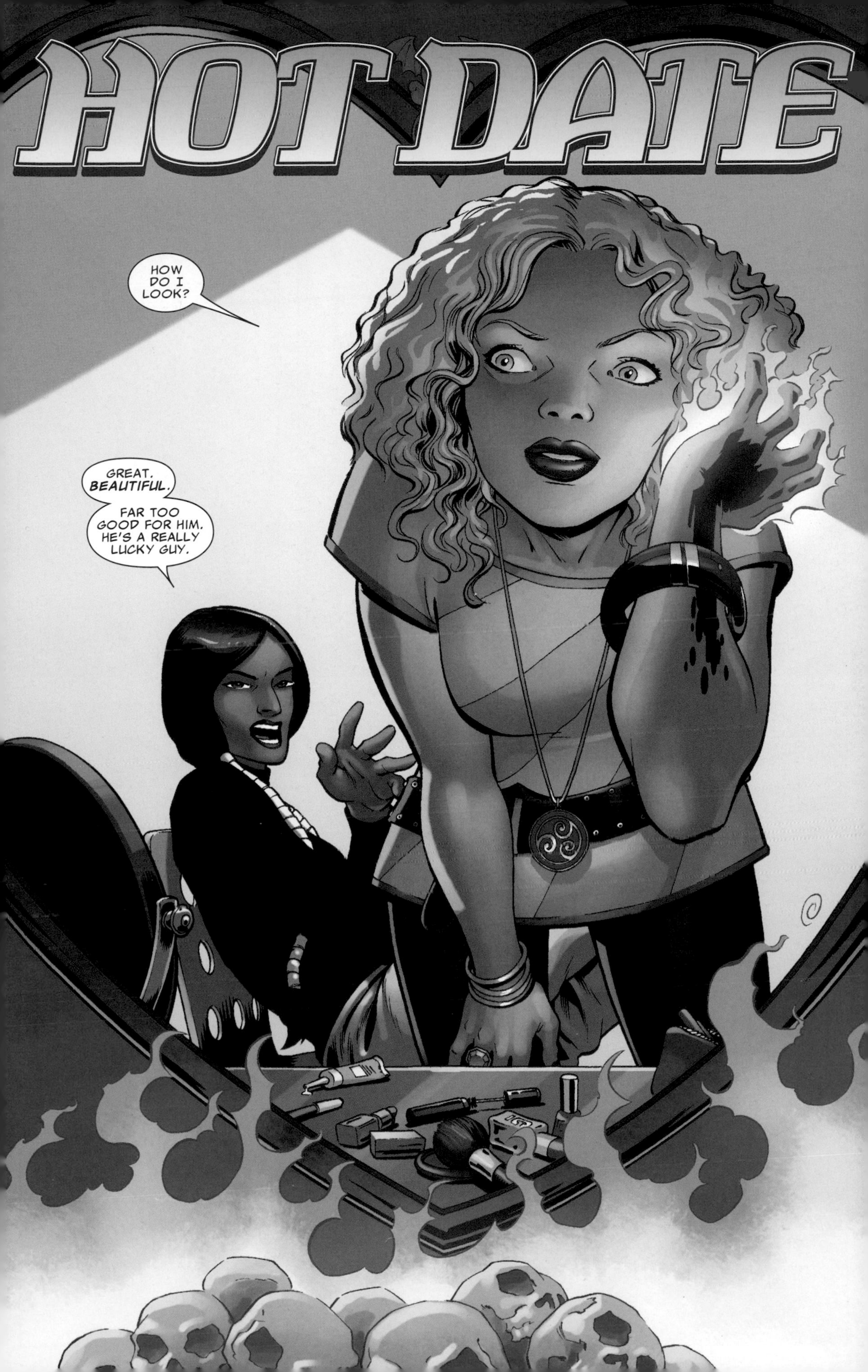
HOT DATE
HOW DO I LOOK?
GREAT. **BEAUTIFUL.**
FAR TOO GOOD FOR HIM. HE'S A REALLY LUCKY GUY.

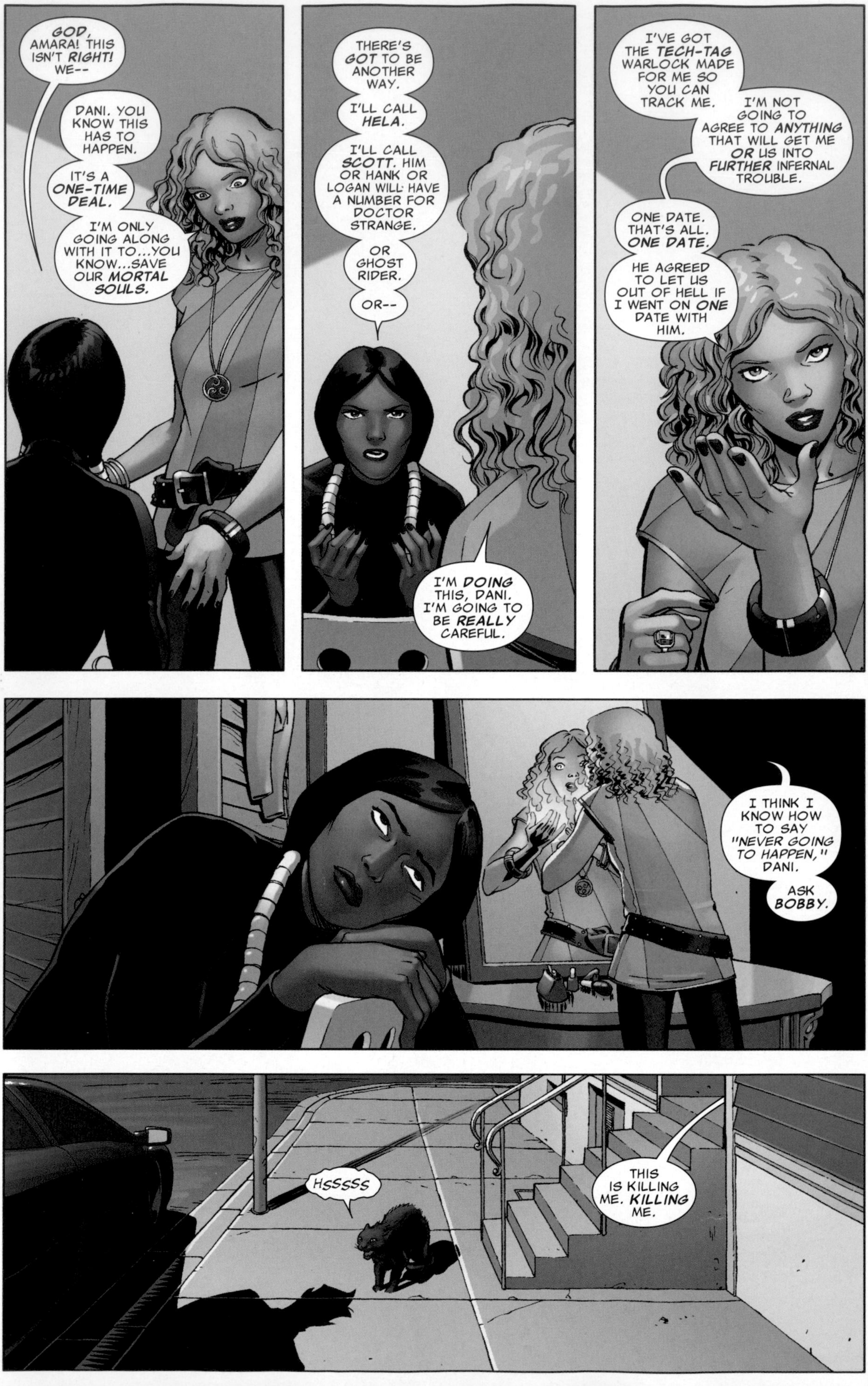
GOD, AMARA! THIS ISN'T RIGHT! WE--
DANI. YOU KNOW THIS HAS TO HAPPEN.
IT'S A ONE-TIME DEAL.
I'M ONLY GOING ALONG WITH IT TO...YOU KNOW...SAVE OUR MORTAL SOULS.
THERE'S GOT TO BE ANOTHER WAY.
I'LL CALL HELA.
I'LL CALL SCOTT. HIM OR HANK OR LOGAN WILL HAVE A NUMBER FOR DOCTOR STRANGE.
OR GHOST RIDER.
OR--
I'M DOING THIS, DANI. I'M GOING TO BE REALLY CAREFUL.
I'VE GOT THE TECH-TAG WARLOCK MADE FOR ME SO YOU CAN TRACK ME.
I'M NOT GOING TO AGREE TO ANYTHING THAT WILL GET ME OR US INTO FURTHER INFERNAL TROUBLE.
ONE DATE. THAT'S ALL. ONE DATE.
HE AGREED TO LET US OUT OF HELL IF I WENT ON ONE DATE WITH HIM.
I THINK I KNOW HOW TO SAY "NEVER GOING TO HAPPEN," DANI.
ASK BOBBY.
HSSSSS
THIS IS KILLING ME. KILLING ME.

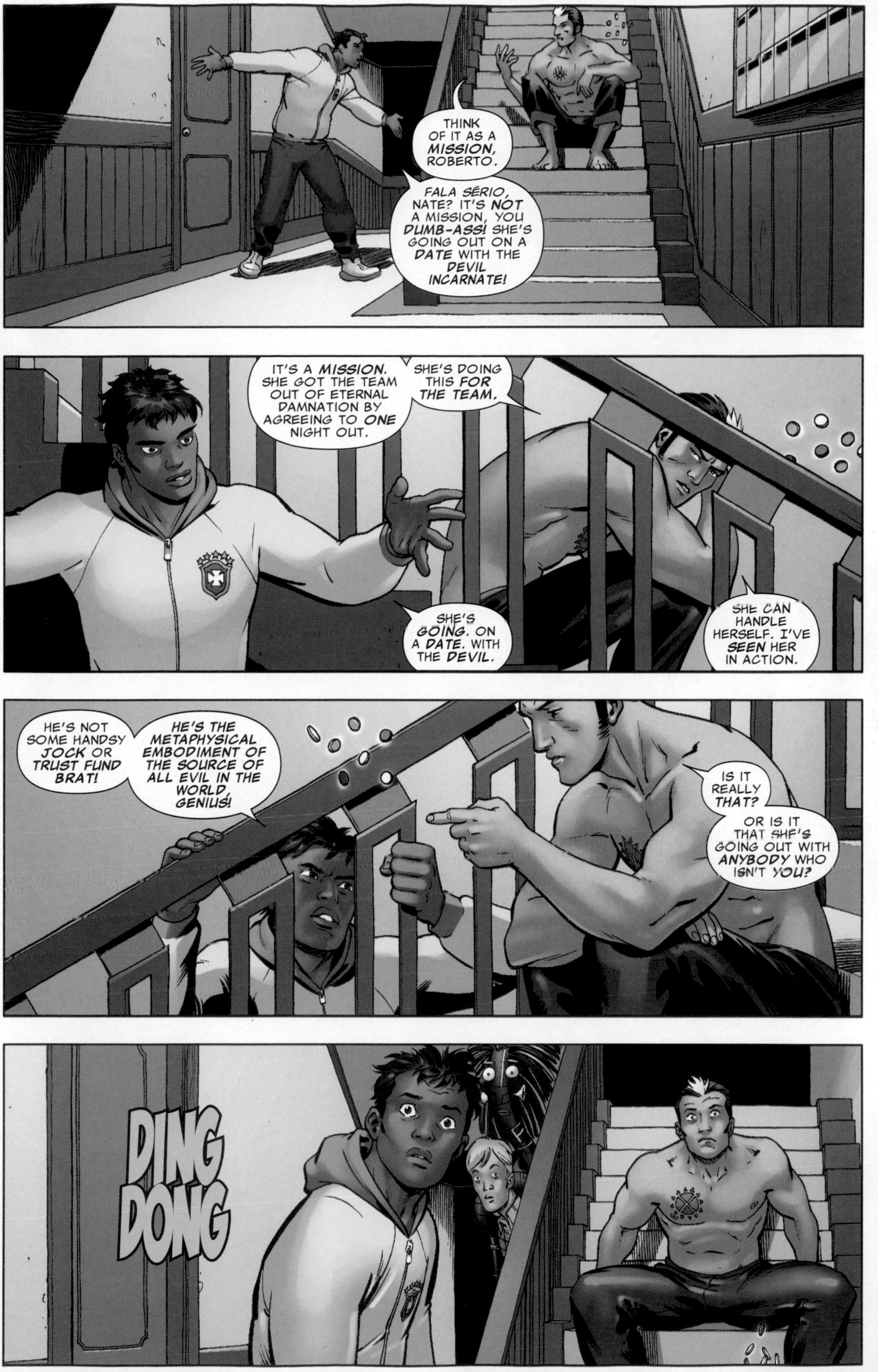
THINK OF IT AS A MISSION, ROBERTO.
FALA SÉRIO, NATE? IT'S NOT A MISSION, YOU DUMB-ASS! SHE'S GOING OUT ON A DATE WITH THE DEVIL INCARNATE!
IT'S A MISSION. SHE GOT THE TEAM OUT OF ETERNAL DAMNATION BY AGREEING TO ONE NIGHT OUT.
SHE'S DOING THIS FOR THE TEAM.
SHE'S GOING. ON A DATE. WITH THE DEVIL.
SHE CAN HANDLE HERSELF. I'VE SEEN HER IN ACTION.
HE'S NOT SOME HANDSY JOCK OR TRUST FUND BRAT!
HE'S THE METAPHYSICAL EMBODIMENT OF THE SOURCE OF ALL EVIL IN THE WORLD, GENIUS!
IS IT REALLY THAT?
OR IS IT THAT SHE'S GOING OUT WITH ANYBODY WHO ISN'T YOU?
DING DONG

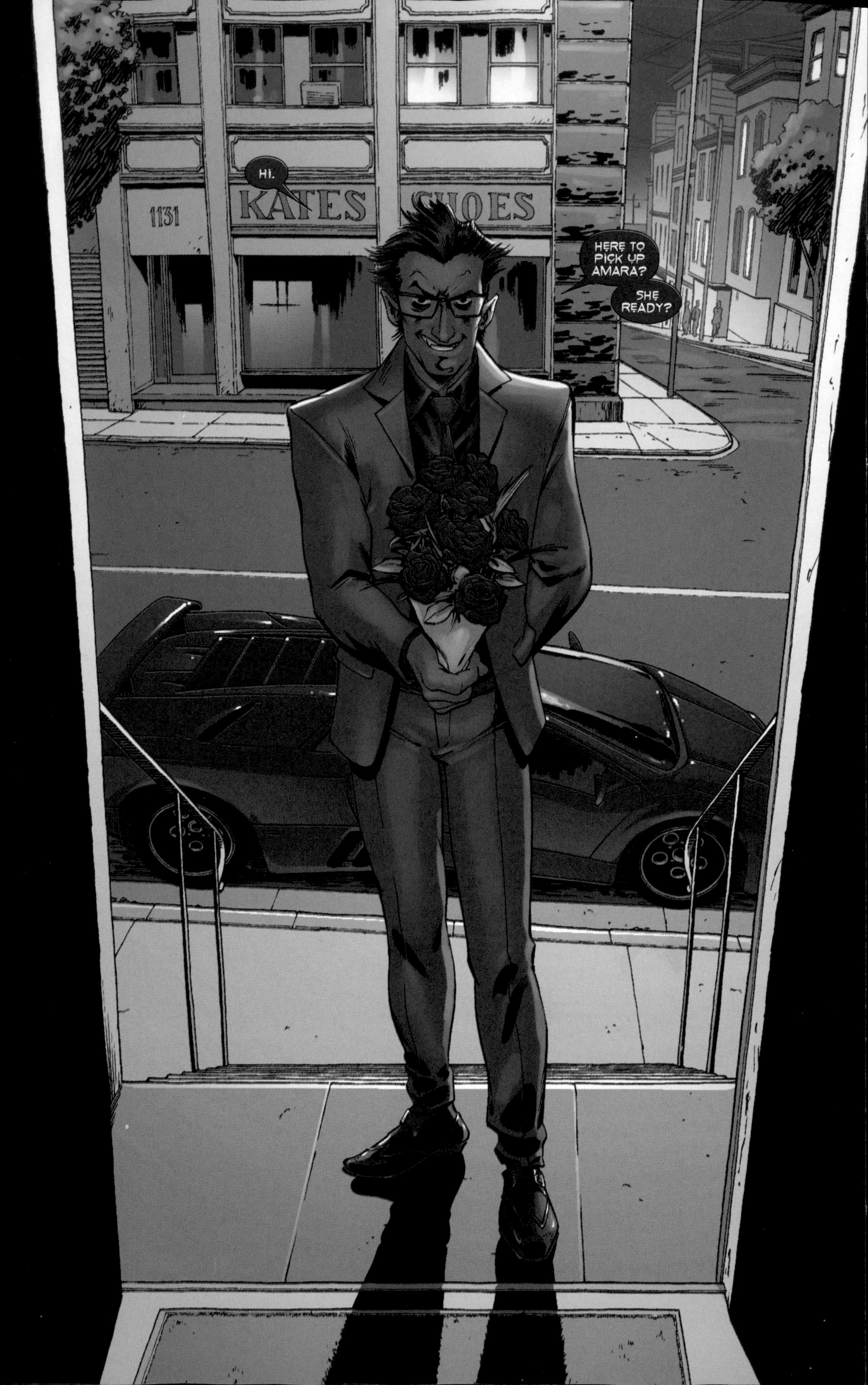
HI.
KATES SHOES
1131
HERE TO PICK UP AMARA?
SHE READY?

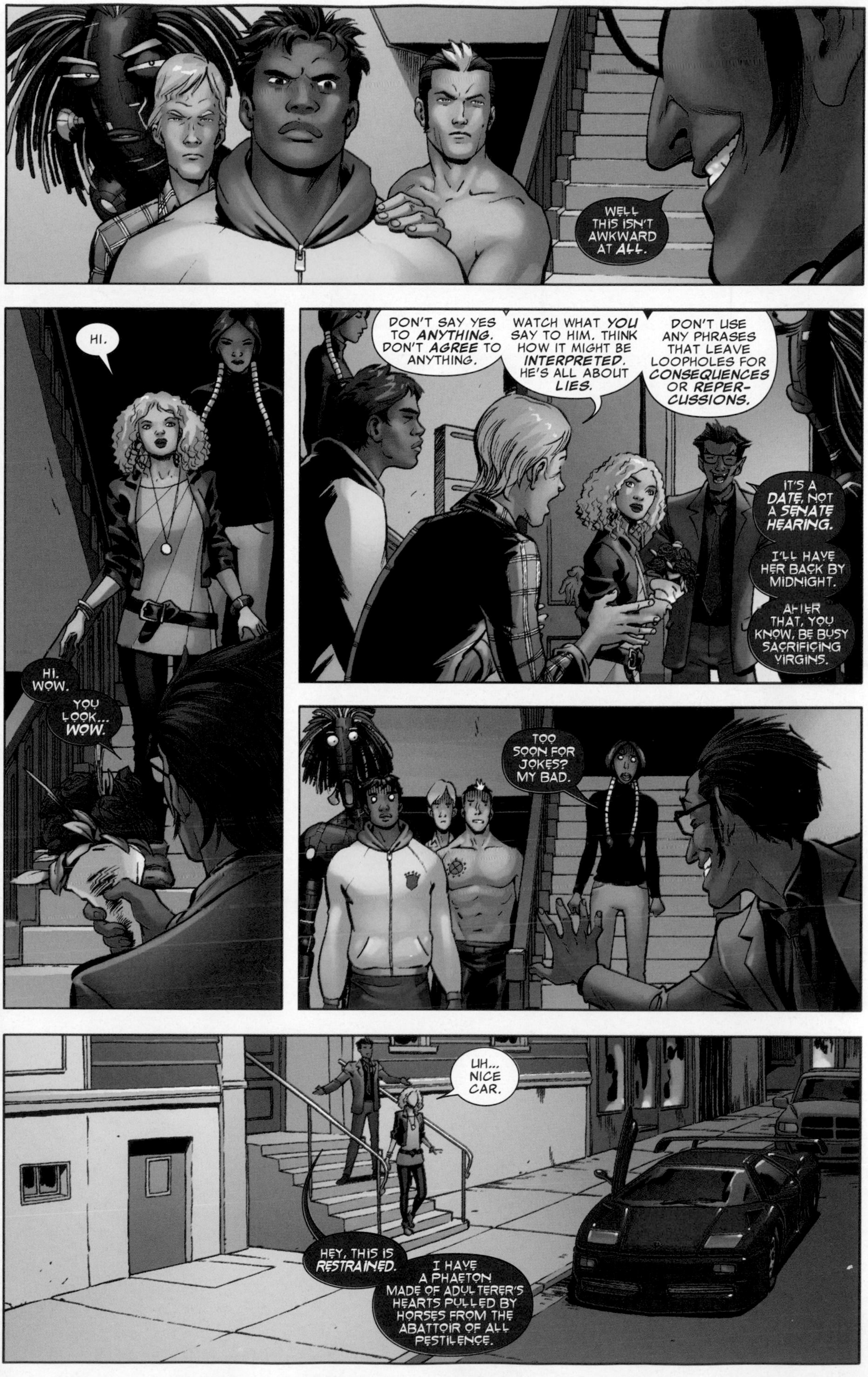
WELL THIS ISN'T AWKWARD AT ALL.
HI.
HI. WOW.
YOU LOOK... WOW.
DON'T SAY YES TO ANYTHING. DON'T AGREE TO ANYTHING.
WATCH WHAT YOU SAY TO HIM. THINK HOW IT MIGHT BE INTERPRETED. HE'S ALL ABOUT LIES.
DON'T USE ANY PHRASES THAT LEAVE LOOPHOLES FOR CONSEQUENCES OR REPERCUSSIONS.
IT'S A DATE, NOT A SENATE HEARING.
I'LL HAVE HER BACK BY MIDNIGHT.
AFTER THAT, YOU KNOW, BE BUSY SACRIFICING VIRGINS.
TOO SOON FOR JOKES? MY BAD.
UH... NICE CAR.
HEY, THIS IS RESTRAINED.
I HAVE A PHAETON MADE OF ADULTERER'S HEARTS PULLED BY HORSES FROM THE ABATTOIR OF ALL PESTILENCE.

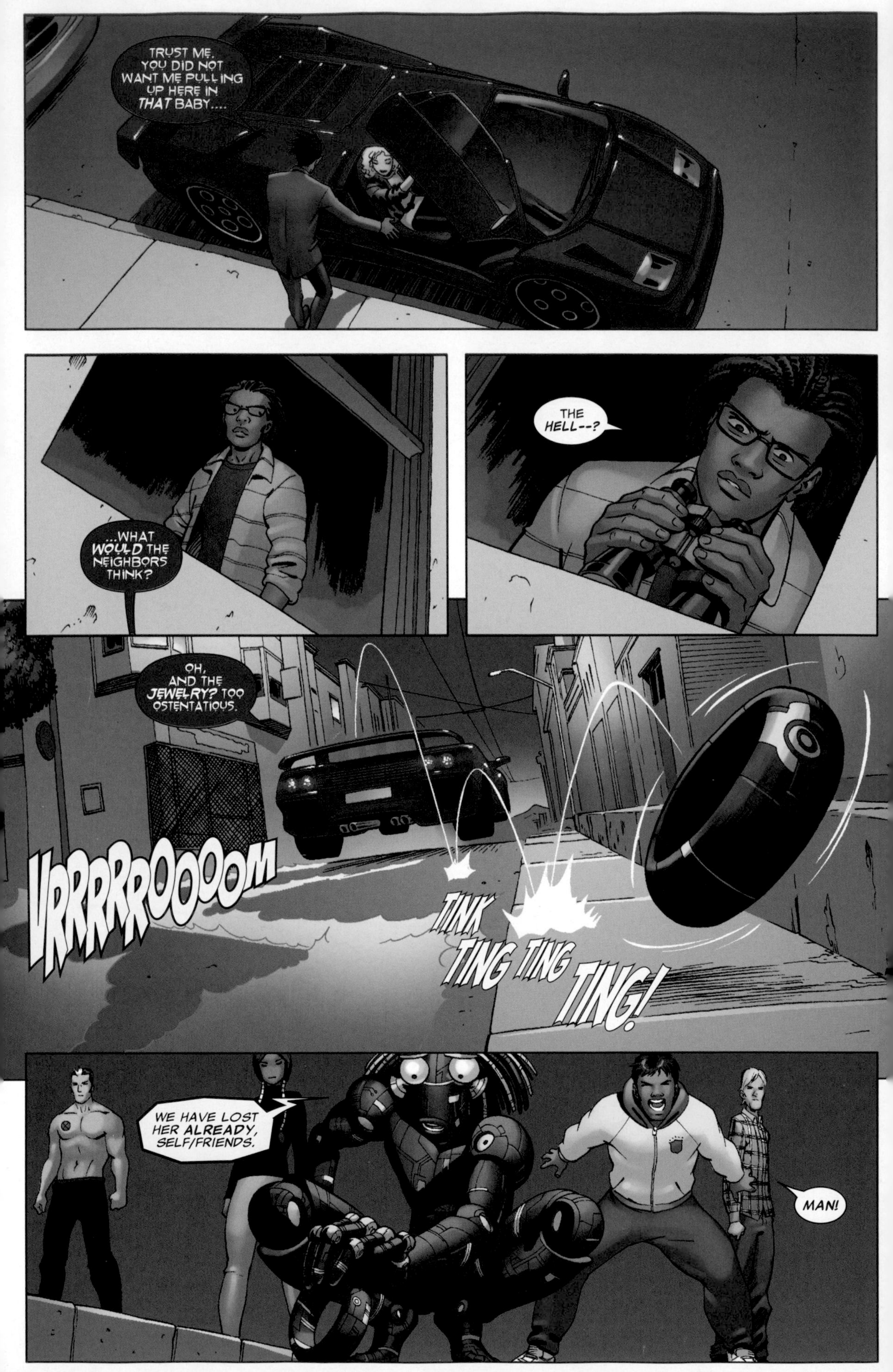

TRUST ME. YOU DID NOT WANT ME PULLING UP HERE IN THAT BABY....
...WHAT WOULD THE NEIGHBORS THINK?
THE HELL--?
OH, AND THE JEWELRY? TOO OSTENTATIOUS.
URRRRROOOOM
TINK
TING TING
TING!
WE HAVE LOST HER ALREADY, SELF/FRIENDS.
MAN!

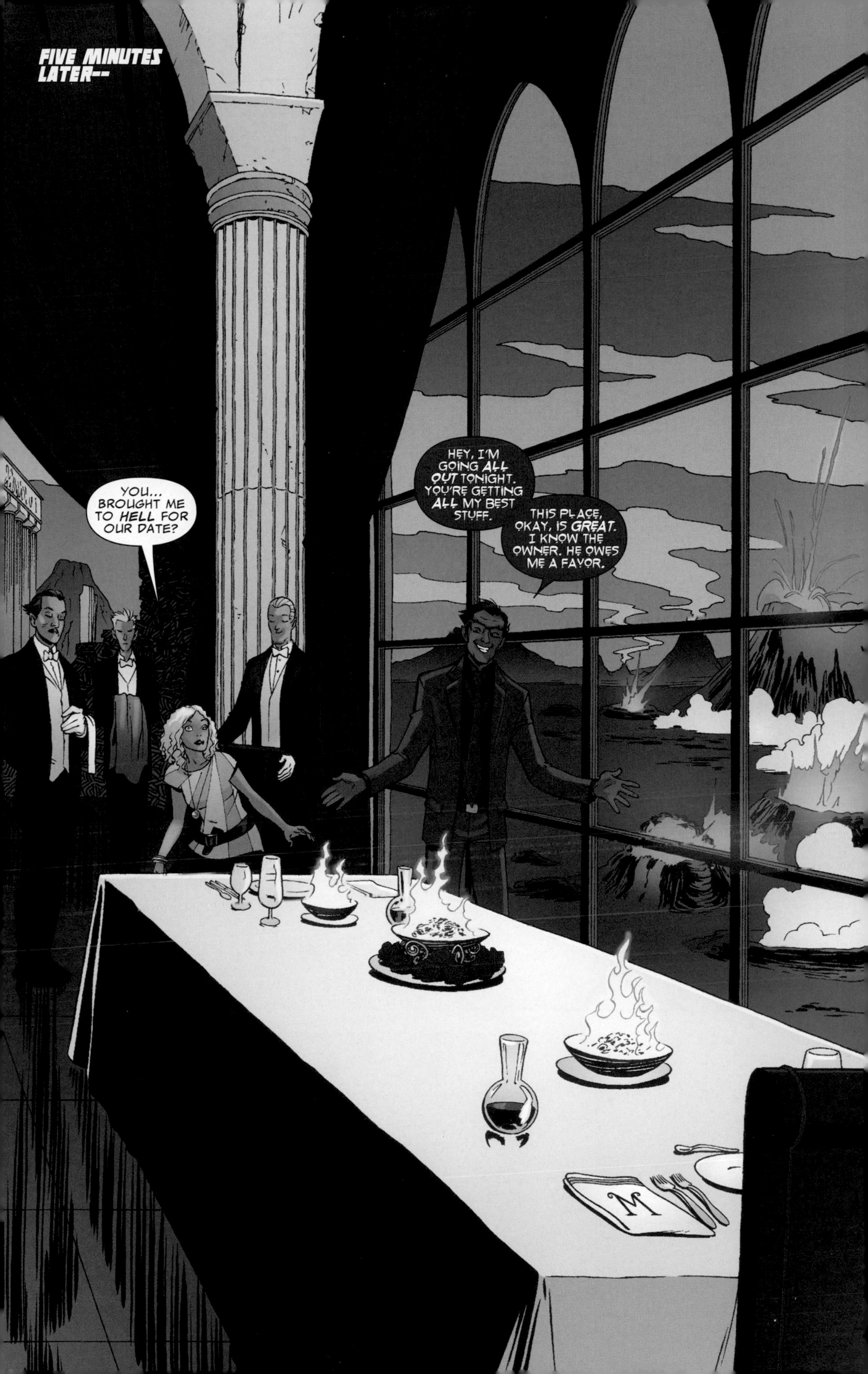
FIVE MINUTES LATER--
YOU... BROUGHT ME TO HELL FOR OUR DATE?
HEY, I'M GOING ALL OUT TONIGHT. YOU'RE GETTING ALL MY BEST STUFF.
THIS PLACE, OKAY, IS GREAT. I KNOW THE OWNER. HE OWES ME A FAVOR.

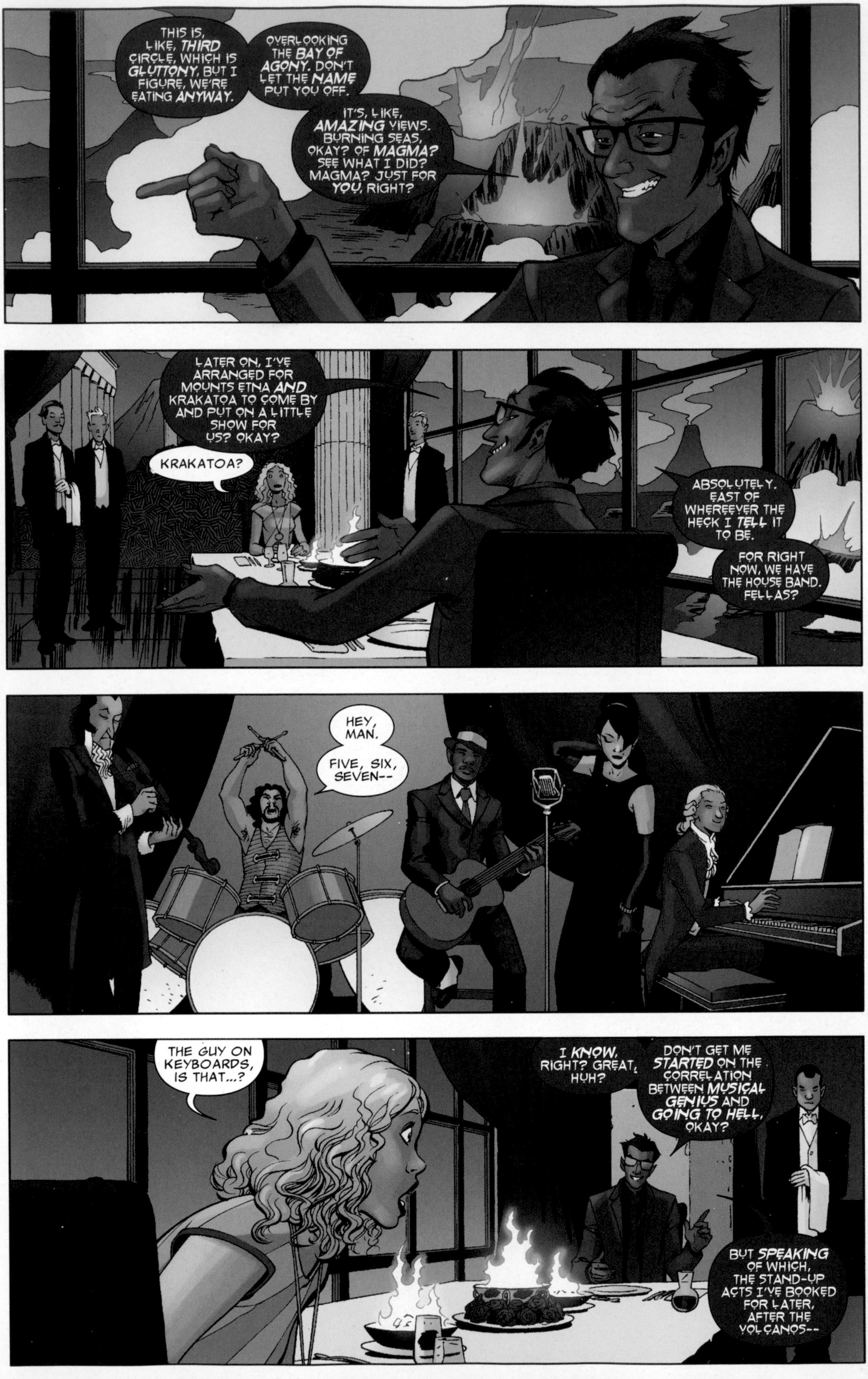
THIS IS, LIKE, THIRD CIRCLE, WHICH IS GLUTTONY, BUT I FIGURE, WE'RE EATING ANYWAY.
OVERLOOKING THE BAY OF AGONY. DON'T LET THE NAME PUT YOU OFF.
IT'S, LIKE, AMAZING VIEWS. BURNING SEAS, OKAY? OF MAGMA? SEE WHAT I DID? MAGMA? JUST FOR YOU, RIGHT?
LATER ON, I'VE ARRANGED FOR MOUNTS ETNA AND KRAKATOA TO COME BY AND PUT ON A LITTLE SHOW FOR US? OKAY?
KRAKATOA?
ABSOLUTELY. EAST OF WHEREEVER THE HECK I TELL IT TO BE.
FOR RIGHT NOW, WE HAVE THE HOUSE BAND. FELLAS?
HEY, MAN.
FIVE, SIX, SEVEN--
THE GUY ON KEYBOARDS, IS THAT...?
I KNOW. RIGHT? GREAT, HUH?
DON'T GET ME STARTED ON THE CORRELATION BETWEEN MUSICAL GENIUS AND GOING TO HELL, OKAY?
BUT SPEAKING OF WHICH, THE STAND-UP ACTS I'VE BOOKED FOR LATER, AFTER THE VOLCANOS--

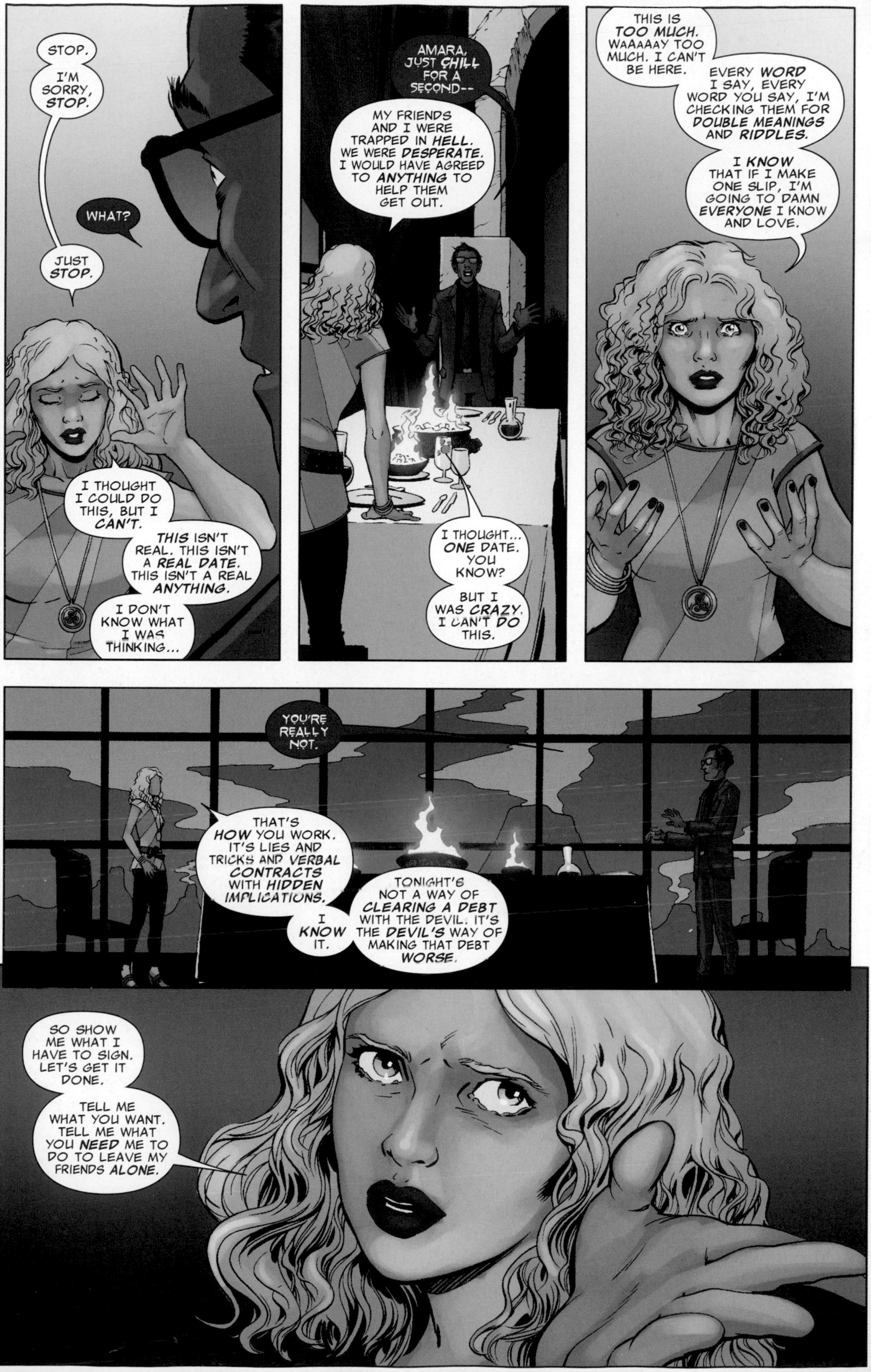
STOP.
I'M SORRY, STOP.
WHAT?
JUST STOP.
I THOUGHT I COULD DO THIS, BUT I CAN'T.
THIS ISN'T REAL. THIS ISN'T A REAL DATE. THIS ISN'T A REAL ANYTHING.
I DON'T KNOW WHAT I WAS THINKING...
AMARA, JUST CHILL FOR A SECOND--
MY FRIENDS AND I WERE TRAPPED IN HELL. WE WERE DESPERATE. I WOULD HAVE AGREED TO ANYTHING TO HELP THEM GET OUT.
I THOUGHT... ONE DATE. YOU KNOW?
BUT I WAS CRAZY. I CAN'T DO THIS.
THIS IS TOO MUCH. WAAAAAY TOO MUCH. I CAN'T BE HERE.
EVERY WORD I SAY, EVERY WORD YOU SAY, I'M CHECKING THEM FOR DOUBLE MEANINGS AND RIDDLES.
I KNOW THAT IF I MAKE ONE SLIP, I'M GOING TO DAMN EVERYONE I KNOW AND LOVE.
YOU'RE REALLY NOT.
THAT'S HOW YOU WORK. IT'S LIES AND TRICKS AND VERBAL CONTRACTS WITH HIDDEN IMPLICATIONS.
I KNOW IT.
TONIGHT'S NOT A WAY OF CLEARING A DEBT WITH THE DEVIL. IT'S THE DEVIL'S WAY OF MAKING THAT DEBT WORSE.
SO SHOW ME WHAT I HAVE TO SIGN. LET'S GET IT DONE.
TELL ME WHAT YOU WANT. TELL ME WHAT YOU NEED ME TO DO TO LEAVE MY FRIENDS ALONE.

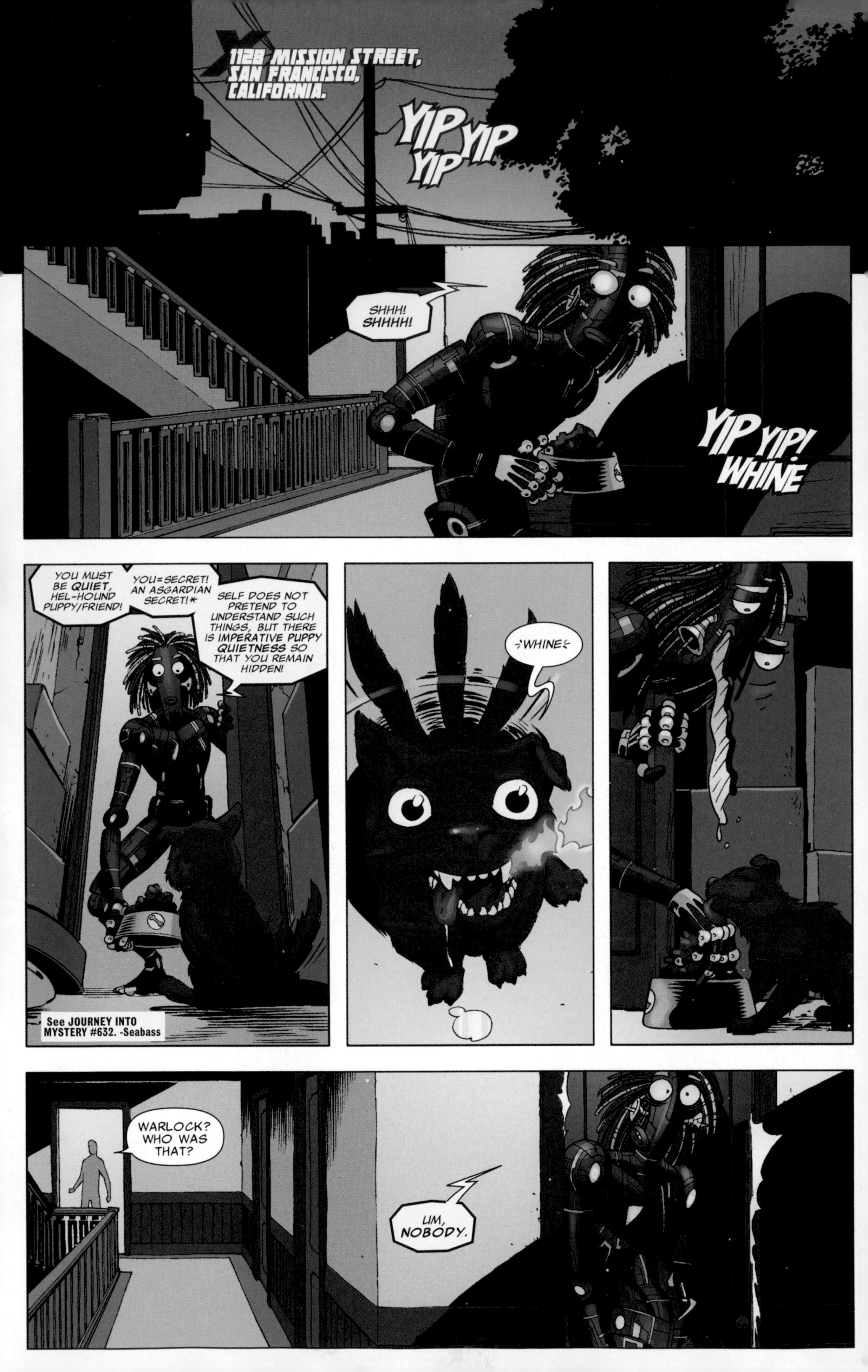
1128 MISSION STREET, SAN FRANCISCO, CALIFORNIA.
YIP YIP YIP
SHHH! SHHHH!
YIP YIP! WHINE
YOU MUST BE QUIET, HEL-HOUND PUPPY/FRIEND!
YOU=SECRET! AN ASGARDIAN SECRET!*
SELF DOES NOT PRETEND TO UNDERSTAND SUCH THINGS, BUT THERE IS IMPERATIVE PUPPY QUIETNESS SO THAT YOU REMAIN HIDDEN!
*See JOURNEY INTO MYSTERY #632. -Seabass
WHINE
WARLOCK? WHO WAS THAT?
UM, NOBODY.

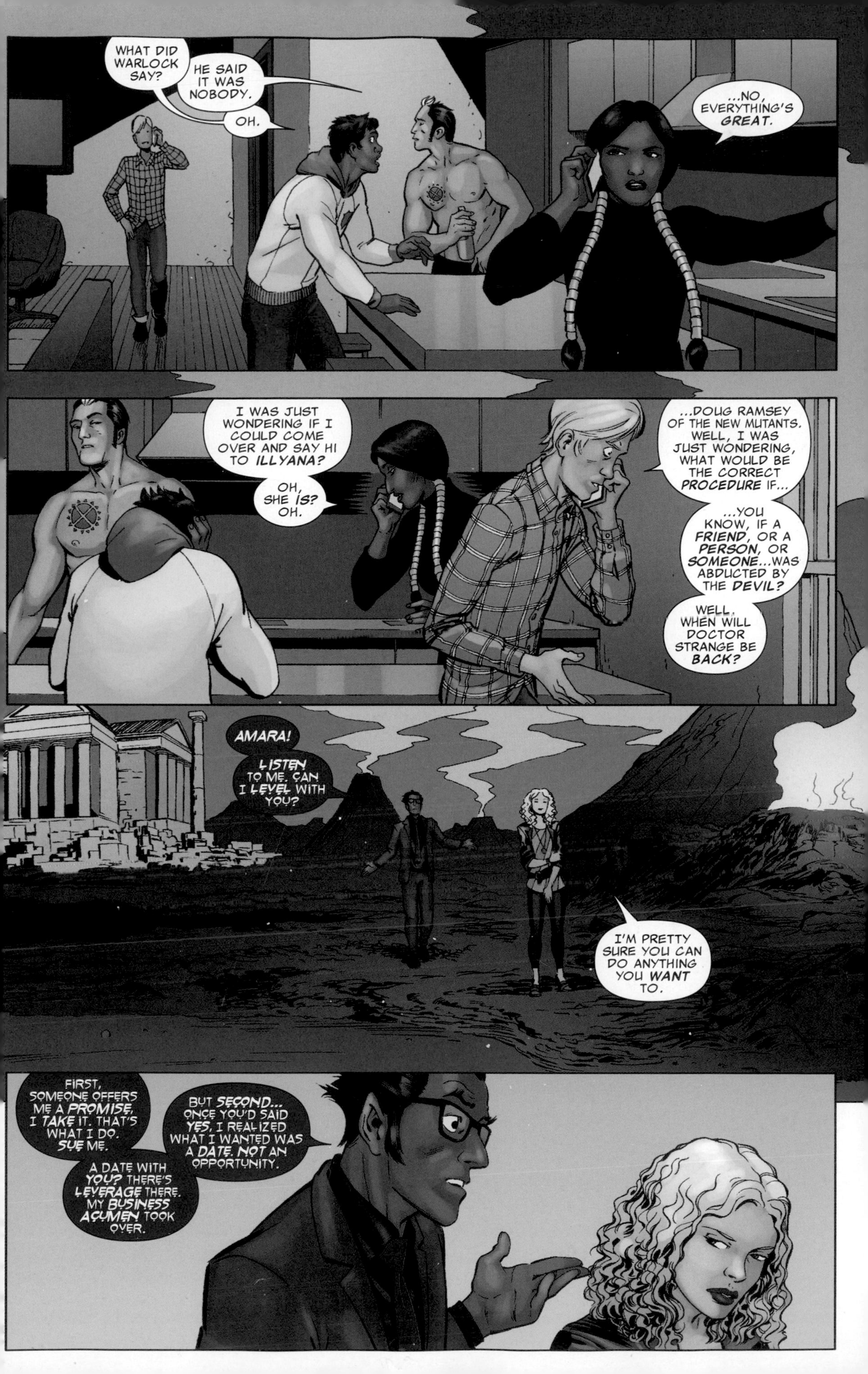

WHAT DID WARLOCK SAY?
HE SAID IT WAS NOBODY.
OH.
...NO, EVERYTHING'S GREAT.
I WAS JUST WONDERING IF I COULD COME OVER AND SAY HI TO ILLYANA?
OH, SHE IS? OH.
...DOUG RAMSEY OF THE NEW MUTANTS. WELL, I WAS JUST WONDERING, WHAT WOULD BE THE CORRECT PROCEDURE IF...
...YOU KNOW, IF A FRIEND, OR A PERSON, OR SOMEONE...WAS ABDUCTED BY THE DEVIL?
WELL. WHEN WILL DOCTOR STRANGE BE BACK?
AMARA!
LISTEN TO ME. CAN I LEVEL WITH YOU?
I'M PRETTY SURE YOU CAN DO ANYTHING YOU WANT TO.
FIRST, SOMEONE OFFERS ME A PROMISE, I TAKE IT. THAT'S WHAT I DO. SUE ME.
A DATE WITH YOU? THERE'S LEVERAGE THERE. MY BUSINESS ACUMEN TOOK OVER.
BUT SECOND... ONCE YOU'D SAID YES, I REALIZED WHAT I WANTED WAS A DATE. NOT AN OPPORTUNITY.

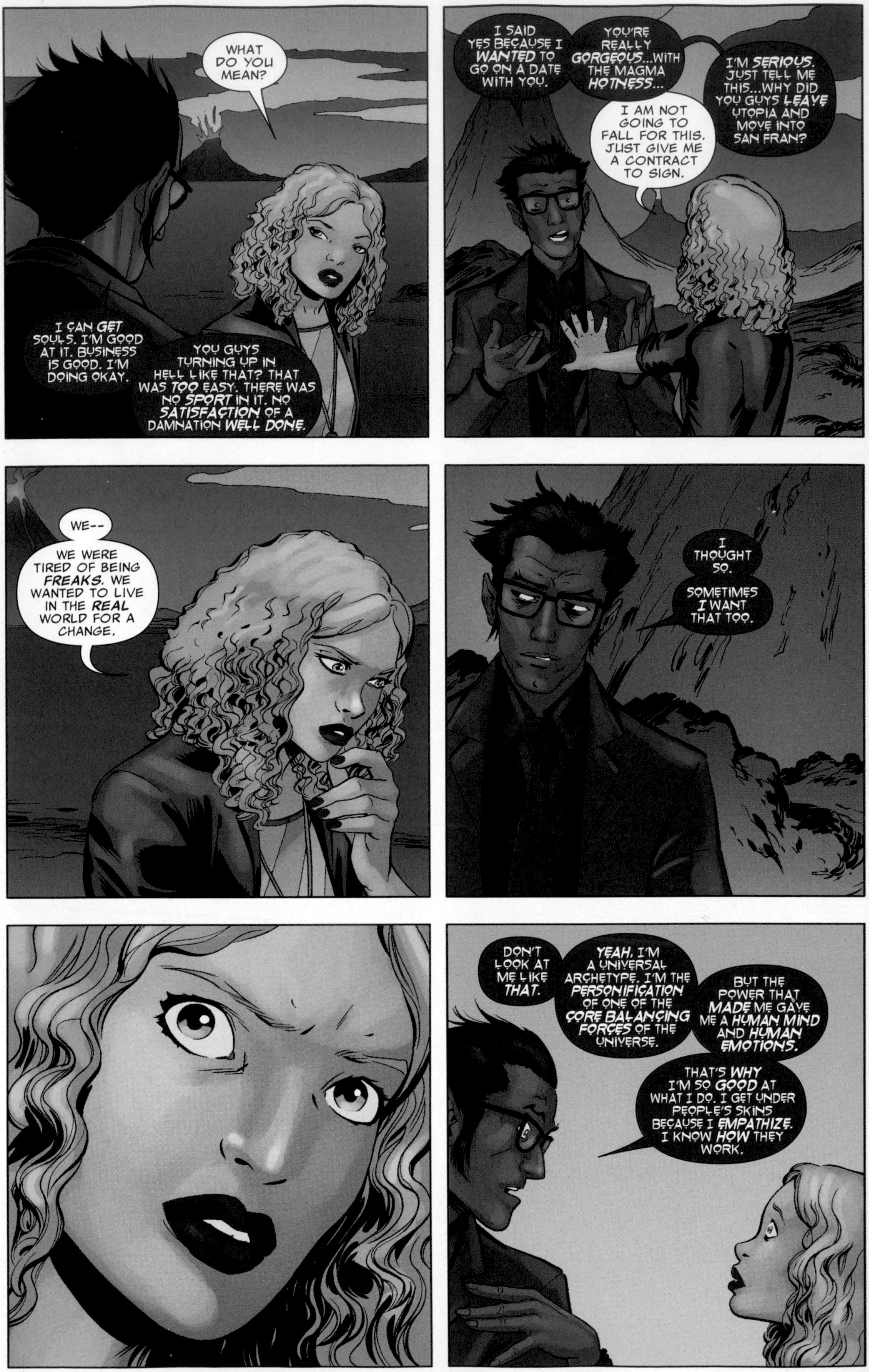
WHAT DO YOU MEAN?
I CAN GET SOULS. I'M GOOD AT IT. BUSINESS IS GOOD. I'M DOING OKAY.
YOU GUYS TURNING UP IN HELL LIKE THAT? THAT WAS TOO EASY. THERE WAS NO SPORT IN IT. NO SATISFACTION OF A DAMNATION WELL DONE.
I SAID YES BECAUSE I WANTED TO GO ON A DATE WITH YOU.
YOU'RE REALLY GORGEOUS...WITH THE MAGMA HOTNESS...
I AM NOT GOING TO FALL FOR THIS. JUST GIVE ME A CONTRACT TO SIGN.
I'M SERIOUS. JUST TELL ME THIS...WHY DID YOU GUYS LEAVE UTOPIA AND MOVE INTO SAN FRAN?
WE--
WE WERE TIRED OF BEING FREAKS. WE WANTED TO LIVE IN THE REAL WORLD FOR A CHANGE.
I THOUGHT SO.
SOMETIMES I WANT THAT TOO.
DON'T LOOK AT ME LIKE THAT.
YEAH, I'M A UNIVERSAL ARCHETYPE. I'M THE PERSONIFICATION OF ONE OF THE CORE BALANCING FORCES OF THE UNIVERSE.
BUT THE POWER THAT MADE ME GAVE ME A HUMAN MIND AND HUMAN EMOTIONS.
THAT'S WHY I'M SO GOOD AT WHAT I DO. I GET UNDER PEOPLE'S SKINS BECAUSE I EMPATHIZE. I KNOW HOW THEY WORK.

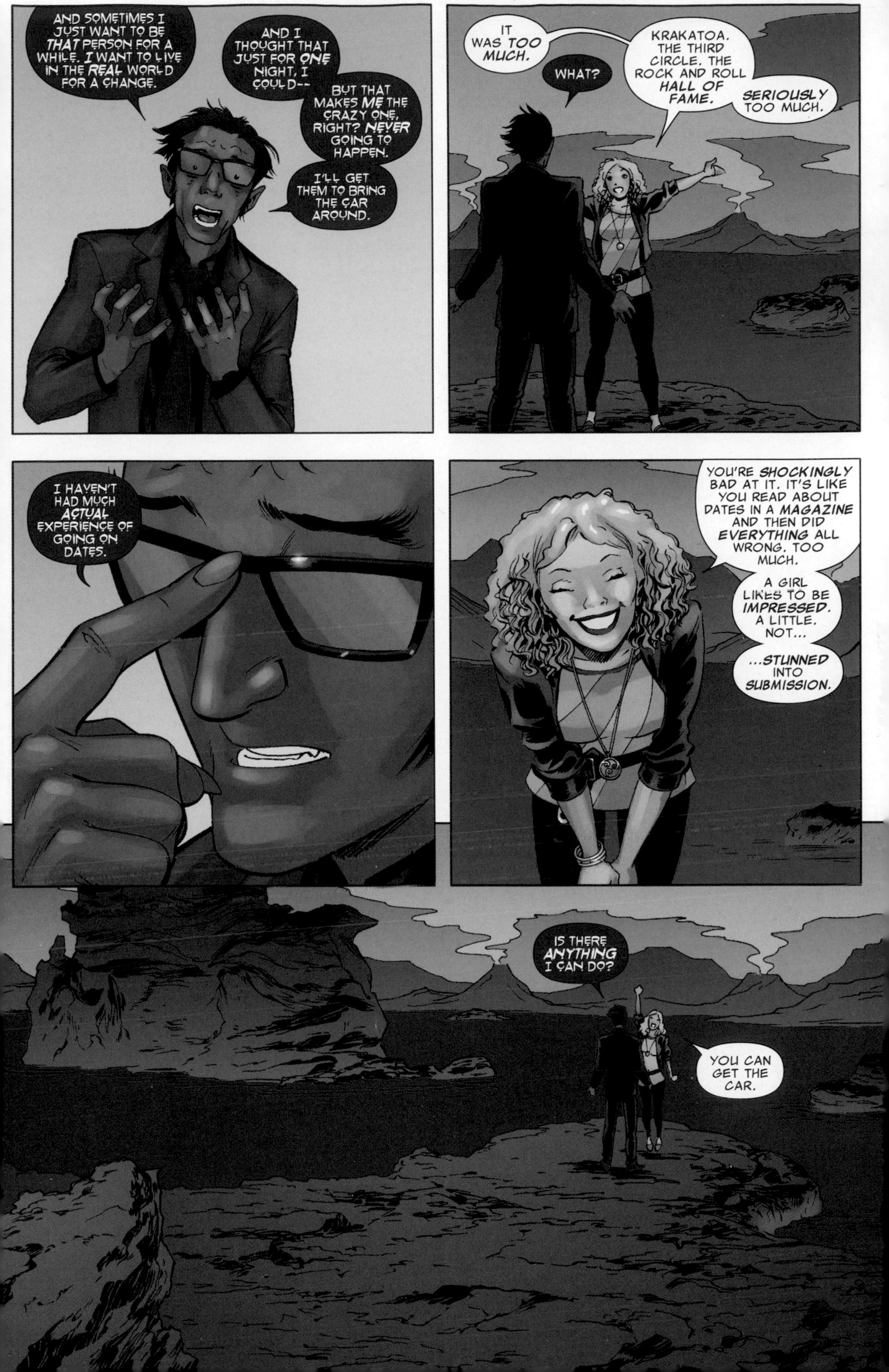
AND SOMETIMES I JUST WANT TO BE THAT PERSON FOR A WHILE. I WANT TO LIVE IN THE REAL WORLD FOR A CHANGE.
AND I THOUGHT THAT JUST FOR ONE NIGHT, I COULD--
BUT THAT MAKES ME THE CRAZY ONE, RIGHT? NEVER GOING TO HAPPEN.
I'LL GET THEM TO BRING THE CAR AROUND.
IT WAS TOO MUCH.
WHAT?
KRAKATOA. THE THIRD CIRCLE. THE ROCK AND ROLL HALL OF FAME.
SERIOUSLY TOO MUCH.
I HAVEN'T HAD MUCH ACTUAL EXPERIENCE OF GOING ON DATES.
YOU'RE SHOCKINGLY BAD AT IT. IT'S LIKE YOU READ ABOUT DATES IN A MAGAZINE AND THEN DID EVERYTHING ALL WRONG. TOO MUCH.
A GIRL LIKES TO BE IMPRESSED. A LITTLE. NOT...
...STUNNED INTO SUBMISSION.
IS THERE ANYTHING I CAN DO?
YOU CAN GET THE CAR.

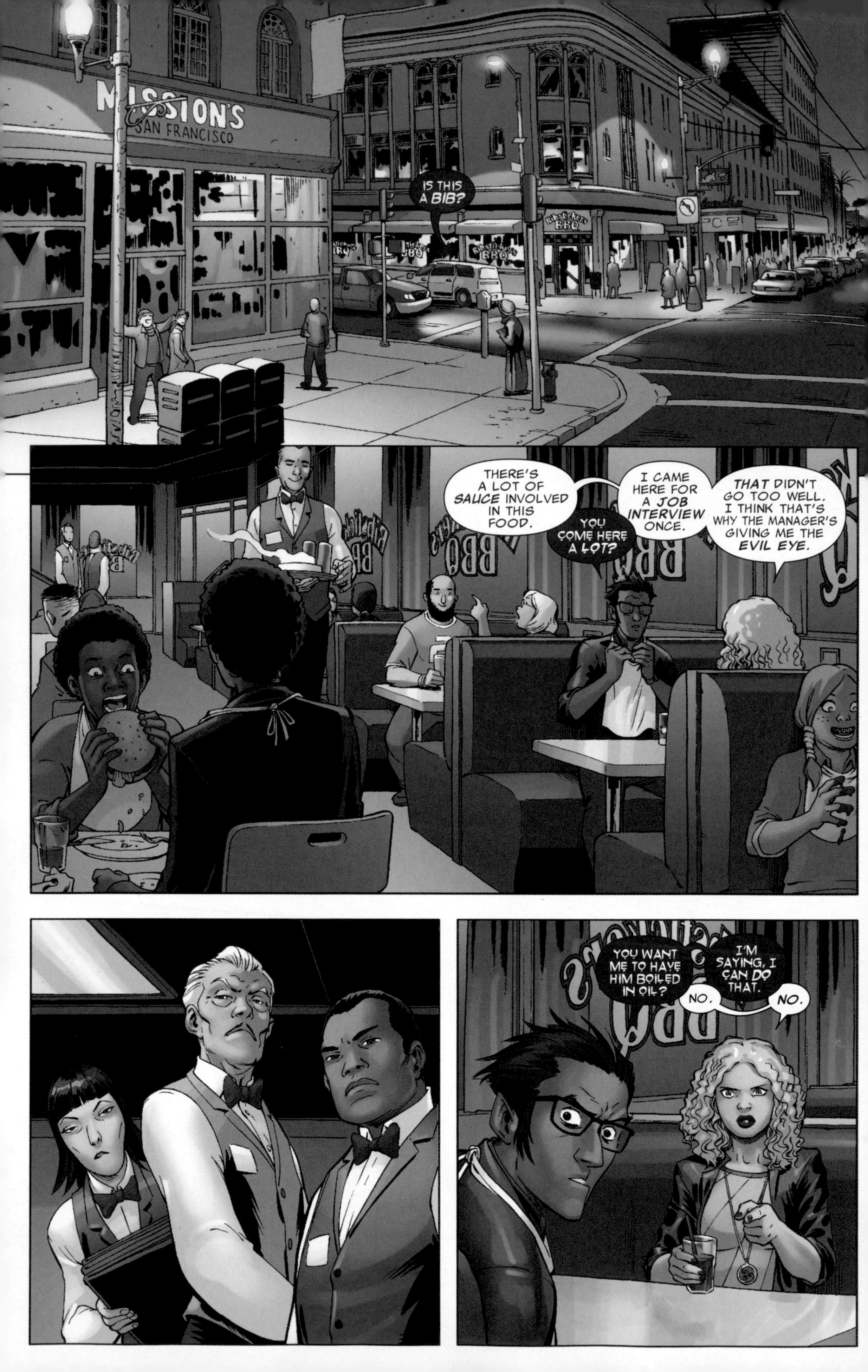

MISSION'S
SAN FRANCISCO
IS THIS A BIB?
THERE'S A LOT OF SAUCE INVOLVED IN THIS FOOD.
YOU COME HERE A LOT?
I CAME HERE FOR A JOB INTERVIEW ONCE.
THAT DIDN'T GO TOO WELL. I THINK THAT'S WHY THE MANAGER'S GIVING ME THE EVIL EYE.
YOU WANT ME TO HAVE HIM BOILED IN OIL?
NO.
I'M SAYING, I CAN DO THAT.
NO.

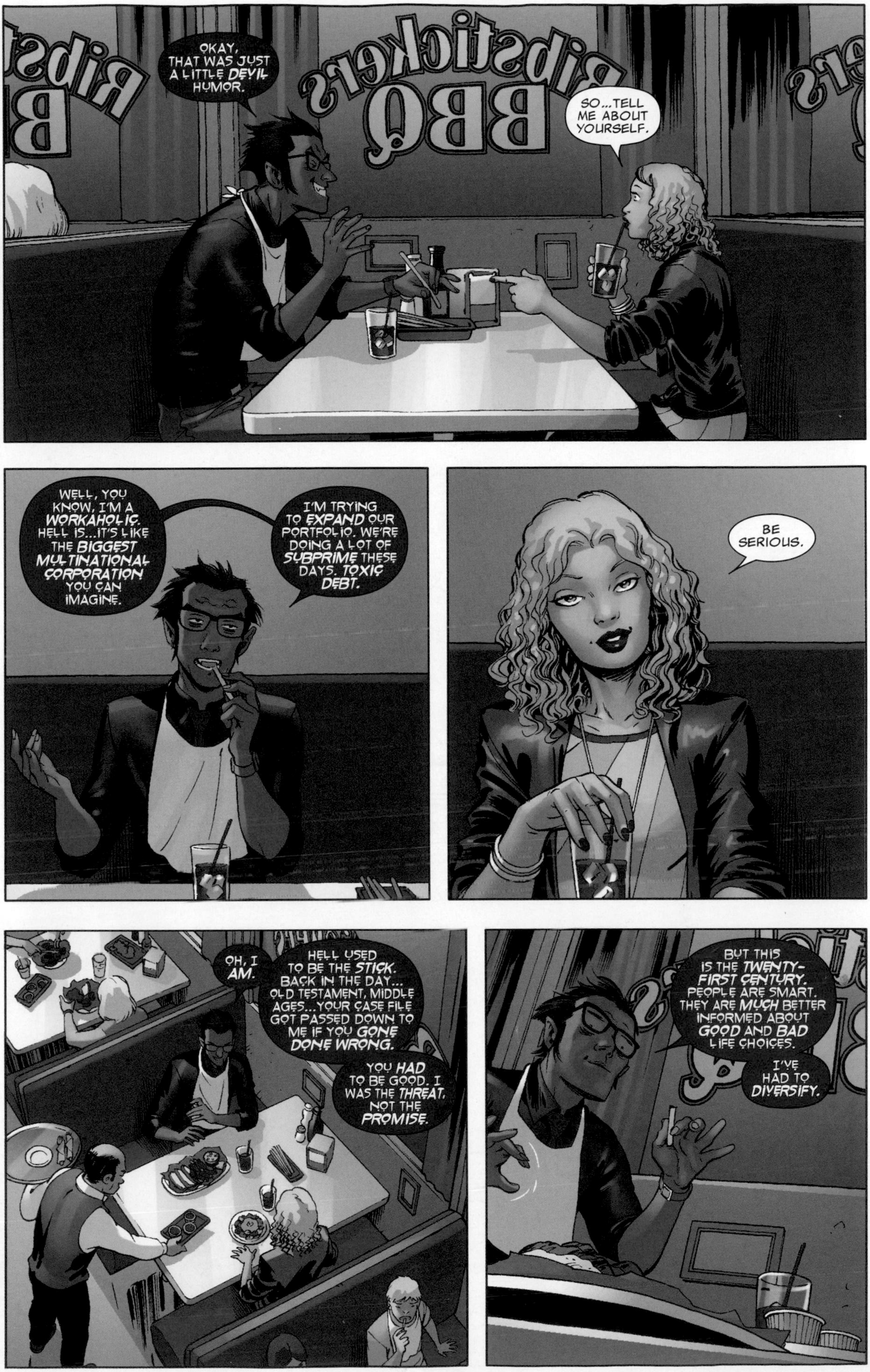
Ribsticker's BBQ
OKAY, THAT WAS JUST A LITTLE DEVIL HUMOR.
SO...TELL ME ABOUT YOURSELF.
WELL, YOU KNOW, I'M A WORKAHOLIC. HELL IS...IT'S LIKE THE BIGGEST MULTINATIONAL CORPORATION YOU CAN IMAGINE.
I'M TRYING TO EXPAND OUR PORTFOLIO. WE'RE DOING A LOT OF SUBPRIME THESE DAYS. TOXIC DEBT.
BE SERIOUS.
OH, I AM.
HELL USED TO BE THE STICK. BACK IN THE DAY... OLD TESTAMENT, MIDDLE AGES...YOUR CASE FILE GOT PASSED DOWN TO ME IF YOU GONE DONE WRONG.
YOU HAD TO BE GOOD. I WAS THE THREAT, NOT THE PROMISE.
BUT THIS IS THE TWENTY-FIRST CENTURY. PEOPLE ARE SMART. THEY ARE MUCH BETTER INFORMED ABOUT GOOD AND BAD LIFE CHOICES.
I'VE HAD TO DIVERSIFY.

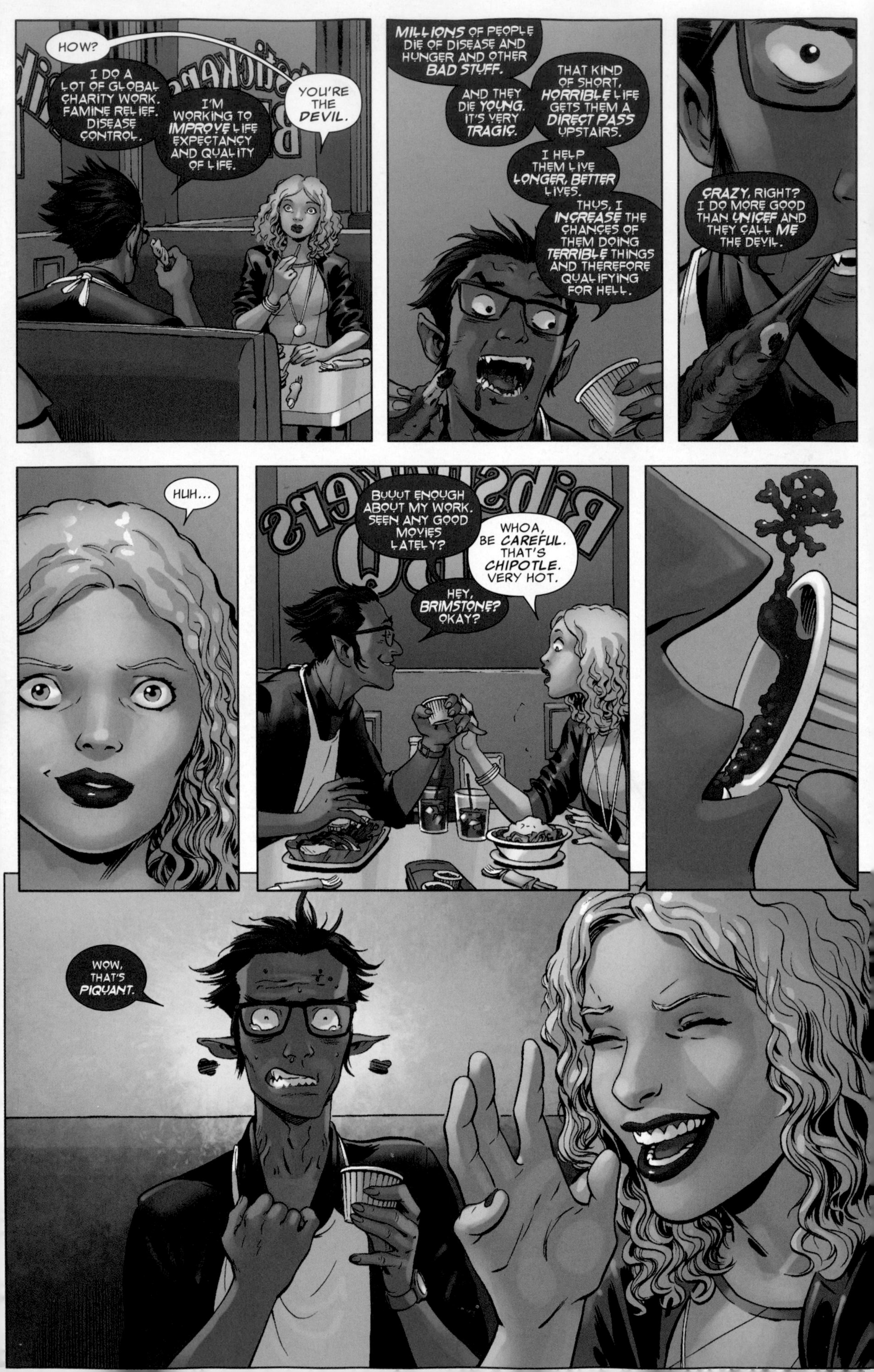
HOW?
I DO A LOT OF GLOBAL CHARITY WORK. FAMINE RELIEF. DISEASE CONTROL.
I'M WORKING TO IMPROVE LIFE EXPECTANCY AND QUALITY OF LIFE.
YOU'RE THE DEVIL.
MILLIONS OF PEOPLE DIE OF DISEASE AND HUNGER AND OTHER BAD STUFF.
AND THEY DIE YOUNG. IT'S VERY TRAGIC.
THAT KIND OF SHORT, HORRIBLE LIFE GETS THEM A DIRECT PASS UPSTAIRS.
I HELP THEM LIVE LONGER, BETTER LIVES.
THUS, I INCREASE THE CHANCES OF THEM DOING TERRIBLE THINGS AND THEREFORE QUALIFYING FOR HELL.
CRAZY, RIGHT? I DO MORE GOOD THAN UNICEF AND THEY CALL ME THE DEVIL.
HUH...
BUUUT ENOUGH ABOUT MY WORK. SEEN ANY GOOD MOVIES LATELY?
WHOA, BE CAREFUL. THAT'S CHIPOTLE. VERY HOT.
HEY, BRIMSTONE? OKAY?
WOW, THAT'S PIQUANT.

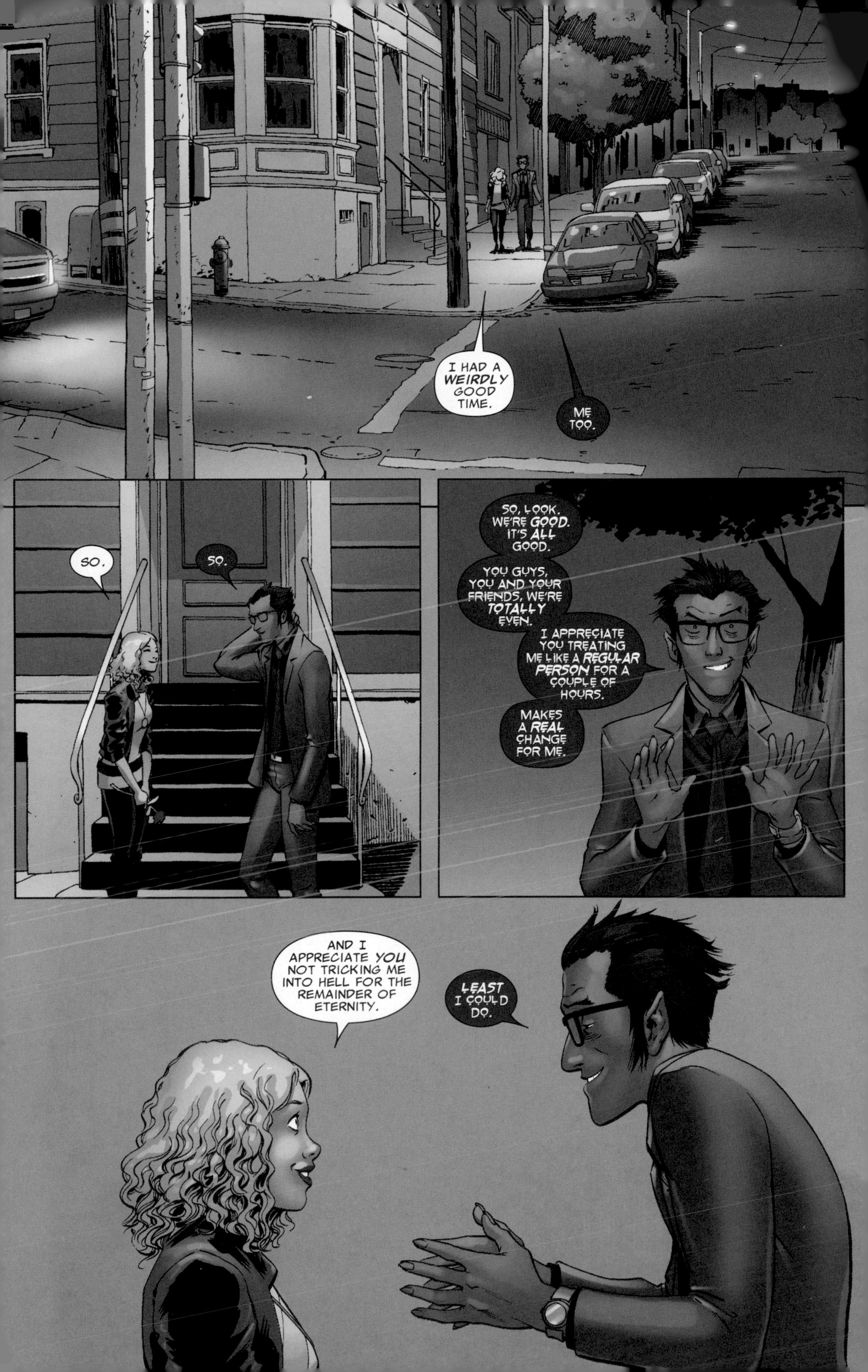
I HAD A WEIRDLY GOOD TIME.
ME TOO.
SO.
SO.
SO, LOOK. WE'RE GOOD. IT'S ALL GOOD.
YOU GUYS, YOU AND YOUR FRIENDS, WE'RE TOTALLY EVEN.
I APPRECIATE YOU TREATING ME LIKE A REGULAR PERSON FOR A COUPLE OF HOURS.
MAKES A REAL CHANGE FOR ME.
AND I APPRECIATE YOU NOT TRICKING ME INTO HELL FOR THE REMAINDER OF ETERNITY.
LEAST I COULD DO.

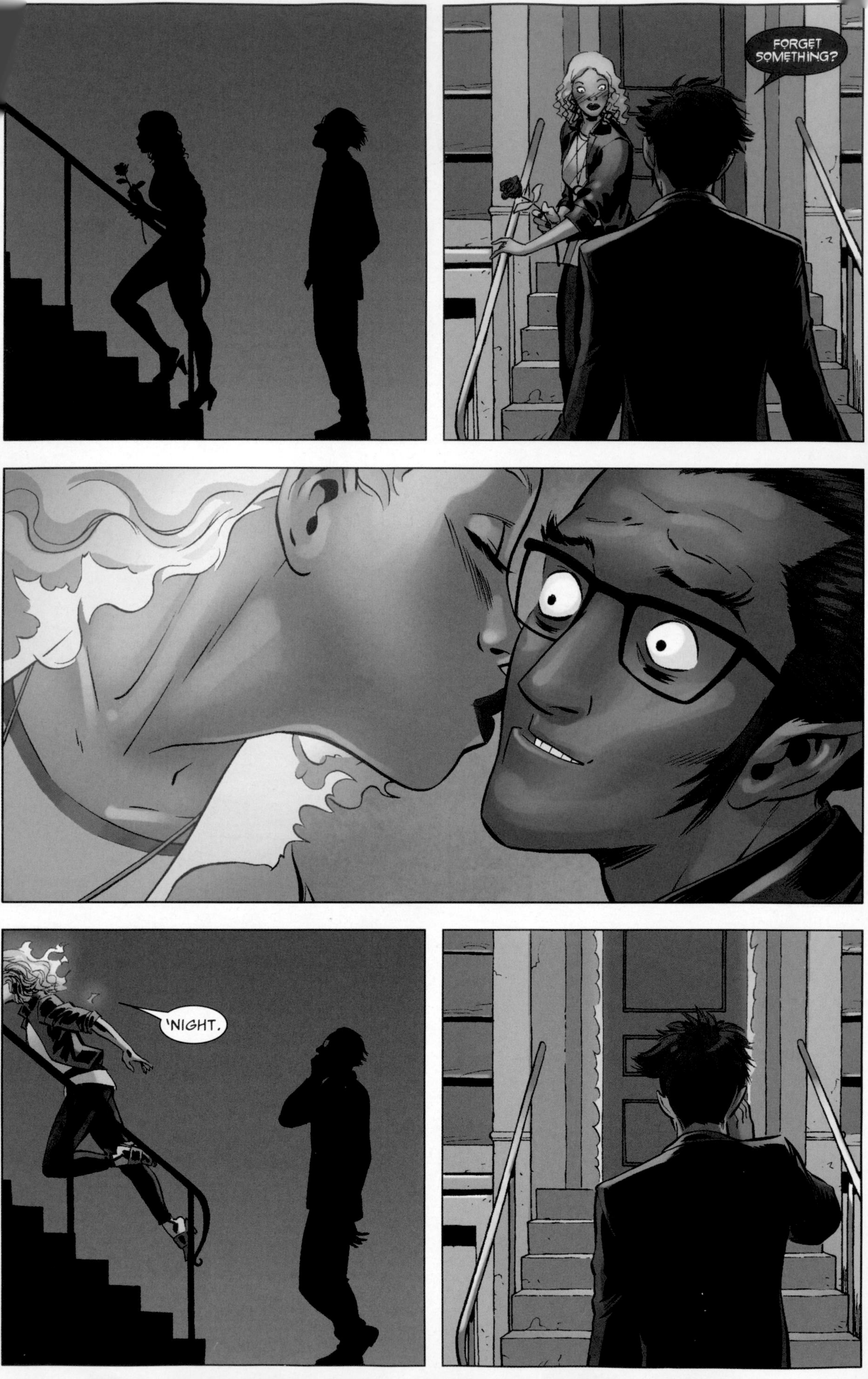
FORGET SOMETHING?
'NIGHT.

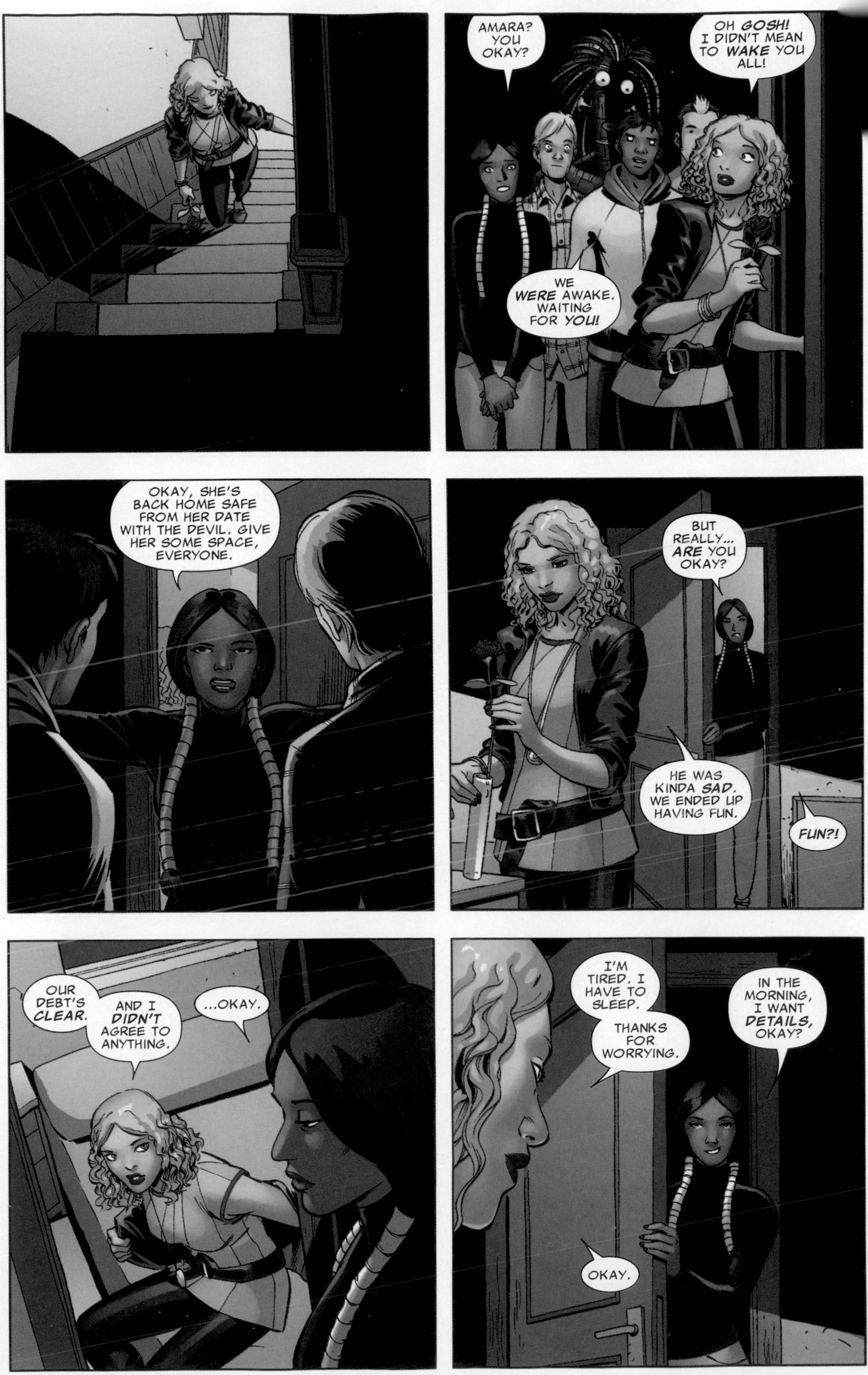
AMARA? YOU OKAY?
OH GOSH! I DIDN'T MEAN TO WAKE YOU ALL!
WE WERE AWAKE. WAITING FOR YOU!
OKAY, SHE'S BACK HOME SAFE FROM HER DATE WITH THE DEVIL. GIVE HER SOME SPACE, EVERYONE.
BUT REALLY... ARE YOU OKAY?
HE WAS KINDA SAD. WE ENDED UP HAVING FUN.
FUN?!
OUR DEBT'S CLEAR.
AND I DIDN'T AGREE TO ANYTHING.
...OKAY.
I'M TIRED. I HAVE TO SLEEP.
THANKS FOR WORRYING.
IN THE MORNING, I WANT DETAILS, OKAY?
OKAY.

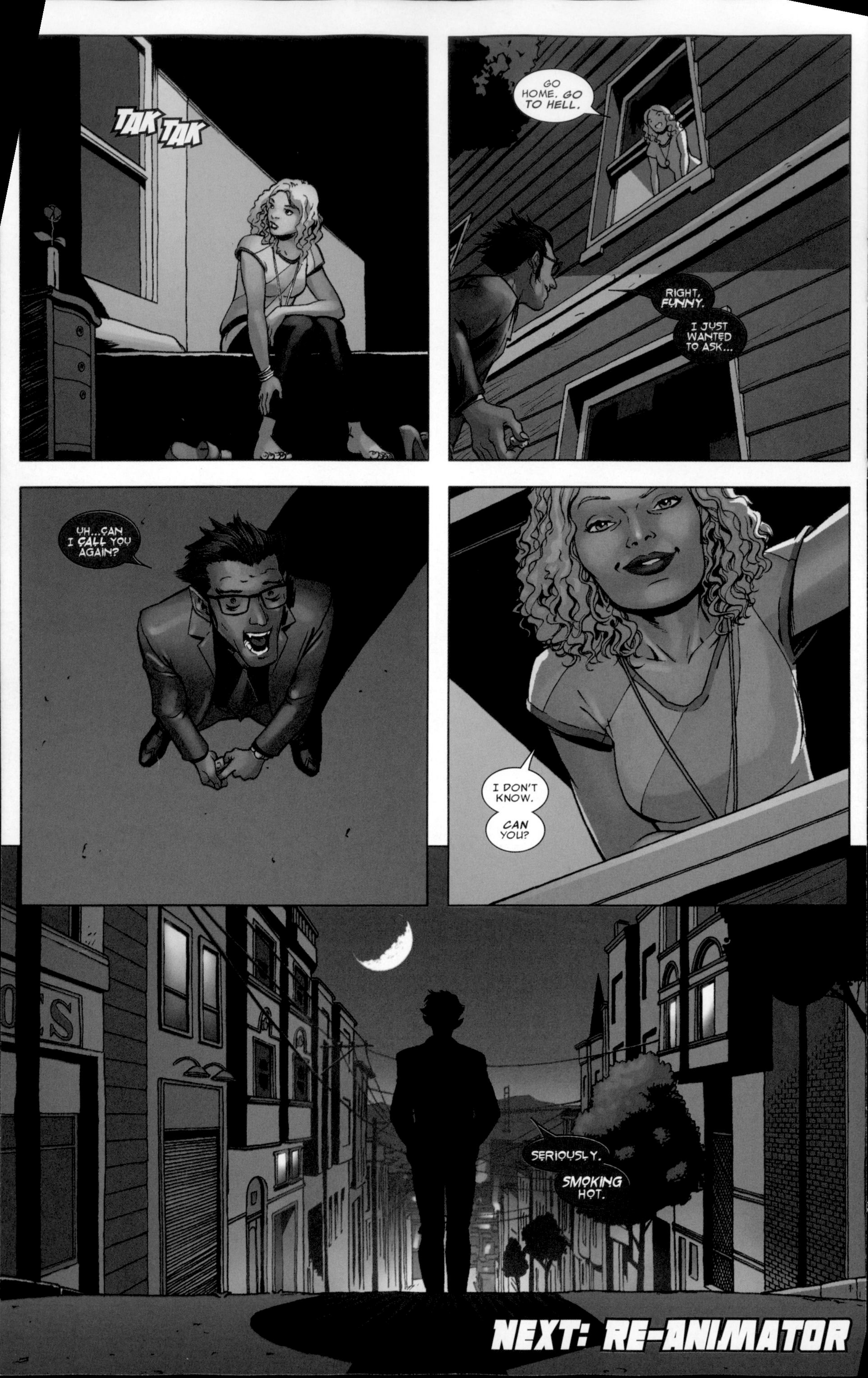
TAK TAK
GO HOME. GO TO HELL.
RIGHT, FUNNY.
I JUST WANTED TO ASK...
UH...CAN I CALL YOU AGAIN?
I DON'T KNOW.
CAN YOU?
SERIOUSLY.
SMOKING HOT.
NEXT: RE-ANIMATOR

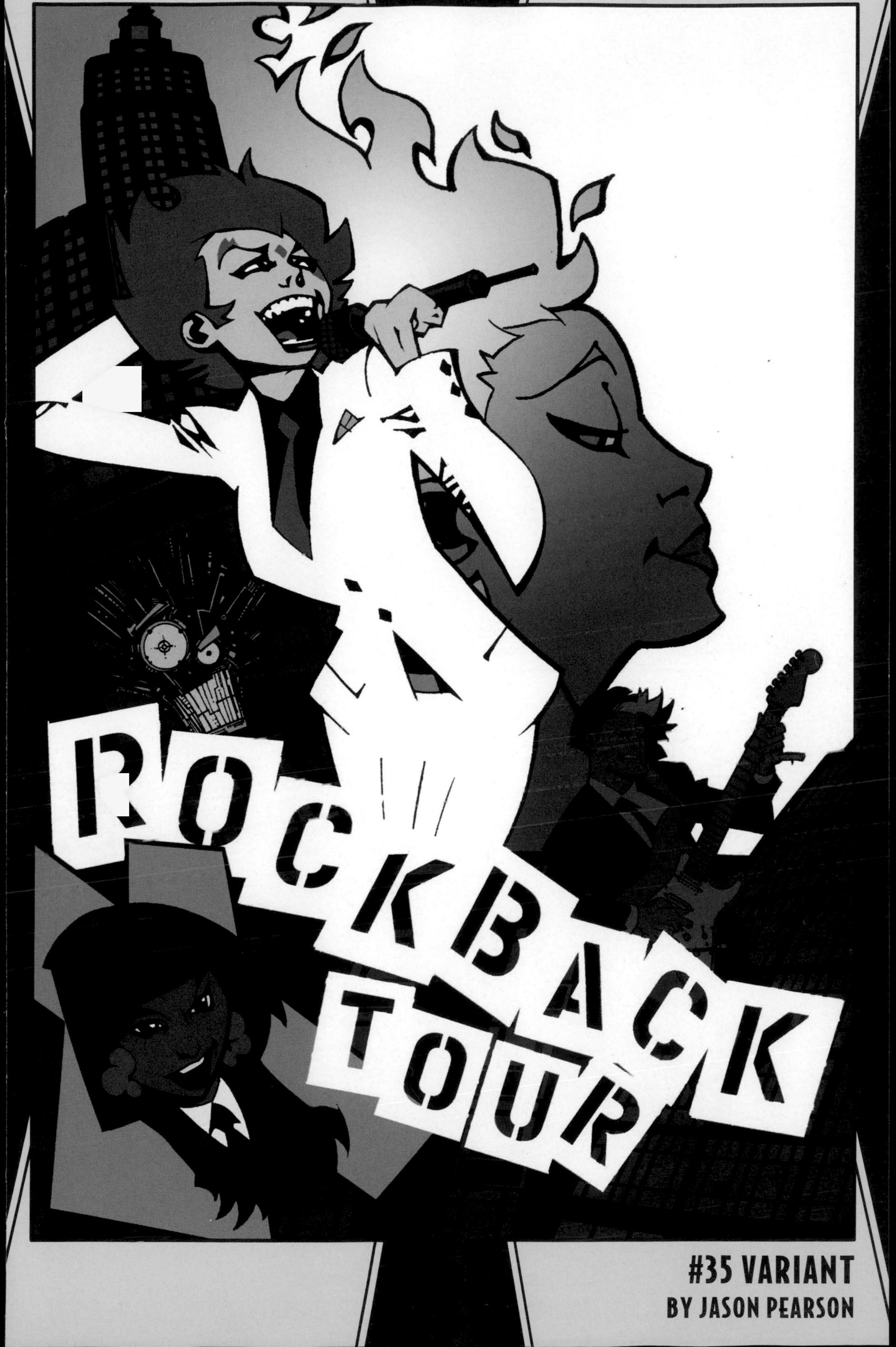
ROCKBACK TOUR

#35 VARIANT

BY JASON PEARSON

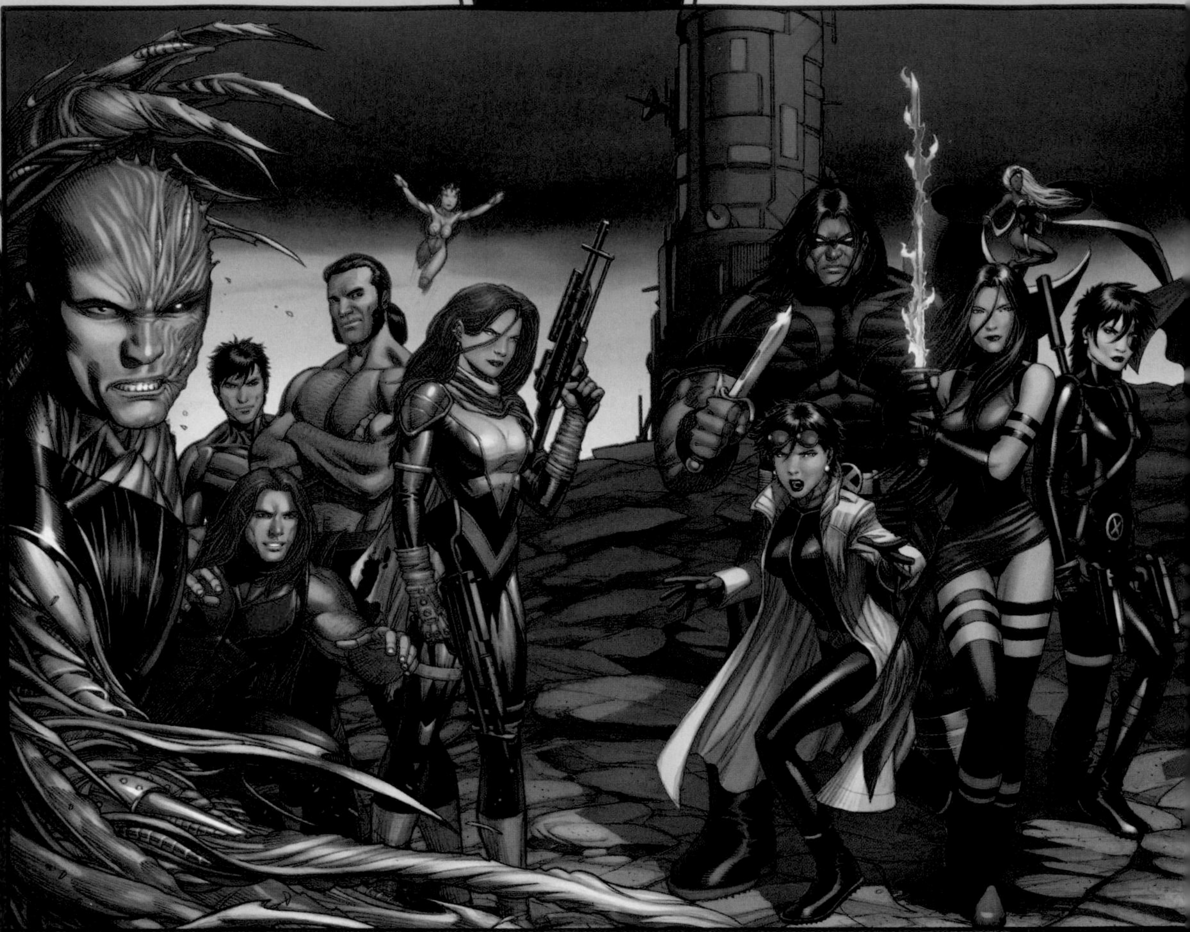

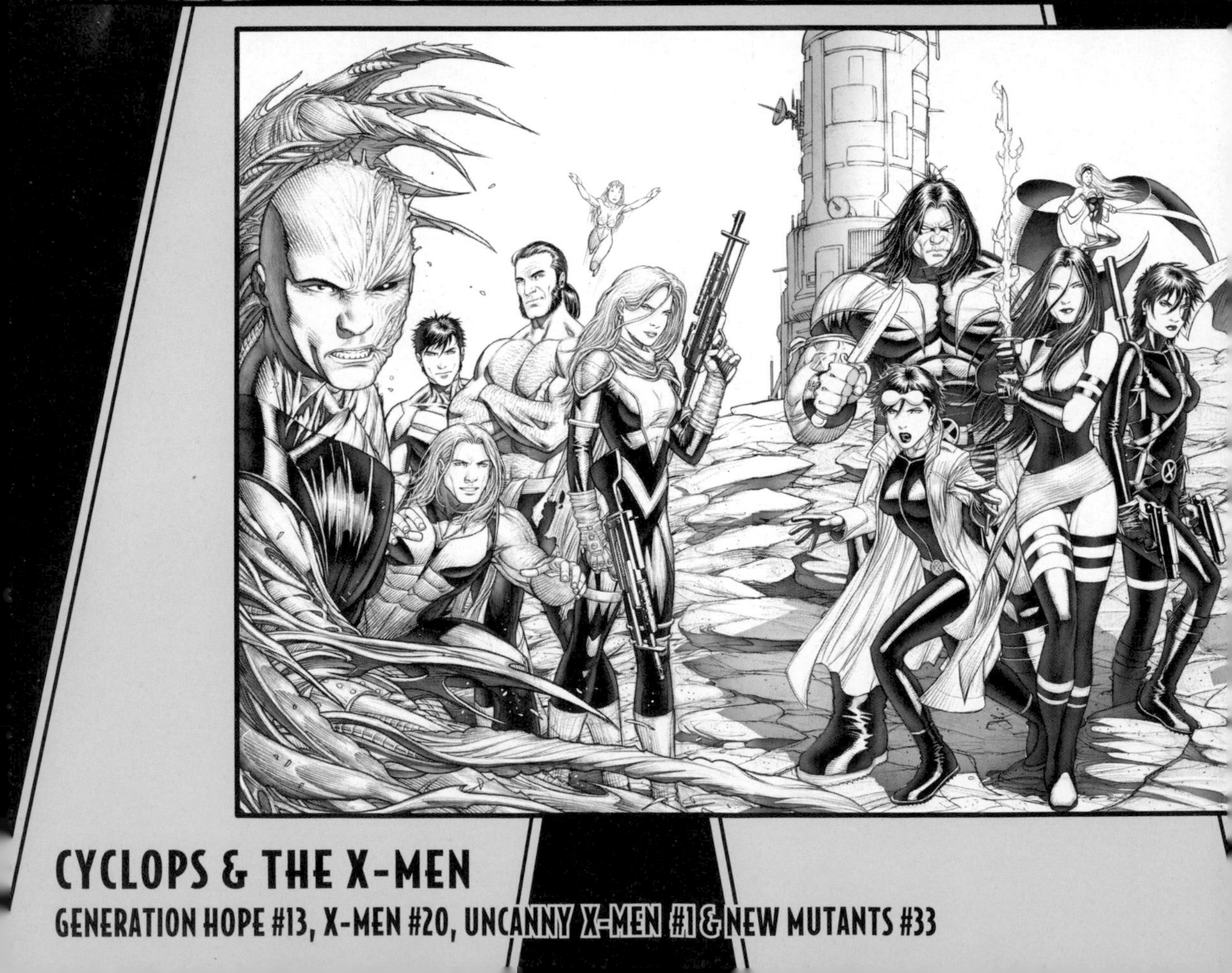

CYCLOPS & THE X-MEN

GENERATION HOPE #13, X-MEN #20, UNCANNY X-MEN #1 & NEW MUTANTS #33

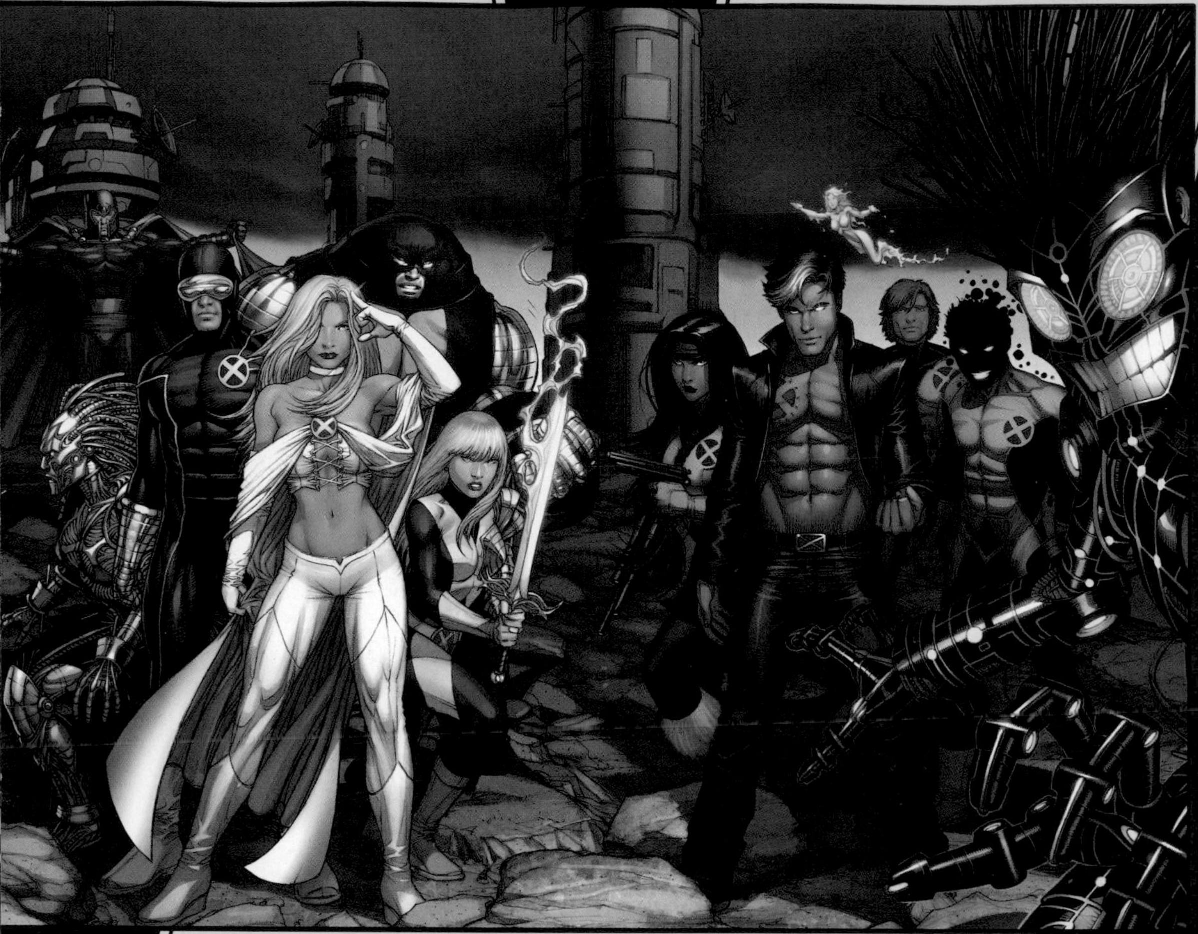

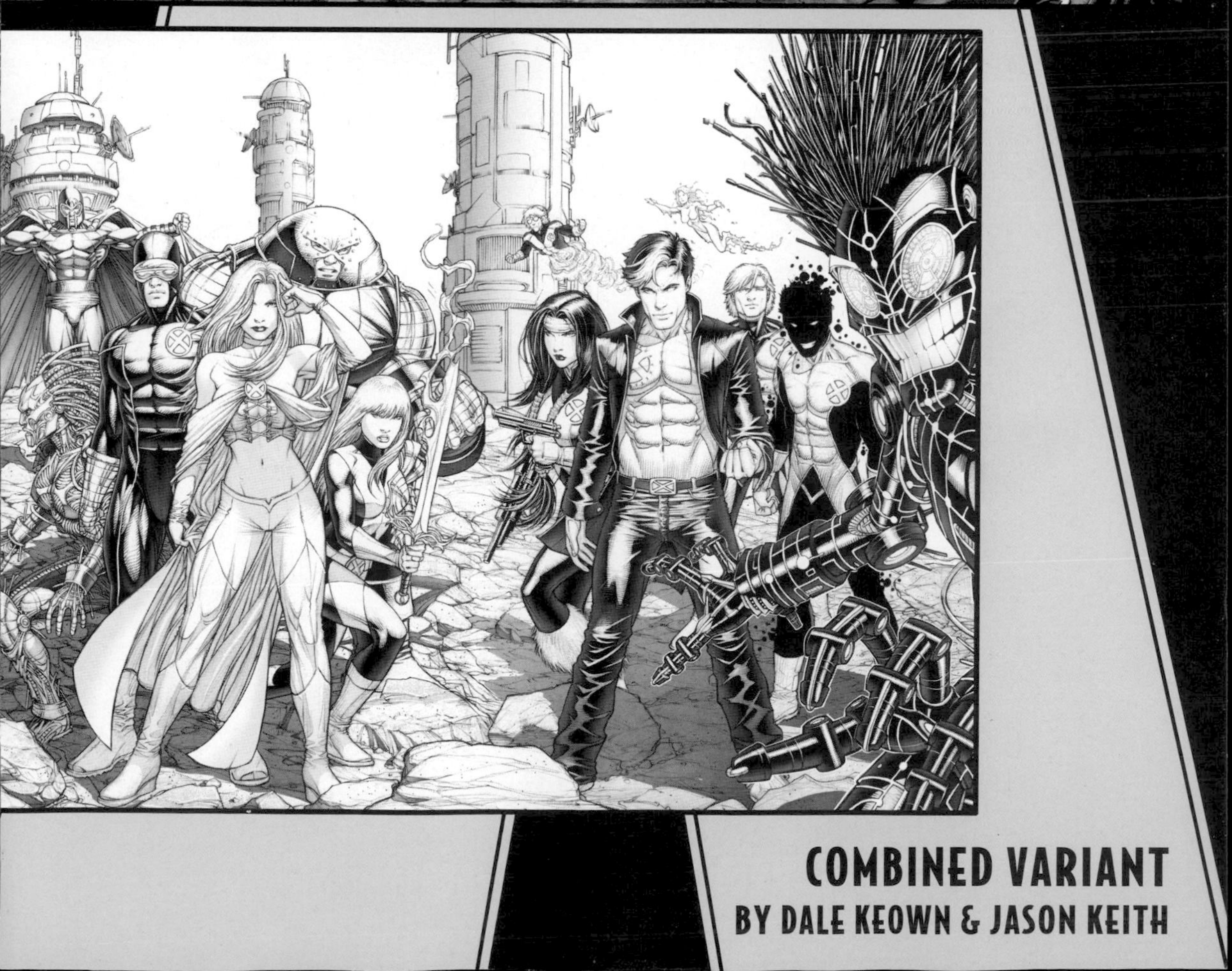

COMBINED VARIANT
BY DALE KEOWN & JASON KEITH

Get caught up with one of Marvel's most critically acclaimed series

NEW MUTANTS

MARVEL PREMIERE EDITION
NEW MUTANTS
RETURN OF LEGION
ZEB WELLS • DIOGENES NEVES • ZACHARY BALDUS

NEW MUTANTS: RETURN OF LEGION PREMIERE HC
978-0-7851-3992-8

MARVEL PREMIERE EDITION
NEW MUTANTS
NECROSHA
WELLS • NEVES • ROBERSON

NEW MUTANTS: NECROSHA PREMIERE HC
978-0-7851-3993-5

MARVEL PREMIERE EDITION
NEW MUTANTS
FALL OF THE NEW MUTANTS
WELLS • KIRK

NEW MUTANTS: FALL OF THE NEW MUTANTS PREMIERE HC
978-0-7851-4583-7

MARVEL PREMIERE EDITION
NEW MUTANTS
UNFINISHED BUSINESS
ABNETT • LANNING • FERNANDEZ • RYAN

NEW MUTANTS: UNFINISHED BUSINESS PREMIERE HC
978-0-7851-5230-9

"I'm pleasantly surprised that this "Regenesis" of the X-Universe has added another mutie book to my reading list." *CBR.com*

On Sale Now

MARVEL
www.marvel.com

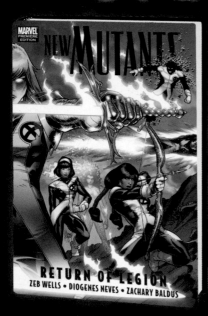

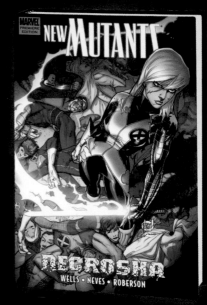

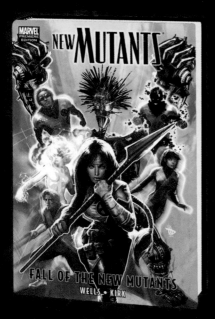

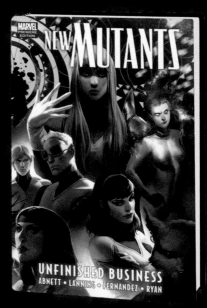